ALSO BY ALEKSANDRA CRAPANZANO

———— • ————

EAT. COOK. L.A.: Recipes from the City of Angels

The London Cookbook: Recipes from the Restaurants, Cafes,
and Hole-in-the-Wall Gems of a Modern City

GÂTEAU

The Surprising Simplicity of French Cakes

Aleksandra Crapanzano

Illustrations by Cassandre Montoriol

SCRIBNER

New York London Toronto Sydney New Delhi

Scribner

An Imprint of Simon & Schuster, Inc.

1230 Avenue of the Americas

New York, NY 10020

Text copyright © 2022 by Aleksandra Crapanzano

Illustrations copyright © 2022 by Cassandre Montoriol

All rights reserved, including the right to reproduce this book or portions thereof in any form whatsoever. For information, address Scribner Subsidiary Rights Department, 1230 Avenue of the Americas, New York, NY 10020.

First Scribner hardcover edition September 2022

SCRIBNER and design are registered trademarks of The Gale Group, Inc., used under license by Simon & Schuster, Inc., the publisher of this work.

For information about special discounts for bulk purchases, please contact Simon & Schuster Special Sales at 1-866-506-1949 or business@simonandschuster.com.

The Simon & Schuster Speakers Bureau can bring authors to your live event. For more information or to book an event, contact the Simon & Schuster Speakers Bureau at 1-866-248-3049 or visit our website at www.simonspeakers.com.

Interior design by Jaime Putorti

Manufactured in Canada
Cover printed in the U.S.A.

1 3 5 7 9 10 8 6 4 2

Library of Congress Control Number: 2022936967

ISBN 978-1-9821-6973-2
ISBN 978-1-9821-6975-6 (ebook)

For my parents, Jane Kramer and Vincent Crapanzano,

who gave me a love of writing,

a passion for good food,

a life without borders and the freedom to dream.

Contents

La Seine

Rue de l'Université

DES GÂTEAUX
ET DU PAIN

Rue du Bac

JEAN-PAUL
HÉVIN

Rue Jacob

Rue Bonaparte

LADURÉE

Bd. St Germain

ANGELINA

MAISON DU
CHOCOLAT

Bd. Raspail

POILÂNE

Rue du Four

Rue de Sèvres

PIERRE
HERMÉ

MULOT

Rue Saint-Sulp

Rue de Babylone

Rue Saint-Sulp

MICHALAK

Rue Bonaparte

LE BON
MARCHÉ

Rue du Cherche-Midi

Rue de Rennes

Rue de Vaugirard

Jardin
du
Luxembourg

Introduction

The idea for this book came to me one weekend by the sea with our friends Delphine and David and their four kids. After several years in New York, they were moving home to Paris, and we were bereft. It was the sort of moment in a deep friendship when you realize how important ritual is in celebrating a bond. We were, that weekend, without knowing it—although we talked about it constantly—happily promising ourselves many more weekends together—weekends that would be all the more poignant, as they would require planning and travel. Ideas of where and when those weekends would take place would drift through our conversations, never far from our thoughts. It was, we sensed, a way of not saying goodbye, but it was also full of the happy certainty that we would tend to our friendship, that it mattered. Of course, little did we know that weekend in the spring of 2020 that more than a year would go by before we'd be able to gather together once more. That next time, a very happy time, would be in Paris, at a long outside table at the restaurant Les Cocottes. But I'm getting ahead of myself. That weekend by the sea in East Moriches, we feasted without fuss. Nobody hovered over a hot stove, nobody fretted about their recipes. And yet somehow by our first supper, Delphine and David's daughter, Lila, and her father had both made fruit tarts. Lila had thinly sliced fruit for a dough Delphine had made and rolled, while David had made a *tarte Tatin*. Nathan, the eldest son, had made *cannelés* in copper molds for a late-afternoon snack, and Lila had put a bowl of *madeleine* batter in the fridge to rest overnight. Delphine had prepared a gorgeous scallop ceviche and had mixed cocktails while simultaneously getting her youngest boys to practice the piano. My husband, John, and I had brought large loaves of *miche*, those great rounds of sourdough, and a tote full of good cheeses from the city. Salads were assembled, fish grilled, wine bottles opened. Verbena leaves picked for a late-night tisane. The next morning brought *café au lait* and piping hot madeleines, straight from the oven. A quick dark chocolate cake was made before a hike that ended with a swim.

There was ease to our meals. Everything was more or less served at room temperature, so there was no rush to the table. We ate with immense relish and pleasure, but all the elements seemed part of a larger ensemble. Bread, wine, cheese, salad and dark chocolate for supper on Sunday after a full day and a long lunch brought a tender close to our three days together. It was only late in bed that last night that I noted the sheer amount of baking that had been done—tarts, cakes, *cannelés*, madeleines, even a batch of *les brownies New Yorkais*. And yet it was almost impossible to remember when any of the measuring and mixing and baking had actually happened.

Having lived in Paris for many years as a child, this didn't surprise me. The French bake at home far more than we imagine. But, maybe more important, they bake far more simply than we imagine, and mostly from a range of classics that lend themselves to seasonal riffing and improvisation. What they don't do is labor over the grand and intricate *pâtisserie* that is what we've come to think of as French baking. They wisely leave pâtisserie to the *pâtissiers* and *pâtissières*—those who, after long apprenticeships, have studied at the venerable schools, such as Ferrandi or l'Institut Paul Bocuse, before honing their skills and building their reputations for decades and then, and only then, opening their own shops. This truly gets to the essence of Parisian home cooking. By and large, the French do not try to compete with their chefs, nor with the *pâtissiers*, *boulangers* or *traiteurs*. But it is equally true that I've never been in the home of a Parisian who was not a natural cook, nor one who didn't finish dinner with a little something sweet, effortlessly made and casually served. And so, while Delphine and David are *particularly* generous hosts, their way of cooking and eating is—remarkably—not altogether out of the ordinary.

The world's captivation with all things French, particularly all things Parisian, is not one I would ever wish to dispel. I fall squarely into the Francophile camp. But having lived there, my perspective is perhaps different—no less enchanted, no less fond, but perhaps a bit savvier as to the inner workings that make what is *charmant* and *délicieux* appear effortless. Whether it is tying a silk scarf or rolling a génoise, far less time is expended than would seem fair for such fabulous results. So allow me to let you in on the secret. It's very simple. The French master the classics. And, by mastering them, they are set free to improvise with confidence and panache.

The trick is having an arsenal of recipes that, once learned, become mere blueprints, allowing for myriad variations, depending on what's in season and what's in the cupboard. It is a practical approach, and the French are nothing if not practical. That, more than anything, is the essence of *savoir faire*, that distinctly Parisian know-how that blends style and functionality in every aspect of life—including popping a *gâteau* in the oven without anyone even noticing. When you know what you're doing, there's no need to overthink it. It looks easy because it *is* easy.

I've written a dessert column for the *Wall Street Journal* for close to a dozen years, and so it is no wonder, I suppose, that I want both to debunk the great myth that Parisians return home after work and whip up a batch of impossibly delicate macarons or, say, layer a mille-feuille, and also to shine a spotlight on the brilliance of French home baking because the classics are, in fact, brilliant. Many of the recipes in this book date back, in some form or another, hundreds of years, some even to the Middle Ages. They've stood the test of time because they are *inratable*—foolproof. (And just to be sure they work in the U.S. with American ingredients, I've tested and double-tested each and every one.)

Whenever I return to France, one of the things that immediately calms me in some inexplicably profound way is the immediacy of the French connection to their history. They are simply less wowed by novelty and more interested in eating what they know and love, and they appreciate it being made well and with skill. This is true throughout the country but, in Paris, there is a playful irreverence mixed in, and an ease with pivoting and changing things up. Paris is where home cooks and chefs alike borrow confidently from all regions of the country and, for that matter, the world. More and more, Parisians bake and cook with a global pantry, reaching one moment for *ras el hanout*, the Moroccan spice mix, and the next for makrut lime leaves from Thailand. The flavors of the Mediterranean—of Italy, Spain, Israel and North Africa—predominate, but the influence of the Middle East, for example, is seen in the use of saffron, floral waters and pistachios from Iran. Often the flavors of vacations—to St. Barts, Corsica, Greece—will find their way into cakes, conjuring sun and sand the way the smell of suntan lotion evokes summer. Recently, an interest in the ancient grains that had fallen from favor after World War II, when white flour became ubiquitous, has gained momentum, but perhaps more in savory dishes than in desserts.

Outside of Paris, France remains deeply differentiated by region. Identity is still profoundly linked to the land. And the gifts of the land, region to region, are notably different—

from the Agen prunes grown in the Aquitaine to the walnuts of Périgord and Grenoble; from the apple orchards of Normandy to the golden mirabelle plums of the Lorraine; from the great lavender fields of Provence to the spicy piment d'Espelette of the Pyrénées. Nearly every French person I know has a kind of agricultural map of France imprinted on their minds. And Paris—in drawing the young from every corner of the country—has, for centuries, adopted the best of these regional specialties.

Needless to say, shopping for food in the French capital is taken very seriously indeed. All the same, Parisians love shortcuts. Walk into, say, La Grande Épicerie de Paris, the great gourmet supermarket in the seventh arrondissement, and you will see shoppers buying prepared puff pastry and freshly ground almond flour, not to mention jars of exquisite fruit suspended in sugar syrup and tender frangipane still a touch warm from the mixer. You will find dried fruit of every variety, and orange rind crystallized, candied and dipped in chocolate. And you will encounter a multitude of sugars, from raw to rock, from the lightest of powders to the moist grittiness of a dark Demerara. Inspiration is never far.

And, yet, the core French recipes remain a comforting constant, often requiring no more than the most basic and least expensive of pantry staples. So we come full circle to the secret of mastering, then riffing on, the classics. I've structured this book around that very premise, as it is at the heart of how the French cook, be it a boeuf bourguignon or a cake. A recipe for *gâteau au yaourt*, for example, is so easy it's taught in nursery school. But add a heady splash of crème de framboise and a pint of raspberries, and suddenly you have a very grown-up dessert. Or substitute some of the all-purpose flour with almond flour, add a few spoonfuls of orange blossom water, and the cake takes on yet another dimension. Or perhaps you want the zest of lemon and the herbal astringency of rosemary. Friends showing up for dinner? Drizzle on a little glaze to dress it up. It really is that easy.

Why cake, you might ask? Although Marie Antoinette didn't actually bark, "Let them eat cake," the French do have a thing for cakes. Even madeleines, *financiers* and *bouchons* are all considered little *gâteaux*, as are nut tortes, savory cakes and celebratory *bûches de Noël*. A French cake will, by and large, have less sugar, as nuance is prized over sweetness. A bit of salt will bloom the flavors. A cup of yogurt might add a moist backstage tang. Vanilla is used sparingly. The pure taste of apples is rarely masked by cinnamon. And the pucker of a lemon cake is not undermined by a thick blanket of frosting. Chocolate is most always dark and bittersweet. Gluten-free cakes abound but are rarely named as such. They simply reflect an appreciation for nuts, toasted and ground, in baking. Parisians tend to be avid tea drinkers. Think of Mariage-Frères, Palais des Thés and the teas of Fauchon and Hédiard.

Simple after-dinner infusions of verbena or mint perfume many a cake. Parisians are highly likely, when baking, to reach for a handy bottle of Calvados, Armagnac, Cognac, eau-de-vie, Poire Williams or crème de cassis and to add a splash—more to impart a depth of flavor than an overt hit of booze. Rose water and orange blossom water add delicate floral notes, as do the buds of chamomile and lavender. The French sometimes macerate fresh fruit in a little leftover white wine to serve alongside a slice of cake, but crème fraîche is more or less *de rigueur*. A cake may be lightly glazed or dusted with cocoa or confectioners' sugar, but rarely heavily iced. These modest cakes have a timeless, understated elegance. No wonder they are classic.

Of course, no book about gâteaux would be complete without many a *gâteau au chocolat*. These cakes tend to be simple affairs, without added distractions. They are decidedly for lovers of dark chocolate, who find frosting too sweet but welcome a thin blanket of ganache and maybe the foil of cool, tangy crème fraîche. These are the cakes of late-night dinner parties and grown-up birthdays. None take longer than fifteen minutes to assemble, but their flavors will linger.

For something lighter and more playful, a dacquoise, with its layers of meringue and Chantilly, is the answer. These are not the dacquoises you might purchase in a pâtisserie or order in a restaurant—those might be intricate things of refined beauty built into perfect circles and filled with alternating flavors of buttercream and coated in a mirrored glaze. Most Parisians would not even think to attempt something so involved, when a better version can be easily bought on nearly every corner! Instead, they take the idea behind a favorite cake and simplify, doing away with decorative flourishes and belabored details. This is also true of layered cakes. At home, this is nothing more than a génoise (spongecake) brushed with a simple syrup and covered in berries, ganache or Chantilly. How you flavor the syrup and Chantilly—these are the only decisions requiring a little thought. The actual baking becomes second nature.

In an age when rituals and traditions have grown scarce and diluted, there is beauty in the very French belief in the power of celebration—and in the fabulous, largely unchanging cakes that embody and express it. I've included a few favorites, from a moist spice cake (see page 90) to a coconut yuzu bûche de Noël (see page 271). Despite being among the most adored of cakes, these yule logs disappear from sight by the first of January—leaving the French to yearn for them for the ensuing eleven months. Or, to make nearly the same thing and call it a *rouleau*. In early summer, this might be filled with tiny *fraises des bois*—wild forest strawberries—and in late summer, with ripe peaches.

And let's not forget savory cakes! *Les cake salés*, as they are called, the French having appropriated the word "cake" for a loaf, sweet or salty. These are ingenious quick breads. Imagine the filling of your favorite sandwich, chopped up and tossed into batter and baked into a flavorful, tender loaf. The good ones are similar in taste and texture to a gougère. In other words, fabulously cheesy. These cakes can be wrapped up for school, for travel, for picnics. They keep for a few days and do well toasted when past their prime. Cut into batons, they are served with aperitifs. Sliced thickly and served with salad, they are supper. Too easy, too good not to include.

My hope, in writing this book, is that you will never again be wracked with baking nerves or find yourself slaving away over impossible feats of pâtisserie in a hot kitchen while everyone else is sipping Sancerre in the cool breeze of a garden. My hope is that you will discover that the Parisian culinary ease that is so chic and astonishing is a choice, not a genetic superpower. All it takes is a little know-how and even less practice. My hope is that the core recipes in this book will set you free to reach, with a sure hand, for whatever fruit, spice, liqueur, nut, chocolate, citrus, flower or herb just happens to meet your fancy, and that you will toss it in your batter with a knowing smile, because your recipe is, well, *inratable*.

Equipment

BLENDERS: I use a Vitamix to grind spices and coffee, and to combine ingredients that don't need to be whisked but should be well integrated, such as yogurt, eggs and vanilla. It's very lazy of me, but I like shortcuts, and a few quick pulses does the trick. If you don't have a blender powerful enough to grind spices, you will need a spice grinder or small coffee grinder. Cardamom, for example, needs to be freshly ground, as do star anise and fennel seeds. The good news is that whole spices last far longer than ground ones, so you will buy them less frequently.

CAKE DOMES: I love these. Most non-iced cakes should sit at room temperature, not in the fridge, as the cold can change their texture, making them denser. This can be an advantage in certain chocolate cakes, but rarely in a cake with a delicate crumb. Enter the dome, that relic of the 1950s. Here's why I love it: it keeps air and bugs out but, unlike aluminum foil or plastic wrap, it never touches the surface of your cake, so your ganache or buttercream stays smooth. My one word of warning: don't cover a cake until it is truly at room temperature, or the trapped warm, moist air will make it soggy.

CAKE PANS: Most of the cakes in this book are made in round pans, loaf pans or on sheet pans. The specialty items you may not have and will, no doubt, want are for madeleines, financiers and bouchons. At a bare minimum, consider the following:

ESSENTIALS

Loaf pans in standard (8½ x 4½ inches) and large (9 x 5 inches)

Round cake pans with diameters of 8, 9 and 10 inches

Springform pans with diameters of 8, 9 and 10 inches

Madeleine molds—metal or silicone

Financier molds—metal or silicone

Bundt pan, 10–12 cups

Half and quarter sheet pans

NONESSENTIALS

French loaf pans (long and skinny)

Savarin or baba au rhum molds

Bouchon molds

Ramekins

Springform pan with a 7-inch diameter

Muffin pan

When in doubt, use metal. USA Pan makes excellent baking pans in aluminized steel, while NordicWare—famous for their Bundt pans—makes an excellent line in cast aluminum.

The French have been baking with silicone for quite some time now. Silpat makes easy-to-release mats and molds, and their products are readily available. For silicone cake pans, I use Silikomart, an Italian line of fanciful and practical molds that I order online. Both Silpat and Silikomart molds need to be set on a baking sheet, as they are flexible. Silicone is non-stick and some brands are dishwasher-safe.

HANDHELD ELECTRIC BEATERS: Even with a stand mixer, I find these indispensable because you can move them about the kitchen. They are sometimes called "handheld electric mixers," but what they really do well is beat. My mother still has the same set she bought long before I was born. We've held it so many times, I think it's molded itself perfectly to the shape of our hands. I use mine for smaller volumes, such as whipping half a cup of cream or beating two or three egg whites or whisking anything over the stove.

OVENS AND OVEN THERMOMETERS: Sometimes I think ovens are like fingerprints, and that no two are ever exactly alike. While this may not be true, what is worth remembering is that gas ovens fluctuate wildly in temperature, as if set on a pendulum. And even the very best are rarely accurate. However, a gas oven is terrific for baking many a French cake, as the recipes are old enough to date back to the hearth. Gas oven heat rises from a base heat source, and that helps a cake rise, particularly those made without leaveners that are relying entirely on the power of eggs to generate lift. Electric ovens tend to be far more accurate, and their convection settings truly circulate an even temperature. My word of warning about electric ovens is in the force of their convection settings. The higher-end models have a professional power to them that is markedly stronger than their basic counterparts. This can mean a difference in baking time of as much as ten minutes. The solution is simple: Buy an oven thermometer. Use it religiously. Set it where you can see it easily through the door, and so without having to open the oven. Check it before you put a cake in to bake and glance at it every ten minutes to see if you need to adjust the settings. If you are using the convection setting in a Viking, Wolf, Gaggenau, Miele, La Cornue or Molteni, for example—and lucky you!—you may need to set your oven temperature twenty degrees lower and start checking for doneness ten minutes earlier than specified. And always trust your nose. If the kitchen smells like cake, the cake is probably fully baked.

PARCHMENT PAPER: I almost never bake anything without inserting a round, square, or rectangle of parchment in the pan. It makes tipping even the stickiest of cakes out of their pans easy and cuts cleanup in half. I don't use waxed paper, however. I prefer the purity of the If You Care line of parchment sheets and rolls. It's a brand I trust and can find at most markets. King Arthur Flour makes very useful pre-cut parchment rounds that fit right in the bottom of cake pans. I keep a supply of these in all sizes. When using these rounds, do make sure to butter not just the sides of the pan but really get into those edges separating the base from the sides. This is often where cakes stick.

RUBBER SPATULA: Essential for folding and for transferring batter. Keep one exclusively for baking, so that it does not absorb odors from garlic and the like.

SCALES: Please buy a scale if you don't have one! Some are no thicker than an iPad and can be tucked away almost anywhere. Baking, even home baking, is as much science as it is art and play. Channel your inner chemist. I include the weight of flour, as everyone measures it a bit differently, and I'd like to remove that variable. The same is true of confectioners' sugar. And chocolate? Only standard chocolate chips can be measured by the cup, and I rarely call for them. I use grams, as that is the standard among pastry chefs here and in France. If you zero your scale after each addition, you can usually add all your dry ingredients without having to dirty lots of measuring cups. All to say, it is an accurate, faster and neater way to measure.

STAND MIXER: I've loved my kitchens—just not their size. Even when we lived in a four-story Brooklyn townhouse, my kitchen was tiny. It had a great big window facing our garden and fourteen-foot ceilings, but not nearly enough counter space for a stand mixer. When Covid locked us all down in terror, we moved to our house in Connecticut—another very small but open kitchen—and I started testing and double- and triple-testing the recipes in this book. It was then that I finally gave in and set a stand mixer on our tiny island, and that is where it will live forever more. I may be late to the fan club, but there's simply no turning back. Being able to walk away and have a machine whisk egg whites into meringue or a pint of cream into Chantilly makes most every cake in this book an easy and quick affair. If you have the room and resources for a stand mixer, buy one and you'll want to hug it for every minute it saves you. And if you don't, your cakes will taste all the sweeter for your efforts. Maybe. French cake batters are, by and large, meant to be whisked. Use the whisk attachment on your mixer as the default for all the recipes in this book. In fact, I almost never take mine off.

Ingredients

BAKING POWDER: Many French cakes rely entirely on the levity of beaten eggs, but when leavener is called for, it's usually baking powder. I use Bob's Red Mill double-acting baking powder. If you don't see it listed, don't worry! It's not a mistake—it merely means you can rely on the eggs to give height.

BUTTER: It is, quite simply, the most essential and most beloved ingredient in any French kitchen. It graces every table, and it is the stuff of all good things, from the eponymous *beurre blanc* to a Breton butter cake. Which butter to buy is a subject taken extremely seriously, with certain regions in Brittany and Normandy holding their own *Appellation d'Origine Contrôlée* to ward off imposters. In these rich, fertile lands, you will find at least a dozen very specific varieties of butter for sale in every *fromagerie* and *laiterie*. And you will, of course—of course, because you are reading a book entitled *Gâteau*—be unable to resist *beurre pâtissier*, with a fat content of no less than ninety-nine-point-eight percent, or *beurre tendre*, a butter that is whipped to tender perfection. American butters generally have around eighty percent butter-fat, meaning that roughly eighteen percent is water and maybe two percent is milk solids. European butters have a higher fat content, with around eighty-two to eighty-six percent butterfat. This difference may seem small, but it is disproportionately large in taste and texture. They are more expensive, but when butter is the star—and, it often is, if only to those paying attention—spring for one when you can. Échiré, Président, Plugrá and Beurre d'Isigny won't disappoint. Looking for a local choice? Vermont Creamery Cultured Butter delivers a smooth finish. When baking, I buy unsalted butter, as it allows me to control the amount of salt in a batter, and even a mere pinch is usually a smart addition. Most often, you'll see that I call for butter to be at room temperature. Thirty minutes won't do the trick. Take it out of the fridge hours in advance or leave it on the counter overnight. *Beurre noisette* is browned butter, made by melting butter in a skillet and then letting it continue to cook until it turns a dark golden hue and smells like hazelnuts. It's frequently used in madeleine and financier batters.

CHOCOLATE: My favorite ingredient. I could write a book about chocolate, but let me say what I need to say in one word: Valrhona. I hate to specify a brand, particularly an expensive one, but it is, hands down, the best baking chocolate and cocoa I know. The quality of your chocolate is often the difference between baking a good cake and a great one. Nearly all my favorite French pâtissiers consider Valrhona's Guanaja as their go-to staple. At seventy percent cacao, it is dark, bittersweet, intense and has a long, velvety finish, like a great Bordeaux. If you are going to keep one chocolate in your pantry, make it this one. For ganache, I'll often switch to Valrhona's Manjari, which at sixty-four percent cacao is still dark but heading toward semisweet. It has the faint undercurrent of dried berries, a sort of sweet and fresh tanginess under a rich blanket. I particularly like it paired with orange or raspberries. Another favorite is Valrhona Caraïbe, which balances a roasted nuttiness with a smooth and deep finish. It's an excellent foil for rum. Milk chocolate was always the one chocolate I could easily resist. Until, that is, I tried Valrhona Dulcey. At thirty-five percent cacao, it is firmly on the milky side, but it has an almost caramel-like depth of flavor and reminds me of my father's camel hair coat: soft, elegant, sophisticated. Not at all like any other milk chocolate I've ever tasted. And no, Valrhona isn't paying me to write this.

Always melt chocolate either in a microwave or in a bain-marie, or double boiler. This simple contraption of one pot or a metal bowl set over a larger pot filled with simmering water is easy to rig. No special equipment needed, so long as you have two smallish pots of different sizes. The chocolate sits in the top pot and is warmed by the rising steam; it should not touch the water. Chocolate burns easily, so it should be gently melted, then immediately removed from heat. And one last pointer: chocolate absorbs other flavors easily, so store it well wrapped in aluminum foil.

EGGS: I use large organic eggs and, unless otherwise specified, that is what is called for in my recipes. The difference in egg sizes may seem insignificant, but it is, in fact, huge in impact. If you have the wrong size eggs, please use a scale to determine how many you will need. A large egg weighs approximately fifty-seven grams. If you buy eggs at a farmers market or have your own chickens, be aware that farm eggs might be grand in flavor, but they are, well, petite in size. Please bake with eggs that are really and truly at room temperature. That means removing them from the fridge at least an hour before starting. Don't have the time? Set the eggs

in a bowl of warm water for ten minutes, adding hot water every few minutes to keep the temperature up. To beat egg whites, your mixing bowl must be clean and dry. If a bit of shell falls in, use a large piece of shell to attract it and remove it. Of course, don't serve uncooked eggs to children, the elderly, the pregnant or the immunocompromised.

EXTRACTS: Unless a cake is meant to taste of vanilla, it should be a mere member of the orchestra, not an overpowering diva who screams diner pound cake and overprocessed packaged cookies. Vanilla is a thing of beauty, as it can either sing sweet ballads solo or hum as backup, stirring up our memories of childhood desserts. It's an emotional ingredient for much of America, less so for the French. Quality is key. I use Nielsen-Massey, generally their Madagascar Bourbon. For fruit desserts, I sometimes switch to Tahitian, for spiced ones, Mexican, but the Madagascar is my pantry staple. When I want to minimize liquid, I'll switch to the seeds of a vanilla bean or vanilla paste, but the extract distributes most evenly through a batter. Almond and coffee extracts are also essential, to boost flavor when only a little liquid can be added, such as when making Chantilly, buttercreams or ganache. Almond cakes benefit from almond extract, particularly when store-bought almond flour, rather than freshly ground almonds, is used.

FLOUR: French flours are many and varied, and each different from American flours. Walk into a French market, and you will find seven standard types of flour, and none will be called anything remotely like "all-purpose." What most Parisians bake with is much closer to cake flour than our all-purpose flour, and so that is what I most often call for in this book. The difference is notable, so go to the small trouble of keeping a jar of cake flour on hand. All the recipes in this book have been tested with King Arthur Flour. Please note that pastry flour and cake flour are not the same thing. When possible, use a scale to measure. If using measuring cups, fluff up the flour with a fork or spoon, then gently spoon it into the cup and, finally, level that off with the flat side of a knife.

NUT FLOURS: I can't open a bag of nut flour without a pang of guilt. When I wrote *The London Cookbook*, my friend and one of the chefs I most admire, Jeremy Lee, referred to these as "tasteless, stale things that should be banished from kitchens entirely." But in the last few years, nut flours have become so popular, thanks to the gluten-free movement and a growing awareness of the health benefits of nuts, that the turnover is now high and the products relatively fresh. I buy either King Arthur or Bob's Red Mill. I keep almond and hazelnut flour, tightly sealed, in the freezer or fridge (depending on where I have room) to preserve their freshness. That said, there's no comparison in taste between freshly ground nuts and store-bought nut flour so, if and when you have the time, put your food processor to work. Use a cold blade and cold nuts so that you end up with nut flour, not nut butter. For cakes, I always use peeled and blanched nuts, as the skin of nuts tends to be bitter.

ORANGE BLOSSOM AND ROSE WATERS: These floral waters are nearly as common in Paris as they are throughout the Middle East. Rose is the flavor of some of the most beloved macarons sold at Pierre Hermé, Ladurée and Fauchon. At home, rose water is routinely sprinkled on fresh strawberries and stirred into yogurt. It perfumes all manner of cakes, from pistachio to berry, usually added to either soaking syrups or glazes, and it can give a hint of fragrance to Chantilly or buttercream. Orange blossom perfumes many a madeleine recipe, offering that ephemeral floral note that lingers on in our memories. A spoonful is often added to almond cakes and orange cakes, to summer stone fruits and to winter citrus. I add a few drops to a spritzer of orange juice and San Pellegrino most every day. Search out natural floral waters. Anything artificial will smell and taste of soap. And go easy at first, as some brands are stronger than others. Nielsen-Massey calls their floral extracts waters, but they are really extracts and only the tiniest amount is needed. As rose water can dissipate in baking, some bakers will turn to a rose extract. I prefer to add rose or orange blossom water to a soaking syrup, brushed on after baking. Go-to brands are Mymouné, Cortas and Ó Florale.

POTATO STARCH, CORN STARCH: Both are used far more frequently in France than they are in the U.S., particularly when baking without gluten. They are remarkably light and delicate and can often be used interchangeably.

SUGAR: Most of my recipes call for white granulated sugar or confectioners' sugar, the latter often being used in the most delicate of cakes, as well as in glazes. French sugar is slightly finer than American granulated sugar, and sometimes you'll find that I call for superfine sugar. But the two are largely interchangeable. When measuring light brown sugar, I do not pack it down. Instead, I measure it the way flour is measured: fluff it up with a fork, spoon it into a metal measuring cup and level off the top with the flat side of a knife. Brown sugar needs to be freshly opened or stored sealed, as it hardens when it loses moisture.

Spirits

———————————————————————

When in doubt, add a splash. That's the motto on booze in French cooking, and for good reason. After roasting a chicken, for example, it's customary to deglaze the pan with a glass of wine or, in the autumn, a good pouring of Calvados. A little Cognac and butter swirled into a pan after searing a steak adds a sumptuous note to a carnivorous pleasure. Salmon is poached in white wine, duck is braised in Armagnac, and bouillabaisse is finished with Pernod. The same principle holds true for dessert. Brush a simple génoise cake with rum or Grand Marnier, and suddenly you're in business. Try swirling a little crème de fraise des bois onto a *fraisier* (page 176) or a little crème de cassis into your whipped cream or a little crème de pêche onto a simple peach yogurt cake. You'll taste the little grown-up lift. The French will also turn to a bottle of liqueur before they'll reach in the cupboard for an extract. For example, instead of almond extract, they'll use Amaretto Disaronno. Instead of hazelnut extract, they'll use Frangelico. Instead of orange extract, they'll instinctively pull out a bottle of Grand Marnier or Cointreau. Generally, replace ¼ teaspoon extract with 2 teaspoons liqueur.

I rarely make intricate cocktails at home, but I do try to keep the following spirits on hand for drinking, cooking and baking. Which leads me to the question of affordability. There's no reason to buy a very expensive bottle of Cognac to use in the kitchen. But don't buy something you wouldn't want to drink. You're adding it, after all, because it tastes good, and so taste good it must.

ABRICOT DU ROUSSILLON: Such a beauty. Add some to Champagne, Chantilly and, of course, apricots.

AMARETTO: This will augment the flavor of almonds in a cake and is delicious in ganache and Chantilly.

ARMAGNAC: A classic with prunes and chestnuts, Armagnac is found in many a winter cake. Everything Armagnac touches seems to become infinitely more French, a sort of exponential magic. Its flavor is refined but also timeless, conjuring centuries of tradition and taste.

CALVADOS: An essential in apple cakes. I say that as someone who spent childhood weekends in Normandy, where to say otherwise would be sacrilegious. The best rival Armagnac in depth and beauty, but the taste of apples sets it apart. It bears almost no relation to applejack, which is too young, too fruity and too fiery to compete. Clear Creek Distillery makes an apple brandy that has been aged eight years and is the closest American option I've found.

CHAMBORD: This black raspberry liqueur is made in the Loire Valley near the famous Château de Chambord, my favorite of the great French castles. It is delicious in a soaking syrup for a génoise topped with fresh berries and Chantilly. Added to buttercream, it complements a lemon cake beautifully.

COGNAC: Cognac offers a rounded, enveloping elegance that gives a complex dimension to even a simple crème Chantilly.

COINTREAU AND GRAND MARNIER: Both are made with oranges, but Grand Marnier, made with bitter oranges, has a brandy base and is aged in oak. Cointreau is sweeter, transparent and livelier, but less complex. If I want that citrusy brightness, I turn to Cointreau. If I want a sophisticated undercurrent of orange, I reach for Grand Marnier.

CRÈME DE CASSIS: It is everywhere, and for good reason. The ruby of a kir, it is what elevates a simple coulis of raspberries as easily as it turns a génoise syrup or buttercream into something exquisitely French.

CRÈME DE FRAMBOISE: Use this as you would crème de cassis whenever the taste of raspberries is desired. Clearly a great match for a bowl of summer berries, in a coulis or added to a chocolate ganache. A tablespoon will lightly scent a batch of madeleines or financiers.

CRÈME DE PÊCHE: Add half an ounce to a glass of Champagne and you will understand why it is on this list. And then there's the issue of peaches. So often, they are lackluster if not bought at a farm stand. A spoonful or two of crème de pêche will offer that peachy mouthful, in a grown-up way.

FRANGELICO: A wonderful alternative to hazelnut extract, Frangelico has notes of vanilla in it as well as a touch of coffee.

LIMONCELLO: I use this Italian lemon liqueur all the time. On a bowl of berries, in Chantilly, as a soaking syrup, in a glaze, brushed on a génoise or brightening a buttercream. Limonsardo is a Sardinian version that is a little less sweet.

POIRE WILLIAMS: This pear liqueur amplifies the pear notes in a pear cake, but, as my mother taught me, it is also lovely in chocolate mousse. Pear and almond are the closest of friends and show up together in everything from simple yogurt pear cakes to frangipane pear tarts.

RUM: Dark rum is as ubiquitous to French cake as vanilla is to American cake. But the quantities used are different. As an extract, vanilla is quite potent. Rum, a little less so. If substituting, add three to four times the amount of rum as you would vanilla. Or add both, as familiar vanilla dances well with the more spirited rum.

ST-GERMAIN OR FLEUR DE SUREAU SAUVAGE: Elderflower likes lemons, limes and roses.

Critical Intel, *aka* Cheat Sheet

All eggs are large and should be at room temperature.

All butter is unsalted and preferably European.

All milk and yogurt should be whole and unflavored.

When measuring flour, the rule is fluff, spoon, level off! If not using a scale, use a fork or small whisk to aerate the flour, then gently spoon it into a metal measuring cup and level off the top with the back of a knife.

Confectioners' sugar should be freshly opened and measured the same way as flour. If using it in a glaze, it may require sifting.

When measuring brown sugar, never pack it in! Never stamp it down! Brown sugar should be freshly opened, lightly spooned into a metal measuring cup and leveled off with the back of a knife.

Nuts and oils go rancid, brown sugar becomes rock solid, spices lose their fragrance, almond paste dries out, baking soda loses power and confectioners' sugar clumps. Check your ingredients and expiration dates.

Citrus zest, unless otherwise specified, should be finely grated on a Microplane.

No two ovens are the same. Invest in an oven thermometer! If using a powerful convection oven, reduce the temperature by ten to fifteen degrees Fahrenheit.

The French use whisks more than any other tool in baking. For the recipes in this book, always use the whisk attachment on your stand mixer, unless otherwise specified.

If using a stand mixer or handheld electric beaters, the rule of thumb is to cream butter and sugar at medium or medium-high speed and to whip egg whites or cream for a crème Chantilly at high speed. If using a KitchenAid stand mixer, that would be speed settings six and eight.

To preserve the texture of their crumb, cakes, unless iced with buttercream, should be kept at room temperature. Some chocolate cakes like a little time to chill. This is particularly helpful when encouraging a molten cake to set without further baking.

Raw eggs should not be consumed by anyone pregnant, elderly, or immunocompromised. And raw honey should not be consumed by babies under the age of one.

Parchment paper will save you from buttering and flouring pans. Keep a roll or two on hand.

Assume most every recipe calls for a dollop of crème fraîche or crème Chantilly. Having a pint of the former in the fridge at all times keeps the sublime within easy reach.

The
SIMPLEST
of the
CLASSICS

Les Gâteaux au Yaourt

Les Quatre-Quarts

Les Cakes

Gâteau au Yaourt

—— Yogurt Cake ——

Every child in France learns this recipe in their *maternelle*, or nursery school, as it could not be easier to memorize or to make. French yogurt is sold in little half-cup jars, and these jars serve as the measuring cups in this recipe. You can find them now in the U.S., or you can use a half-cup measuring cup.

The yogurt and oil make this a forgiving and moist recipe. It will be as good on day two as day one, if well wrapped once it comes fully to room temperature. To dress a yogurt cake up, glaze it or dust with confectioners' sugar. For inspiration, look to the variations I offer for Quatre-Quarts (page 19). But my biggest advice is not to overlook this simplest of recipes. I can't tell you how many times French friends have made a last-minute *gâteau au yaourt* from memory, adding whatever citrus zest or fruit they have on hand, maybe sneaking in a splash of rum or kirsch for good measure, or perhaps coating the surface in a little warm apricot jam. The cake offers a tasty trip down Nostalgia Lane, for sure, but it makes easily as many appearances at casual dinner parties as it does in the classroom.

Before baking powder became a cake staple, eggs provided the lift. They'd be whisked with the yogurt and sugar until pale and thick, but never so much so that I'd recommend using electric beaters. Likewise, vanilla is a more recent addition and, by recent, I mean in the last hundred or so years. Amazingly, you can add the ingredients in whatever order you'd like, but never let egg yolks sit long on sugar, as they will form a skin. When in doubt, I remember this recipe as 1, 2, 3, then 1, 2, 3.

I'm including two basic versions, the traditional and an ever-so-slightly more involved version.

VERSION 1

- 1 jar / ½ cup / 125 grams whole plain yogurt
- 2 jars / 1 cup / 200 grams granulated sugar
- 3 large eggs, at room temperature
- 1 jar / ½ cup neutral oil, such as canola or grapeseed
- 2 teaspoons baking powder
- 3 jars / 1½ cups / 180 grams all-purpose or cake flour

Preheat the oven to 350°F. Butter and flour an 8½ x 4½-inch loaf pan.

Empty the yogurt from its little jar into a mixing bowl. Add the eggs and whisk to combine. Using the yogurt jar as a measuring cup, add 2 jars of sugar. Whisk well. Whisk in 3 jars of flour, the baking powder, then 1 jar of oil. Whisk until homogenous.

Pour into the prepared pan and bake for 35–45 minutes, or until a knife inserted in the center comes out clean.

VERSION 2

- 1 jar / ½ cup / 125 grams whole plain yogurt
- 3 large eggs, at room temperature
- 1 teaspoon vanilla extract or paste
- The grated zest of one lemon, lime or orange
- 2 jars / 1 cup / 200 grams granulated sugar
- 3 jars / 1½ cups / 180 grams all-purpose or cake flour
- 2 teaspoons baking powder
- ¼ teaspoon fine sea salt
- 1 jar / ½ cup neutral oil, such as canola or grapeseed

Preheat the oven to 350°F. Butter and flour an 8½ x 4½-inch loaf pan.

Whisk the yogurt and eggs together. Whisk in the vanilla extract and lemon zest. Add the sugar and whisk to thoroughly combine. Add the flour, baking powder and salt and whisk just to combine. Add the oil and whisk until homogenous.

Pour into the prepared pan and bake for 35–45 minutes, or until a knife inserted in the center comes out clean.

Note: This recipe can also be made in an 8-inch springform or a 9-inch round cake pan. A 9-inch cake will only take around 30–35 minutes to bake, whereas an 8-inch round will take closer to 40 and a medium loaf between 35 and 45.

Gâteau au Yaourt Citron-Thym

—— *Lemon Thyme Yogurt Cake* ——

A few herbs and a little less sugar drive this classic yogurt cake just shy of the border between sweet and savory. It's definitely still on the sweet side, but the herbs give it a faint herbaceous note and the olive oil a little extra character. That said, choose a mild, fruity, or buttery extra-virgin olive oil, not a green one, which would be too overpowering. I've included lemon thyme leaves here, but plain thyme, rosemary, verbena or tarragon may be substituted. Rosemary is potent, so reduce the amount to one teaspoon, then mince it.

CAKE

1½ jars / ¾ cup / 150 grams granulated sugar

The grated zest of 1 lemon

1 jar / ½ cup / 125 grams whole plain yogurt

3 large eggs, at room temperature

3 jars / 1½ cups / 180 grams all-purpose or cake flour

2 teaspoons baking powder

¼ teaspoon fine sea salt

1½ teaspoons fresh lemon thyme leaves

1 jar / ½ cup extra-virgin olive oil

GLAZE

Juice of 2 lemons or the juice of 1 lemon plus 1 tablespoon limoncello

¼–½ cup / 30–60 grams confectioners' sugar

Lemon thyme leaves, for decoration, or a rosemary sprig or two.

CAKE

Preheat the oven to 350°F. Butter and flour an 8½ x 4½-inch loaf pan.

Combine the sugar and lemon zest in a bowl and, using your fingertips, rub them together to distribute the citrus oils.

Whisk the yogurt and eggs together. Add the zesty sugar and whisk to thoroughly combine. Add the flour, baking powder, salt and lemon thyme and whisk just to combine. Add the oil and whisk until homogenous.

Pour into the prepared pan and bake for 35–45 minutes, or until a knife inserted in the center comes out clean.

GLAZE

Prepare the glaze by mixing the lemon juice and confectioners' sugar together until smooth. Drizzle this over the cake once it has come to room temperature. Scatter the lemon thyme leaves, for decoration.

Note: This recipe can also be made in an 8-inch springform or a 9-inch round cake pan. A 9-inch cake will only take around 30–35 minutes to bake, whereas an 8-inch round will take closer to 40 and a medium loaf between 35 and 45.

Gâteau au Yaourt pour le Dîner

— *Dinner Party Yogurt Cake* —

A few small changes, including a Grand Marnier soaking syrup and a rum glaze turn a childhood favorite into a dinner party classic. If you like candied orange peel, chop up a handful and add it.

CAKE

2 jars / 1 cup / 200 grams granulated sugar

The grated zest of 1 orange

1 jar / ½ cup /125 grams whole plain yogurt

3 large eggs, at room temperature

1 teaspoon vanilla extract

3 jars / 1½ cups / 180 grams all-purpose or cake flour

2 teaspoons baking powder

¼ teaspoon fine sea salt

1 jar / ½ cup neutral oil, such as canola or grapeseed

SOAKING SYRUP

2 tablespoons Grand Marnier

2 tablespoons orange juice

¼ cup / 50 grams superfine sugar

GLAZE

¾ cup apricot jam or marmalade

2 teaspoons rum or water

CAKE

Preheat the oven to 350°F. Butter and flour an 8½ x 4½-inch loaf pan.

Combine the sugar and orange zest in a bowl and, using your fingertips, rub them together to distribute the citrus oils.

Whisk the yogurt and eggs together. Add the zesty sugar and vanilla and whisk to thoroughly combine. Add the flour, baking powder and salt and whisk just to combine. Add the oil and whisk just until homogenous.

Pour into the prepared pan and bake for 35–45 minutes, or until a knife inserted in the center comes out clean.

SOAKING SYRUP

Prepare the syrup by heating the Grand Marnier and orange juice in a microwave until warm, but not hot. Stir in the sugar to dissolve. Drizzle this over the cake while still warm.

GLAZE

To make the glaze, warm the jam with the rum over low heat. Strain. Brush onto the cake once it has cooled to room temperature.

Note: *This recipe can also be made in an 8-inch springform or 9-inch round cake pan. A 9-inch cake will only take around 30–35 minutes to bake, whereas an 8-inch round will take closer to 40 and a medium loaf between 35 and 45.*

Gâteau au Yaourt à la Farine d'Amande

—— *Almond Yogurt Cake* ——

Almond flour has been a pantry staple in Paris for as long as anyone can remember. It happens to be less expensive than it is in the U.S. and, perhaps because of the turnover, usually quite fresh. In the States, it's still seen primarily as an alternative to flour for people with gluten sensitivity or for the health conscious, who like it for its protein content. Almond flour provides texture and taste, and it keeps a cake moist, as almonds are naturally high in fat. The downside is that almond flour cakes don't rise quite as high. Perhaps it is for this reason that this ubiquitous cake is made with equal portions of all-purpose flour and almond flour, capturing the best of both worlds. It is light, tender and moist and lasts for days. Like the classic yogurt cake, it plays well with spices, extracts, liqueurs, syrups and floral waters. Add a little zest, some sliced almonds for crunch, perhaps a brushing of honey while still warm from the oven.

2 large eggs, at room temperature	1 cup / 100 grams almond flour
1 cup whole yogurt	1½ teaspoons baking powder
1 cup / 200 grams granulated sugar	½ teaspoon baking soda
⅓ cup vegetable or grapeseed oil	½ teaspoon fine sea salt
1 teaspoon vanilla extract or 2 teaspoons dark rum	1 cup / 120 grams all-purpose flour
The grated zest of 1 lemon, lime or orange	

Preheat the oven to 350°F. Butter and flour a 9 x 5-inch loaf pan.

In a large mixing bowl, whisk together the eggs, yogurt, sugar, vegetable oil, vanilla and lemon zest until smooth. Add the almond flour, baking powder, baking soda and salt and whisk thoroughly until completely smooth. Sprinkle the all-purpose flour onto the batter and fold it in with a rubber spatula until no streaks of flour remain.

Pour into the prepared pan and bake for 40 minutes, or until a knife inserted in the center comes out clean. (If your oven runs hot, start checking after 35 minutes.)

VARIATIONS

Add ¼ teaspoon almond extract when adding the vanilla extract.

Replace the vanilla with 1 tablespoon of Amaretto Disaronno.

Scatter ⅓–½ cup sliced almonds evenly over the top of the cake before baking it.

Warm ½ cup apricot jam with 1 teaspoon water. Strain and brush over the cake once it has cooled to room temperature.

Gâteau au Yaourt et aux Poires

———— Yogurt Cake with Pears ————

Whenever I needed this cake, it was there for me. The day we sold our house in Brooklyn, which we'd lived in for eighteen years. The memories flooded me. Our son Garrick's first steps replayed in my mind like a cherished home movie on repeat. No thought of the future could shake me out of the past. Sometimes the weather seems right in sync with one's state of mind, and that day was gray, biting and blustery. When I set out for a walk, it started to hail. Then an icy snow whipped about, in every which direction. And so I baked this cake. It's not a new recipe. In fact, it is a classic yogurt cake, but I'd always made it with apples. And it is terrific with apples. But made with Anjou pears and a generous pour of Poire Williams, it left all of us defenseless. Of course, we were already defenseless. But a slice of this still warm from the oven—and you must try it warm from the oven—nurtured us back to a state of grace.

If you are in France, you can, of course, measure out the ingredients using a yogurt jar. One yogurt jar of yogurt, two yogurt jars of confectioners' sugar, three yogurt jars of flour. This cake is baked in an eight-inch springform pan and does get quite tall. The beauty of it lies in the sweet freshness of the pears, baked until they are just starting to soften into the batter. The Poire Williams doesn't read as boozy, but instead seems only to augment the taste of the pears. Speaking of pears, use either Anjou or Comice. Ripe, but only just. When making it with pears, I recommend slices that are a fourth to a third of an inch thick and placed so that they are snuggled up next to each other. Apples, however, can be sliced quite thinly and the slices should overlap each other in concentric circles. Resist the urge to add Calvados or spice. This cake is meant to be the pure and delicate expression of whichever fruit you choose.

- ½ cup / 125 grams whole yogurt
- 1 cup plus 1 tablespoon / 120 grams confectioners' sugar, plus more for dusting, optional
- 2 large eggs, at room temperature, lightly beaten with a fork
- 1½ cups plus 1 tablespoon / 190 grams all-purpose flour
- 2 teaspoons baking powder
- ¼ teaspoon fine sea salt
- ½ cup mild oil, such as vegetable, canola, grapeseed, sunflower or safflower
- 1 tablespoon Poire Williams
- ½ teaspoon vanilla extract
- 2–3 just-ripe Anjou or Comice pears
- Apricot jam, for glazing, optional

Preheat the oven to 350°F. Generously butter an 8-inch springform pan and dust it with flour.

Spoon the yogurt into a good-sized mixing bowl. Add the confectioners' sugar and the eggs. Using a whisk, a rubber spatula or handheld electric beaters, whisk until the batter is homogenous and smooth. Fold in the flour, baking powder and salt. Pour in the oil, Poire Williams and vanilla. Give the mixture a thorough whisking.

Pour the batter into the prepared cake pan.

Peel, core and slice the pears ¼- to ⅓-inch thick. Arrange them in concentric circles on the batter. Don't push them in, just set them on top.

Bake the cake for 55–65 minutes, or until a knife inserted in the center of the cake (avoiding a slice of pear) comes out clean.

If glazing, heat about 2 tablespoons of apricot jam, strain it and brush it over the surface of the cake. This will give it a little sheen but is not necessary. Likewise, a late and faint showering of confectioners' sugar is a lovely touch. But not both, as the jam would make the sugar sticky.

Allow the cake to cool for 10 minutes, then serve still warm or at room temperature.

APPLE VARIATION: Replace the pears with apples that will not lose their shape when baked. Gala, Golden or Honeycrisp are all good options. Eliminate the Poire Williams. Instead, increase the vanilla to 1½ teaspoons and, if you'd like, add 2 teaspoons dark rum.

Gâteau au Miel et à la Fleur d'Oranger

—— *Orange Blossom Honey Cake* ——

A gentle cake, subtly sweet and floral, drizzled with a honey glaze. Yogurt and almond flour will keep it moist overnight.

CAKE

- 1½ cups / 180 grams cake flour
- ¾ cup / 75 grams almond flour
- 1½ teaspoons baking powder
- ½ teaspoon baking soda
- ¼ teaspoon fine sea salt
- 8 tablespoons / ½ cup unsalted butter, at room temperature
- ½ cup / 100 grams granulated sugar
- 2 large eggs, at room temperature
- ¼ cup honey, preferably orange blossom or wildflower
- The grated zest of 2 organic oranges, Meyer lemons, mandarins or clementines
- 1 cup whole yogurt or crème fraîche
- 2–3 teaspoons orange blossom water

GLAZE

- 1 large organic lemon or clementine
- 2 tablespoons unsalted butter
- 5 tablespoons honey
- ½ teaspoon vanilla extract
- 2 teaspoons orange blossom water

CAKE

Preheat the oven to 350°F. Butter the sides of a 9-inch cake pan and line the bottom with a round of parchment.

Whisk the cake flour, almond flour, baking powder, baking soda and salt to thoroughly combine.

In a stand mixer or using a handheld electric beaters, cream the butter and sugar together until pale and fluffy. One by one, add the eggs, beating well after each addition. With the mixer still running, drizzle in the honey and add the orange zest and the yogurt.

Using a rubber spatula, gingerly but decisively fold in the dry ingredients in two or three batches, just until no streaks of flour remain. Fold in the orange blossom water.

Pour the batter into the prepared pan and bake for 30–40 minutes, or until a knife inserted in the center comes out clean.

Set on a cooling rack for about 10 minutes before unmolding onto a cake plate. Glaze the cake while still warm.

GLAZE

Finely zest and juice the lemon and set aside.

In a small saucepan, melt the butter. Drizzle in the honey and stir in the vanilla and zest. Remove from heat and stir in the citrus juice and, right before using, the orange blossom water.

Drizzle the glaze over the warm cake. Serve at room temperature with a dollop of crème fraîche.

Gâteau au Yaourt, à la Verveine et aux Pêches

—— Lemon Verbena Peach Yogurt Cake ——

Look in most any Parisian herb assortment, be it a tiny box by a windowsill or a treasured garden, and you will find a disproportionately large cluster of lemon verbena growing. The leaves are plucked in the evening to make a tisane, perhaps sweetened with a bit of raw sugar. Chopped finely, the leaves are mixed into cakes, both simple and extravagant. In ice cream, its tender perfume is enveloped in cool, rich cream. In sorbet, it offers a slightly lemony, slightly floral note that pairs deliciously with stone fruit. It's perhaps the least herbaceous of the common herbs, which may explain why it is rarely found in savory dishes.

This casual yogurt cake is moist and not meant to be dolled up with Chantilly. It's served in thick slices after school, packed into lunch boxes and picnic baskets, set out with a pot of tea in the afternoon. It's an everyday, any-time-of-day cake that is, conveniently, best at room temperature. Use either fresh or frozen fruit. Peaches or blackberries are verbena's favorite dance partners, but strawberries come in at a close third. If using fresh peaches, choose fruit that is just ripe, but not overly so, or they may not hold their shape when baked.

I use a full quarter cup of verbena leaves, as I drink a *tisane à la verveine* more or less nightly. I want its familiar scent front and center. In fact, sometimes I omit the fruit altogether. For a subtler cake, reduce the amount to three tablespoons. If you don't have easy access to fresh verbena, use two tablespoons of crushed dried verbena, often sold as tea.

If serving this after dinner, try laying a few leaves on the bottom of a buttered 9-inch round cake pan before adding the batter. When you flip the cake, you will find a decorative pattern imprinted in the surface.

- 1⅓ cups / 265 grams granulated sugar
- ¼ cup packed lemon verbena or verbena leaves, finely chopped
- The grated zest of 3 organic lemons
- 1⅔ cups / 200 grams all-purpose flour
- ¼ teaspoon fine sea salt
- ½ teaspoon baking soda
- 1 teaspoon baking powder
- 1 cup / 250 grams whole yogurt, ideally creamline
- ½ cup neutral oil, such as canola, safflower or grapeseed
- 2 large eggs, at room temperature
- 1¼ cups cubed (½ inch) peeled peaches

Preheat the oven to 350°F. Butter a 9 x 5-inch loaf pan.

In a large mixing bowl, using your fingertips, rub the sugar with the verbena and lemon zest to release the citrus and herbal oils. Add the rest of the dry ingredients and whisk to thoroughly combine.

In a small mixing bowl, whisk the yogurt, oil and eggs together. (I sometimes do this in a blender or using handheld electric beaters.) Pour this into the bowl of dry ingredients and, using a rubber spatula, thoroughly stir the two together. Add the fruit and stir gently to combine.

Pour the batter into the prepared pan and bake for 60–75 minutes. (It will be done on the earlier side if using fresh fruit and the later side if using frozen.) A knife inserted in the center of the cake should come out clean. Set the cake on a cooling rack and allow it to come to room temperature before unmolding and serving it.

Le Gâteau au Yaourt avec des Fraises, de l'Eau de Rose et un Zeste de Citron

——— *Yogurt Cake with Strawberries,* ———
Rose Water and Lemon Zest

Imagine a bowl of summer strawberries warmed by the sun, brightened by the zest of a lemon. A soft breeze has just blown a rose petal onto the thick dollop of rich yogurt that tops the berries. Its perfume lingers in the air, then grows faint. Now imagine the marriage of these flavors in a moist, light cake. Baking concentrates the taste of the strawberries. Lemon keeps it lively. Yogurt offers a tangy richness. And rose water hovers in the background, discreet but seductive.

Rose water has perfumed desserts for centuries. Descriptions of cakes dating back to the Middle Ages suggest it was a delicacy reserved for the nobility. And while it has never disappeared, its popularity continued primarily in the Middle East until quite recently. Or, to be more precise, 1987, when *pâtissier extraordinaire* Pierre Hermé first sprinkled it into the batter of a raspberry macaron and launched a frenzy in Paris. Parisians waited in line for these macarons in rain, in hail, in torrential downpours. And Parisians *never* wait in line. They leave that to the tourists. Hermé was as taken with his discovery as anyone. More than twenty years later, he altered the recipe to include lychee, called it an Ispahan macaron after a hybrid damask rose and published a book on the subject.

Parisians took note and began incorporating rose water into their homemade cakes. Raspberry is the usual berry of choice for this recipe, but when wild strawberries come to the market in June, they are used in abundance. Use whatever berry meets your fancy. Simply adjust the amount of sugar as needed. As I crave this simple cake all year long, I've taken to using frozen berries. Picked at their peak, they tend to have more of that strawberry essence we love. Avoid those sitting in plastic boxes in the supermarket. You know the ones. They are beautifully red and utterly tasteless.

The choice of rose water matters. Choose a natural or organic brand, with no artificial flavoring. The taste should be delicate, more of a pink tea rose than the sultry red long-stemmed variety. Mymouné makes a lovely rose water that is easily found online. Use it sparingly. A little goes a long way. If you are not a fan of rose water, simply omit it and add a teaspoon of vanilla extract or ground cardamom.

This cake, like all yogurt cakes, can be dressed up with a dusting of confectioners' sugar. A scattering of rose petals—fresh, dried or candied—is ravishing.

Continued

- 10 ounces strawberries or other berries, fresh or frozen
- 1⅓ cups / 265 grams granulated sugar
- The grated zest of 1 large organic lemon
- 1⅔ cups / 200 grams all-purpose or cake flour
- 1 teaspoon baking powder
- ½ teaspoon baking soda
- ¼ teaspoon fine sea salt
- 1 cup whole yogurt
- ½ cup canola oil
- 2 large eggs, at room temperature, lightly broken up with a fork
- 1–3 teaspoons rose water or to taste, or 1 teaspoon vanilla extract
- 1 tablespoon confectioners' sugar, optional
- A handful of rose petals, fresh, dried or candied, optional

Preheat the oven to 350°F. Line the bottom of a 9-inch springform pan with a round of parchment. Butter the sides of the pan.

Combine the sugar and lemon zest in a large mixing bowl and rub them together with your fingertips to release the oils of the zest. Add the flour, baking powder, baking soda and salt to the bowl. Whisk to combine.

In a second mixing bowl, whisk the wet ingredients until thoroughly combined. Pour the wet ingredients into the dry and whisk until there are no streaks of flour visible and the mixture is smooth. Fold in the strawberries.

Pour the batter into the prepared pan and bake for 50–60 minutes, or until a knife inserted in the center of the cake comes out clean. (If you hit a berry, try again, as it will leave the tester a bit wet.)

Let the cake cool in the pan for 10 minutes or so before transferring it to a cake plate. If using the confectioners' sugar, wait until the cake has come to room temperature and, right before serving, lightly dust it with the sugar. If using rose petals, scatter them over the cake and give it a second, light dusting of confectioners' sugar.

Note: *If using frozen strawberries, remove them from the freezer just as you start preparing the cake batter. This is not meant to thaw them—they're best used frozen—just to soften them enough to slice them in half. If using raspberries or blackberries, leave them whole.*

Quatre-Quarts

——— Pound Cake ———

There are two recipes that every child in France memorizes in school. One is for a gâteau au yaourt and the other is for this gâteau quatre-quarts, which translates roughly as four-fourths. The principle is much the same as in an American pound cake, which traditionally called for a pound each of butter, flour, sugar and eggs. In a quatre-quarts, the eggs are weighed first in their shells, and then the butter, flour and sugar are each weighed to match that number. The true difference, however, between these two very similar cakes is in the technique used to make the batter.

When making a pound cake, butter and sugar are creamed together. In the last step, flour is folded in gently and swiftly to keep the crumb delicate. The French have an altogether different approach. For starters, they use melted butter. This coats the flour in fat, preventing the formation of gluten, which leads to a tough cake. Gluten forms when the flour is exposed to the water in egg whites and the stress of mixing. The high fat content in the butter shields the flour from the water in the egg whites and creates a moist batter that requires minimal mixing. It is about as foolproof as a recipe can be, and it lends itself to nearly any adaptation you can imagine. The French add nuts, chocolate, coffee, spices, zest, extracts, crystallized ginger, liqueurs and floral waters. A quatre-quarts doesn't need a glaze but is happy to have one. It is moist but can absorb a syrup. And, like a pound cake, it is partial to fruit.

A quatre-quatre can be made in a loaf pan, a round pan or a square one. As it is not so much a recipe but rather a ratio of equal parts, it is easily halved or doubled. The lack of a leavener such as baking powder or baking soda is not a mistake. It is simply not needed, as the eggs provide the lift. This cake couldn't be easier to make, but here are a few pointers.

Eggs. Large eggs, still in their shell, weigh about 57 grams. (Without their shell, they weigh closer to 50 grams.) But some can run small, notably fresh farm eggs. When in doubt, weigh them. You may need an extra half or full egg. If you need only half an egg, whisk the egg and add half when you add the yolks. Give the other half to your wonderful dog, who will have smelled the butter melting and will, therefore, be in need of a treat.

Flour. Either all-purpose flour or cake flour can be used. Both work nearly equally well, given that there is little chance for gluten to form when mixing the batter. That said, the equivalent of all-purpose flour in France has a percentage of protein that is somewhere between our cake flour and our all-purpose flour. Using cake flour or half cake and half all-purpose flours does seem to yield a particularly tender crumb. If you have cake flour on hand, use it. If you don't, no matter.

Butter. Yes, butter. The French have a lot to say about butter, and for good reason. In a nutshell, theirs is better. French butter has a higher fat content and gives baked goods an added layer of indulgence. If you feel like splurging, use it. If you decide to brown the butter, increase the amount you use by a tablespoon, as some of the liquid will evaporate during the browning. The French often use a slightly salted butter when baking. But as we rarely do, I've added salt to the recipe.

Vanilla. The French don't reach for vanilla when baking with quite the same habit as we do in the States. They are as likely to reach for rum or Cognac. The age-old traditional recipe for a quatre-quarts doesn't call for vanilla or any flavoring, in fact. But today, in Paris, it will most likely contain vanilla or rum and the zest of either a lemon or an orange. And that is how I've come to love it.

4 large eggs, weighing roughly 200 grams in their shells

1 cup / 200 grams granulated sugar

14 tablespoons unsalted butter, preferably European, melted and slightly cooled

2 teaspoons vanilla extract

The grated zest of 1 lemon or orange

1½ cups plus 1 tablespoon / 200 grams cake flour

½ teaspoon fine sea salt

Preheat the oven to 350°F. Butter and flour a 9 x 5-inch loaf pan.

Separate the eggs and let them come to room temperature. In a good-sized mixing bowl, whisk the egg yolks to break them up a bit. Add the sugar and whisk until they are thick and pale. Add the melted butter, vanilla and lemon zest and whisk until smooth. Add the flour and stir with a rubber spatula until no streaks remain.

Using electric beaters or in a stand mixer, beat the egg whites until they form soft peaks. Add the salt and beat until they form stiff peaks. Stir a quarter of the whites into the yolk mixture to lighten it. Then gently fold the remaining egg whites into the batter.

Pour the batter into the prepared pan and bake for 55 minutes, or until a knife inserted into the center of the cake comes out nearly clean. Allow the cake to cool for 10 minutes in the pan, then remove to a wire rack.

Serve at room temperature. If not eating the cake until later, allow it to cool all the way to room temperature, then wrap it in plastic and store at room temperature.

VARIATIONS

AGRUMES (CITRUS): Reduce the vanilla to 1 teaspoon and use the grated zest of 1 orange and 2 lemons.

ALMOND: Reduce the vanilla extract to 1½ teaspoons and add ½ teaspoon almond extract. Add ½ cup lightly toasted sliced almonds to the batter before folding in the egg whites.

ANISEED: Eliminate the vanilla. Replace the lemon zest with orange zest. Add 1½ teaspoons freshly ground anise seeds when adding the melted butter.

APPLE AND CALVADOS: Reduce the vanilla to 1 teaspoon. Add ¾ cup chopped peeled apples and 2 tablespoons Calvados, applejack or apple cider (either hard or not) to the batter before folding in the egg whites.

ARMAGNAC AND PRUNE: Eliminate the vanilla. Warm 3 tablespoons Armagnac. Pour onto ½ cup chopped prunes. Add to the batter before folding in the egg whites.

BASIL: Eliminate the vanilla. Increase the zest to that of 2 lemons and add 1 tablespoon lemon juice or limoncello. Add ¼ cup julienned basil leaves to the batter before folding in the egg whites. (This combination is terrific combined with the strawberry jam option on page 23.)

BEURRE NOISETTE: Increase the amount of butter to 15 tablespoons. Brown the butter. Be sure to use all the good dark bits on the bottom of the pan.

BLOOD ORANGE: Replace the lemon zest with the zest of 1 blood orange, and add 1 tablespoon of its juice or 2 teaspoons Solerno, a Sicilian liqueur made from blood oranges.

BOOZY: Eliminate the vanilla. Add 1½ tablespoons of the spirit of your choice, such as dark rum, Cognac or Armagnac, or bourbon.

CARDAMOM: Eliminate the vanilla. Replace the lemon zest with orange zest. Add 1½ teaspoons freshly ground cardamom seeds from green cardamom pods when adding the melted butter.

CARDAMOM COFFEE: Eliminate the zest. Add 1½ teaspoons freshly ground cardamom seeds from green cardamom pods and 2 teaspoons espresso powder when adding the melted butter.

CHAI: Add 1 tablespoon chai spice mixture to the melted butter. Infuse for 30 minutes and strain. Alternatively, use 2 teaspoons ground chai spice mixture and add it to the melted butter.

CHAMOMILE: Steep 20 dried chamomile flowers in the melted butter for 30 minutes. Strain, discarding the flowers. This is particularly good with a honey-lemon glaze.

CHERRY: Reduce the vanilla to 1½ teaspoons. Add ½ teaspoon almond extract. Plump ⅔ cup dried cherries in boiling water for 2 minutes. Strain and discard the water. Toss the cherries in 1 tablespoon kirsch and add to the batter before folding in the egg whites. You may also want to add ½ cup lightly toasted almond slices.

CHOCOLATE: Unfortunately, chocolate chunks will sink, but you can add 1 cup mini chocolate chips to the batter before folding in the egg whites. Toss them in 2 teaspoons flour before adding them. For a mocha version, add 2 teaspoons espresso powder when adding the melted butter.

CINNAMON: Reduce the vanilla to 1 teaspoon. Add 2 teaspoons cinnamon powder when adding the melted butter or directly into the melted butter.

CINNAMON APPLE: Reduce the vanilla to 1 teaspoon. Add 2 teaspoons cinnamon powder when adding the melted butter. Add ⅔ cup chopped peeled apples to the batter before folding in the egg whites. Consider adding ½ cup toasted walnut pieces as well.

COFFEE: Eliminate the zest. Add 2 teaspoons espresso powder or ½ teaspoon coffee extract when adding the melted butter.

DATE: Replace the lemon zest with orange zest. If the dates are very dry, plump them in boiling water for 2 minutes, then drain them. Add ⅔ cup chopped dates before folding in the egg whites. Dates pair well with rose, almonds and cardamom. Combine this version with any or all of those.

ELDERFLOWER: Replace the lemon zest with the zest of 3 Key limes. Add 1½ tablespoons St-Germain liqueur to the batter before folding in the egg whites.

FENNEL, ORANGE AND GOLDEN RAISIN: Reduce the vanilla to 1 teaspoon. Replace the lemon zest with orange zest. Add 1½ teaspoons freshly ground fennel seeds when adding the melted butter. Add ⅔ cup golden raisins to the batter before folding in the egg whites. If, by any chance, you have Lucknow fennel seeds, use them! They are terrifically fragrant and sweet.

FIORI DI SICILIA: Reduce the vanilla to 1 teaspoon. Add ½ teaspoon Fiori di Sicilia extract.

GINGER: Reduce the vanilla to ½ teaspoon. Add 2 teaspoons freshly grated ginger root or 1 teaspoon ground ginger when adding the melted butter. Add ½ cup chopped crystallized ginger to the batter before folding in the egg whites.

GRAPEFRUIT: Replace the lemon zest with the zest of ½ grapefruit.

HIBISCUS ROSE: Reduce the vanilla to 1 teaspoon. Replace the lemon zest with orange zest. Steep 1 tablespoon dried hibiscus petals and 1 tablespoon dried rose petals in the melted butter for 30 minutes. Strain, discarding the petals. You may want to add a touch of natural pink food coloring and a rose glaze.

JAM: Once the cake is baked and has come to room temperature, slice it horizontally into three layers. Brush each layer with 2 teaspoons crème de framboise and cover with ¼ cup raspberry jam. Dust the reassembled cake with confectioners' sugar. For a strawberry version, use strawberry jam and crème de fraise des bois. For blackberry, use blackberry jam and crème de mûre. For apricot, use apricot jam and amaretto liqueur or Abricot du Roussillon. For cherry, use cherry jam and kirsch.

JASMINE ORANGE: Replace the lemon zest with orange and use a few drops of culinary-grade essential oil of jasmine. This combination also works terrifically with ginger, so consider adding ½ cup finely chopped crystallized ginger to the batter before folding in the egg whites.

LAVENDER: Reduce the vanilla to 1 teaspoon and use a few drops of culinary-grade essential oil of lavender or 1 teaspoon ground lavender flowers. Alternatively, steep 1 tablespoon dried lavender flowers in the melted butter for 45 minutes. Discard the lavender before proceeding with the recipe. Consider combining this with the blackberry jam version.

LEMON CURD: Once the cake is baked and has come to room temperature, slice it horizontally into three layers. Spread 3 tablespoons lemon curd onto each layer. Dust the reassembled cake with confectioners' sugar.

LEMON THYME: Eliminate the vanilla. Increase the zest to that of 2 lemons. Add 1 tablespoon minced lemon thyme leaves when adding the melted butter. Alternatively, steep the lemon thyme leaves in the melted butter for 45 minutes. Discard the leaves before proceeding with the recipe.

LIME: Replace the lemon zest with the zest of 2 limes and add their juice. You can also add 1 tablespoon silver tequila. You may also want to add ⅔ cup shredded dried coconut or 2 teaspoons coconut liqueur.

LIME AND MAKRUT LIME: Replace the lemon zest with the zest of 2 limes and add their juice. Steep 15 fresh makrut lime leaves in the melted butter for 30 minutes. Discard the leaves before proceeding with the recipe.

LIMONCELLO: Eliminate the vanilla. Increase the zest to that of 2 lemons and add 1 tablespoon limoncello.

MAPLE: Replace the granulated sugar with maple sugar.

MATCHA: Reduce the vanilla to 1½ teaspoons. Add ½ teaspoon almond extract. Add 1 tablespoon matcha powder with the flour.

MARMALADE: Once the cake is baked and has come to room temperature, slice it horizontally into two layers. Brush the bottom layer with ¼ cup orange, lime, grapefruit or ginger marmalade. Dust the reassembled cake with confectioners' sugar. (I suggest two layers, not three, as marmalade is an intense flavor.)

MEYER LEMON: Increase the zest to that of 2 Meyer lemons and add 1 tablespoon of their juice.

NUTMEG: Replace the lemon zest with orange zest. Replace the regular melted butter with beurre noisette. Add ¼ teaspoon freshly grated nutmeg.

ORANGE AND CLOVE: Add ¼ teaspoon freshly ground cloves to the melted butter and use the zest of 1 orange.

PASTIS: Reduce the vanilla to 1 teaspoon. Add 2 tablespoons pastis. Go-to labels are Ricard and Pernod.

PEAR: Reduce the vanilla to 1 teaspoon. Add ⅔ cup chopped peeled pears and 1½ tablespoons Poire Williams to the batter before folding in the egg whites.

PEPPER: Add ½ teaspoon freshly ground black peppercorns or ¾ teaspoon freshly ground pink peppercorns. Both of these can be combined with the strawberry jam version.

POPPY SEED: Eliminate the vanilla. Add 1 tablespoon poppy seeds. They are good with either lemon or orange zest.

RAS EL HANOUT: Reduce the vanilla to 1 teaspoon. Replace the lemon zest with orange zest. Add 2 teaspoons ras el hanout and ½ teaspoon cinnamon when adding the melted butter. For a coffee version, use 1 teaspoon ras el hanout, ½ teaspoon cinnamon and 1 teaspoon espresso powder.

ROSE: Eliminate the vanilla. Add ¼ teaspoon rose extract instead. (Rose water will not remain potent through baking.) Alternatively, grind dried culinary rose petals to a fine powder and use 1 teaspoon of the powder. Another option is to brush the cooked cake with rose syrup.

ROSEMARY: Eliminate the vanilla. Add 2 teaspoons minced fresh rosemary. Increase the lemon zest to that of 2 lemons and add 1 tablespoon lemon juice or limoncello.

RUM RAISIN: Eliminate the vanilla. Heat 3 tablespoons dark rum. Pour onto ½ cup dark raisins. Add to the batter before folding in the egg whites.

SAFFRON: Reduce the vanilla to ½ teaspoon. Replace the lemon zest with orange zest. Add ¼ teaspoon crushed saffron threads to the melted butter. Allow to infuse for 10 minutes. Do not remove the saffron threads. Add 1 teaspoon freshly ground cardamom seeds from green cardamom pods. This is delicious with a rose water syrup or glaze. A scattering of chopped pistachios is lovely, too.

TURMERIC AND GINGER, FRESH: Add 1 tablespoon grated or minced fresh turmeric and 1 tablespoon grated or minced fresh ginger to the melted butter.

TURMERIC AND GINGER, DRIED: If possible, use the zest and juice of 2 Meyer lemons instead of the zest of 1 regular lemon. Add ¾ teaspoon dried turmeric (preferably Alleppey turmeric), 2 teaspoons ground ginger and ¼ teaspoon freshly ground black pepper. This is also terrific with ½ cup minced crystallized ginger folded in as a final step. This recipe really sings if your Alleppey turmeric is quite fresh. The fresher the turmeric, the more floral and citrusy its fragrance.

VANILLA: Instead of the vanilla extract, use 2 teaspoons vanilla paste or the seeds of 2 vanilla pods.

VERBENA: Reduce the vanilla to 1 teaspoon. Steep 20 fresh or 15 dried verbena leaves in the melted butter for 45 minutes. Discard the leaves before proceeding with the recipe.

Gâteau Weekend Parfumé à la Lavande

———— Lavender Lemon Weekend Cake ————

I cannot pass a lavender bush without swirling my fingers around the flowering tip of a stem, just enough to release its oils but never to crush its small buds. For the next hour or so, I'll give my fingers a furtive sniff here and there, my own private source of bliss. When Garrick was little, I'd show him how, and we'd share a secret smile as we found odd reasons to justify putting our fingers to our noses for far longer than the scent even lasted. Now that Garrick is a teenager, it's Griffin, our great Bouvier des Flandres, who stops to sniff the scent on my fingertips. Had we not named him Griffin, his name would surely have been Ferdinand for the Spanish bull who wisely preferred to stop and smell the roses rather than chase a posturing bullfighter with a lethal sword round and round a walled ring. For years, I kept flowering stems of lavender in my sunglass case so that whenever I'd open it, the scent would travel me home to my parents' summer house and the lavender my father had planted. Great bushes of it, interspersed with rosemary and sage, ushers one up to the stone path that leads to the farmhouse they lovingly restored. Early on, I learned that keeping a shallow bowl of dried lavender by the window would deter scorpions and that sniffing it at night would produce an almost-Pavlovian response, putting me instantly to sleep. In France, lavender was everywhere. It was in bubble bath and soap and lotion. It was in tea and candles. It was in ice cream and pastilles. And, it was in cake.

There are many schools of thought on how best to bake with lavender, but it all comes down to season and access. The longer lavender sits, the more its flavor diminishes. It will still smell good weeks after it has lost its culinary potency. (And color, which you may want to supplement with a few drops of natural food dye.) In much of France, Italy and California, it's easy to find fresh lavender at farmers markets. Elsewhere, you'll need to source dried buds. Many bakers like to include these little purple buds in the batter. I do not. They are pretty, but their texture is unappealing. I'll scatter some about for visual effect, but that's it. For imparting flavor, my preferred approach is to pulverize the fragrant buds with granulated or raw sugar in the food processor. This coats the sugar in the flower's essential oils. If a recipe calls for milk or cream, infuse it with the flower. To do this, warm the milk or cream to a bare simmer. Remove from heat. Stir in a few spoonfuls of lavender buds and set aside for half an hour. Strain before using. This approach also works with simple syrup.

Continued

If all this sounds imprecise, rest assured that you can also buy excellent lavender extract online and proceed with the confidence that you will produce a fragrant cake, exactly to your liking. Try a half teaspoon in the batter and a quarter teaspoon in the glaze. I do this throughout the colder months. If I want a lavender hue, I tend to crush a few blackberries and use their juice in the glaze, as a natural alternative to food dye.

How much lavender to include? This is the dreamy part. If you want a faint wisp of its scent, use two teaspoons of buds. If you want a faint but recognizable aroma, use three. If you want to feel like you are standing in a lavender field in Provence—and who doesn't?— use four teaspoons. If you're not sure, start small, taste and ease your way up. The lavender should be fresh or recently dried, purple and highly scented. If it is gray, it is past its prime and needs to be tossed. Best, then, to pivot and turn this into a lemon cake.

Note: If using fresh or dried lavender, source flowers that haven't been sprayed with pesticides. Essential oils can be dangerous to ingest. Purchase lavender extract, not lavender oil.

CAKE

- 1 cup / 200 grams granulated sugar
- 1 tablespoon fresh or dried lavender buds, or to taste
- The grated zest of 3 lemons, in strips, juice reserved for the glaze
- 7 tablespoons unsalted butter, preferably French
- 1⅔ cups / 200 grams all-purpose or cake flour
- 1¼ teaspoon baking powder
- ½ teaspoon fine sea salt
- 3 large eggs, at room temperature
- ½ cup crème fraîche or sour cream

GLAZE

- 1 cup / 114 grams confectioners' sugar
- 3 tablespoons lemon juice
- 4 blackberries, optional
- ¼ teaspoon lavender extract, optional
- 1 teaspoon fresh lavender buds, optional

CAKE

Preheat the oven to 350°F. Butter an 8½ x 4½-inch loaf pan and dust it with flour.

Combine the granulated sugar, lavender and lemon zest in a food processor and pulse until the zest and lavender have been broken down and are barely visible. If time is on your side, leave the mixture in the processor for half an hour or so to allow the citrus oils and lavender perfume to infuse the sugar. In a rush? Keep going.

Melt the butter and set aside.

In a large mixing bowl, whisk the flour, scented sugar, baking powder and salt to combine.

In a smaller mixing bowl, whisk the eggs to break them up a bit. Add the crème fraîche and whisk to combine.

Pour the melted butter over the dry ingredients and give it two or three stirs with a rubber spatula. Immediately add the egg and cream mixture and stir to combine until no streaks of flour remain. Avoid overmixing.

Pour the batter into the prepared pan and bake for 40–45 minutes, or until a knife inserted in the center of the cake comes out clean.

Place on a cooling rack for about 10 minutes, then unmold the cake and let it continue to cool on the rack. It should be at room temperature before being glazed.

GLAZE

To make the glaze, combine the confectioners' sugar, lemon juice and the strained juice of the blackberries, if using them, and lavender extract, if desired. Stir well to liquefy. Pour the glaze over the cake. If using, the lavender buds can be scattered over the glaze for visual effect. Serve, if you'd like, with a dollop of crème fraîche.

To store the cake overnight, wrap it in plastic or enclose it in an airtight container once it is truly cool to the touch. If it is hot, it will steam and alter the cake's delicate texture.

VARIATIONS: Rose, rose geranium, elderflower, orange blossom, lime blossom, marigold and chamomile work beautifully here, as do smaller quantities of fresh herbs, such as lemon verbena, basil, tarragon, makrut leaves, mint, lemon thyme and rosemary.

Note: *For this recipe, it's best to zest the lemon with a vegetable peeler, taking care not to include any of the white pith, which is quite bitter. The large strips of zest will preserve the oils.*

Gâteau au Miel
—————— *Honey Loaf Cake* ——————

The rue Cler, in the seventh arrondissement, is decidedly my favorite shopping street in Paris for all things food. My friend Delphine lives close by, and we can easily spend an entire afternoon never venturing past the end of the block. There's a Mariage Frères for tea, two exceptional chocolate shops, the famous pâtisserie À la Mère de Famille, several grocers competing to see who can procure Comice pears with the finest blush and muscadine grapes that are sweeter than nectar. There's one of the finest charcuteries in Paris, called Davoli and beloved for its choucroute. While Charcuterie Jeusselin, just across the street, is known for its exceptional sausages. There's a florist with buckets of flowers spilling out over the sidewalk. There is also a shop devoted only to roses. Four good wine shops—this is France, after all. A *crêperie*, should we need a snack and find the cafés too crowded. An Asian traiteur. An excellent bookstore. A cookie shop called La Fabrique. A terrific *glacier*. A salmon shop. Yes, there is also a *poissonnerie*, but here you will find only salmon and the finest imaginable. A fromagerie that is one of my two favorites in the city—the other one being Barthélémy. And—you will smile at this—Maison de la Chantilly. Yes, whipped cream. In puff pastry, in hot chocolate, in a cone with berries. What is missing? Honey, of course. And that is to be found as well, at Famille Mary.

Famille Mary has all the usual suspects: acacia, wildflower, eucalyptus, orange blossom, lemon blossom, lime blossom, chestnut, rosemary, thyme and lavender. And then, depending upon the season, you might notice, say, their Miel de Noël, with notes of mandarin and lemon. But what I most love to peruse (euphemism for "purchase") are the regional honeys. There is honey from the forests of Anjou and also from the sunflowers of Anjou. This will be different from the honey from the sunflowers of Charente-Maritime, a region dear to me because it is the birthplace of our dog family of Bouviers des Flandres. There is lavender honey from the Luberon and blackberry honey from Les Landes. Honey from the forests of the Lorraine and the hills of the Jura and the mountains of Haute-Savoie. There is chestnut honey from the Dordogne and from the wildflowers of the Marne. Alfalfa honey from the Ardennes and an irresistible honey with fleur de sel de Guérande.

Besides buying honey for toast, honey for tea, honey for colds, honey that is so precious it requires a silver spoon, I also pick out honeys for this cake. Honey is the star of this cake, and what honey you choose will be its leading note. I find it a delicate cake and shy away from the darker, stronger honeys. But I also want a pronounced flavor that will be audible, so to speak, in each bite. For this recipe, try to take a step up from the supermarket variety in the plastic bear, but, of course, save the most exquisite honeys for eating raw or slathering on thick slices of fresh bread.

1¾ cups / 210 grams cake flour	3 large eggs, at room temperature
½ teaspoon fine sea salt	4 additional large egg yolks, at room temperature
1 teaspoon baking powder	
½ cup plus 1 tablespoon / 112 grams granulated sugar	½ cup honey
	1¼ teaspoons vanilla extract
1 cup plus 2 tablespoons unsalted butter, at room temperature	The grated zest of 1 organic lemon, preferably a Meyer lemon

Preheat the oven to 350°F. Butter and flour a 9 x 5-inch loaf pan.

In a stand mixer or using handheld beaters, whisk the flour, salt, baking powder and sugar together until thoroughly combined. Add the butter in pieces and beat, at medium-high speed, until pale in color.

In a small bowl, whisk the whole eggs, egg yolks, honey, vanilla and zest until homogenous.

With the mixer running on low, add the egg mixture, a little at a time, to the butter mixture, until combined. Don't overmix.

Pour the batter into the prepared pan and bake for 50–60 minutes, or until a knife inserted in the center comes out clean.

Wait 5 minutes before transferring the cake to a plate. It will be hard to resist warm, but, at room temperature, the flavors will be more apparent. It's best the day it is made but is still good on day two, and on day three, it can be toasted and lavished with salted butter for breakfast.

Le Weekend Cake au Yuzu

—— *Yuzu Cake* ——

Yuzu is one of the most beautifully perfumed members of the citrus family. To use a wine phrase, it offers a mouthful. A sort of smooth, rounded, fragrant fullness with an almost floral pucker. It's been a favorite in Paris for some time, but the recent influx of Japanese chefs in the city has grown its popularity.

The French used to take Wednesday and Saturday afternoons off and, of course, Sundays. The idea of *le weekend* wasn't introduced until the middle of the twentieth century, when, in 1936, the forty-hour, five-day workweek became legally mandated after a series of protests. The idea and the name, however, had already taken hold among those who had crossed the Channel to England or the ocean to the United States. The Anglo-Saxon term was adopted, as was the newfound ability to leave town Friday afternoon and return late Sunday. Of course, a cake was created to suit the occasion. Le Weekend Cake is meant to last three days without drying out. Crème fraîche keeps it moist.

CAKE

8 tablespoons unsalted butter

2¼ cups / 270 grams all-purpose flour

1½ teaspoons baking powder

½ teaspoon fine sea salt

1½ cups / 300 grams granulated sugar

5 large eggs, at room temperature

¾ cup crème fraîche

½ cup yuzu juice

The grated zest of 2 lemons or
    tangerines

The grated zest of 2 limes

GLAZE

1 cup confectioners' sugar

2½ tablespoons yuzu juice

CAKE

Preheat the oven to 350°F. Butter two 9 x 5-inch loaf pans.

Melt the butter in a small saucepan and set aside somewhere warm.

In a small mixing bowl, lightly whisk the flour, baking powder and salt to combine, then set aside.

In a stand mixer, using handheld electric beaters or a simply a good old whisk, combine the granulated sugar and eggs at medium speed until starting to lighten, about 3–5 minutes. Add the crème fraîche and whisk until homogenous. Reduce the speed to low and add the dry ingredients, then the yuzu juice, then the lemon zest and finally the melted butter. Stop when smooth.

Pour the batter into the prepared pans and bake for 50–55 minutes, or until a knife inserted in the center of a loaf comes out clean. Transfer to a rack to cool to room temperature before glazing.

GLAZE

In a small mixing bowl, whisk together the confectioners' sugar and yuzu juice until smooth. Pour over the cakes.

Gâteau au Citron

—— *Lemon Cake* ——

M y friend Marguerite is over six feet tall and moves with astonishing grace and elegance. This is something I had observed for many years with, I have to say, quite a bit of envy but which became even more remarkable to me when I saw her bake for the first time. We have a dinner date once every season—this may seem strange, but this plan has kept us in touch even during the busiest of years. Usually we meet at a quiet restaurant where the management won't balk if we stay three or four hours, so long as we order a good bottle of wine. But when we meet at her house, she always makes this favorite cake of mine. It has a tender, moist crumb and a terrific burst of lemon. It is that lemon cake recipe you will turn to again and again, as it will never fail you. I love perching on a kitchen stool and watching Marguerite make the batter, which she does with swift ease, never checking the recipe, never doubting her movements, never pausing in our conversation. I wouldn't exactly call it a weekend cake or gâteau de voyage, as it is fragile, but it does keep well overnight, wrapped or sealed in an airtight container. If we're having friends over to dinner, I'll serve this with some berries tossed with a little limoncello and sugar and maybe a dollop of whipped cream or crème fraîche, but not because it needs their help. It doesn't.

CAKE

½ cup butter, at room temperature	1 teaspoon baking powder
1 cup / 200 grams granulated sugar	½ teaspoon fine sea salt
2 large eggs, at room temperature, lightly beaten with a fork	½ cup whole milk
1½ cups / 180 grams all-purpose flour	

GLAZE

The juice of 1 very large extra-juicy lemon or 2 medium ones	½ cup granulated sugar

CAKE

Preheat the oven to 375°F. Butter and line an 8½ x 4½-inch loaf pan with parchment.

In a stand mixer or using a handheld electric beater, cream the butter and sugar together until pale and fluffy. Add the eggs and beat another minute or two to thoroughly incorporate them.

In a small bowl, whisk the dry ingredients until well-mixed.

Fold half the dry ingredients into the butter-sugar-egg mixture, then half the milk. Follow with the remaining dry ingredients and then the remaining milk. Using a rubber spatula, mix with a gentle, but thorough, folding motion until you see no streaks of flour.

Pour the batter into the prepared pan and bake for 50–55 minutes.

GLAZE

Mix the lemon juice and sugar together. I find leaving it in a ceramic container on top of the stove, so the oven warms it a bit, works well. You want the sugar to dissolve, and the glaze pours best when slightly warm. The glaze is meant to be somewhere between a soaking syrup and a glaze, so don't worry if it seems runny. It should be.

Remove the cake from the oven and immediately pierce the top a half-dozen times with a sharp knife. Pour on the glaze. Let the cake thoroughly absorb the glaze before removing the cake from the pan.

ORANGE CAKE: To make this an orange cake, add the zest of an orange to the cake batter. Also add the zest of a second orange to the glaze and allow it to infuse while the cake is baking. Pour it through a sieve, pressing on the solids, and discard the zest.

Cake au Yaourt d'Avoine d'Apollonia

—— *Apollonia's Oat Yogurt Loaf Cake* ——

My first visit to Poilâne, easily the best-known bread bakery in the world, occurred when I was ten years old, and my family had just moved down the street from the bakery. It was a few days before the start of the school year; I was an American girl about to enter the École Bilingue, and I was twitchy with nerves and the thoughts of all the things I didn't know and had never tasted. I followed my father down the rue du Cherche-Midi—so named, he had just been telling me, because of the singular beauty of afternoon sunlight on the gentle curve of its trajectory through the 6th arrondissement—and into a bakery, where I was immediately struck by an enveloping, heady smell that I could not have named then, but which I later came to understand was a magic eau-de-vie of butter, sourdough, cooked apples, toasted walnuts and the faint after-aroma of slightly burnt sugar and browned butter.

It was unlike anything I'd known, and yet I recognized in it something timeless, something profoundly French that had existed long before us and would live long after us. In a kind of trance, I found myself at the register, where a middle-aged woman was looking at me from behind the counter. I would come to know her very Parisian mix of precision and warmth. She was proper, formal and, perhaps to an American sensibility, even officious, but there was a great well of kindness behind her brisk, constant greetings of "Monsieur, Madame, Mademoiselle," and the quickness with which she counted out centimes and francs with the unerring exactitude of a calculator.

That day, Madame nodded to a long basket of plain cookies that were slightly and unevenly brown at the edges. "*Prenez-un*," she offered. And so, I tried one. The cookie—called, with perfect French irony, *punition*—yielded upon being bitten, but not without putting up a little fight, a little resistance, giving it more character than shortbread, say, or sugar cookies. Its flavor was not pronounced but was the simple expression of high heat and good ingredients, exquisite butter above all. The edges were just short of burned, and that tiny hint of bitterness seemed only to make the cookie sweeter.

Number 8, rue du Cherche-Midi was and remains the literal hearth of Poilâne. The wood-burning oven in the basement is still used, just as it was in 1932, when Pierre Poilâne opened the bakery. Several times a day, I'd walk by the shop, my dog, Romeo, in tow and stop for *punitions* or for a little apple tart or a brioche. And always for the loaf of bread that was my family's daily staple, the heart of our breakfast, lunch and my after-school snack. If we were having cheese, we'd add a Poilâne walnut loaf to the mix, but that was about as far off-course as we'd deviate.

In the morning, I'd eat slices of the *miche* toasted with a thick slathering of butter from Fromagerie Barthélémy. Poilâne bread is amazingly dense and substantial, and the cool, slightly salted layer of rich butter would take a moment before melting into the toast. The yeasty, heady smell of toasted sourdough and wheat seemed then, and still, to be rooted in *terroir*, with much the same depth as you might expect from a venerable Bordeaux.

Many now know the story of Lionel and Irena Poilâne's sudden and tragic deaths in a helicopter crash in 2002, when their daughter, Apollonia, was only eighteen. But few know that she had been learning the ins and outs of her father's (and, before him, her grandfather's) bakery from an early age. She once told me, with still-vivid frustration, of having to wait for her hands to grow large enough to work the dough; but there was little else she wasn't doing by the time she was tall enough to stand at the work table.

Tragedy put her at the helm decades earlier than anyone would have wished, but she was well prepared, and the bakery has thrived under her watchful, active care. That she is both practical and eminently capable and yet still awed by the mysterious ways of bread— of wheat and yeast and heat—means she might discuss the science of milling grains one moment and, the next, the visual poetry of the letter *P* as it is written in the flour that tops every loaf.

Most notably, she's honored the recipes and techniques that are Poilâne, resisting all pressures to modernize, expand too rapidly, or sell, but she has added items that reflect a contemporary appreciation of different grains, such as her *sablés au seigle* (rye cookies) and *sablés au riz* (rice flour cookies). When I asked her to contribute a recipe to this book, she created this moist oat yogurt cake, and she wrote to tell me that she'd carried pints of Oatly yogurt over from London to Paris to be sure to test with a yogurt my readers would be able to get in the United States. I couldn't help but smile—it was so very Apollonia, thoughtful, practical, hardworking. And, of course, a wise marriage of old and new.

While Apollonia suggested lemon as an accent in this cake, something about the rich, comforting quality of oats beckoned for cinnamon when I first tried the recipe, perhaps because it's what I sprinkle on hot oatmeal. And that is how I most love this cake. This is a good recipe for bold spice blends as well, such as a chai blend or a ras el hanout. A little orange zest would keep the brightness, and a handful of chocolate chips would not be amiss.

Continued

½ cup oat yogurt, such as Oatly

1¼ cups / 150 grams all-purpose flour

¾ cup / 150 grams granulated or ¾ cup / 90 grams light brown sugar

3 large eggs, at room temperature

¼ cup neutral oil, such as canola, grapeseed or sunflower

The grated zest of 1 lemon or 1 teaspoon cinnamon

1 teaspoon baking powder

Preheat the oven to 350°F. Generously butter a 9 x 5-inch loaf pan.

Combine the yogurt, flour and sugar in a large mixing bowl and whisk to combine. Add the eggs and whisk to thoroughly incorporate. Add the oil and lemon zest and whisk to incorporate. Add the baking powder and whisk until you have a smooth, homogenous batter.

Pour the batter into the prepared pan and bake for 35–40 minutes, or until a knife inserted in the center comes out clean.

Bring to room temperature on a cooling rack.

Gâteau au Sucre Roux, au Rhum et aux Pépites de Chocolat

—— Cake with Brown Sugar, Rum and Chocolate Chips ——

This is a deeply flavored cake that I make in the autumn or winter. It's loosely based on one I tore out of French *Elle* many years ago and have since lost. In that recipe, a tablespoon of coffee extract was used, not rum. This balance of ingredients, here, seems to become one warming, boozy note, which I prefer. The honey and brown sugar add depth and the crème fraîche gives it a slight tangy richness. Like most French cakes, it is made with melted butter and is not too sweet. Toasted walnuts would be the classic addition, but the American in me opts for chips or chunks of dark chocolate. If you prefer not to use alcohol, replace the rum with strong espresso. Use a honey that is not overly floral. Or choose a stronger honey, but not one that will compete with the rum. Buckwheat, for example, would be too domineering, but chestnut would add an intriguing depth.

¾ cup unsalted butter, preferably European

2 cups plus 2 tablespoons / 255 grams cake flour

2 teaspoons baking powder

⅔ cup / 120 grams light brown sugar

3 large eggs, at room temperature

⅓ cup honey

2 teaspoons vanilla extract

⅞ cup crème fraîche or whole Greek yogurt

⅓ cup dark rum

1 cup chocolate chips or 1 cup chopped toasted walnuts or pecans tossed in 1 teaspoon flour

Preheat the oven to 350°F. Generously butter a 10-cup Bundt pan. Set in the fridge until the butter is cold. Dust with cocoa powder.

Melt the butter and set aside somewhere warm.

Place all the dry ingredients in a small mixing bowl and whisk to combine.

In a larger mixing bowl, combine the eggs, melted butter, honey, vanilla, crème fraîche and rum. Using electric beaters on low speed, whisk to thoroughly combine. The purpose is to integrate the ingredients, not add air, so only a minute or two is necessary.

Tip the dry ingredients and the chocolate chips into the wet and fold to combine using a rubber spatula.

Pour into the prepared pan and bake for approximately 40 minutes, or until a knife inserted in the center comes out clean. (If you insert the knife into a chocolate chip, try again.)

Cake à la Farine d'Épeautre
au Chocolat et au Café

——— *Spelt Chocolate and Coffee Cake* ———

November 2019. I sniff. I stop. I smell another health food store. But it's not the horrible health food store smell that is holier than thou, it is a nutty, grainy smell that is quite enticing. But something else strikes me, too. It's the third health food store I've passed in a very short walk near St-Germain-des-Prés. Paris has fallen for wellness with a *coup de foudre*. This has me worried. But then, through the window, I see the dairy section and a display of butters, and I rest easy. *Plus ça change*. I'm all for smart choices, just not all the time. The shop turns out to be a mecca of healthy grains, raw honeys, tisanes, tahini and homemade Nutella. And the shoppers? Glowing skin and lipstick blotted to a barely visible kiss of color. It could be Los Angeles, except that the shop clerks are wearing lab coats and, instead of feigning intimacy, they are confident, quick and somewhat bossy with their recommendations. For some reason, this has always inspired absolute trust in me, and I leave the shop with a neat packet of spelt flour and instructions (more or less) on how to make this cake. I am also told that the yogurt may be replaced with crème fraîche—a sign that I am definitely not in Los Angeles.

The ganache is optional, but delicious. Add a touch of cardamom or cinnamon, should you want some spice. If not making the ganache, sprinkle the batter with muscovado or raw sugar before baking it, to add a sweet crunch.

CAKE

- ⅔ cup unsalted butter, at room temperature
- 1½ cups plus 2 tablespoons / 300 grams light brown sugar
- 2 tablespoons granulated sugar
- 2 teaspoons vanilla extract or paste
- 2 large eggs, at room temperature
- 1¾ cups / 200 grams spelt flour

- 1 cup / 100 grams almond flour
- ¾ cup plus 1½ tablespoons / 85 grams cocoa powder
- 1½ teaspoons baking soda
- ½ teaspoon fine sea salt
- ⅔ cup plus 1 tablespoon whole Greek yogurt
- ¾ cup espresso, still warm

OPTIONAL GANACHE

- ½ cup heavy cream
- 1 tablespoon honey
- 2 teaspoons instant espresso powder

- ½ cup / 100 grams bittersweet chocolate, finely chopped

Preheat the oven to 350°F. Line a 9 x 5-inch loaf pan with parchment or butter it and dust it with cocoa powder.

In a stand mixer or using electric beaters, whisk the butter, brown sugar and granulated sugar until light and fluffy, about 6 minutes. With the mixer running, add the vanilla and the eggs, one at a time, until fully incorporated.

Sift half the dry ingredients directly into the wet batter, then fold in half the yogurt. Repeat. With the mixer on low, whisk in the coffee, and continue to mix until the batter is perfectly smooth.

Pour the batter into the prepared pan and bake for 50 minutes, or until a knife inserted in the center comes out clean. Allow the cake to cool for a few minutes in its pan before transferring it to a cooling rack to come to room temperature.

If you're making the ganache icing, bring the heavy cream to a simmer in a double boiler. Stir in the honey, espresso powder, and chocolate. Stir until smooth. Remove from heat and pour over the cooled cake. Wait about 20 minutes for the ganache to set before serving the cake.

Gâteau Simple au Noisette

—— *Hazelnut Cake* ——

Here, butter is melted to a nutty beurre noisette, a taste I've augmented with a little hazelnut flour. Tangy crème fraîche, plenty of vanilla and a bit of brown sugar round out the flavor. This not-too-sweet loaf is most definitely *à goûter*, not for dessert. I tend to bake this Sunday night, at the start of a busy week. A quick slice with a strong coffee on the run on Monday morning, then toasted on Tuesday and Wednesday and given a smear of butter and a drizzle of honey—and, done. Breakfast accomplished. It is a moist loaf, but a strong crust and crumb makes it easy to nibble on the way to school without leaving a Hansel and Gretel trail. It may not be the protein-packed breakfast of champions, but the French are rightly loath to eat processed cereal at breakfast and packaged granola bars in the afternoon, preferring instead to have a taste of something made by hand. What is baked with love is always the most nourishing.

Note: If you don't have hazelnut flour, simply use 1¾ cups all-purpose or cake flour. Likewise, if you don't have light brown sugar, simply use 1¼ cups granulated.

1 cup unsalted butter

¾ cup / 150 grams granulated sugar

½ cup / 60 grams light brown sugar

4 large or extra-large eggs, at room temperature

½ cup / 50 grams hazelnut flour

½ teaspoon fine sea salt

1 teaspoon baking powder

½ cup crème fraîche

1 tablespoon vanilla extract

1½ cups / 180 grams cake or all-purpose flour

Preheat the oven to 350°F. Line the bottom of a 9 x 5-inch loaf pan with parchment and butter the sides.

Brown the butter in a frying pan until it has the color and nutty fragrance of hazelnuts. Pour into a mixing bowl and set aside to cool for 10 minutes.

Add the granulated sugar and brown sugar to the warm-but-not-hot butter and beat with electric beaters for a few minutes to integrate the ingredients and further cool the butter. One by one, add the eggs, beating well after each addition. Add the hazelnut flour, salt and baking powder and beat to combine. Add the crème fraîche and vanilla and continue to beat until the batter is homogenous and smooth. Using a rubber spatula, fold in the cake flour, using a decisive but gentle motion, until no streaks of white remain.

Pour into the prepared pan and bake for 1 hour, or until a knife inserted in the center of the cake comes out clean. Due to the brown butter, hazelnut flour and brown sugar, the cake will be a bit darker than most, so don't judge doneness by color. Unmold the cake after about five minutes and allow it to come to room temperature. If not eating within a few hours, wrap the cake in plastic or store in an airtight container once truly at room temperature. There's no need to refrigerate it.

Gâteau à la Cardamome

—— Cardamom Cake ——

About a dozen years ago, Copenhagen became a chic place for Parisians to go for a long weekend. And for good reason, as it's a fantastic city. First came the widespread discovery of Danish design and its pared-down beauty. Then a small bare-bones restaurant by the name of Noma became the most celebrated restaurant in the world, and its chef René Redzepi's fabulously unpredictable mash-up of foraged foods and exquisite technique brought culinary pilgrims to his wooden tables and benches. And somewhere along the way, foraging French tourists fell in love with the city's ubiquitous cardamom cakes. (Cardamom is used by the Danes with much the same frequency as we use cinnamon.) Danish bread with its chewy, grain-studded texture and cardamom cake with its heady perfume started popping up in Paris. The bread trend didn't last, but soon enough Parisians were baking a cross between the little yeasted cardamom cakes of Denmark and their own very French weekend cakes. I'm a little cardamom-crazy, so this came as good news. Cardamom happens to be a stimulant, which might explain the chai frenzy and certainly explains my own habit of sniffing the pods when I need a little boost. Of course, it also has a hauntingly beautiful scent.

Grinding cardamom to order is essential, as it quickly loses its fragrance when stored. To do this, press down on green cardamom pods with the flat side of a knife to release the black seeds inside. Grind the seeds to a powder in a spice grinder, coffee grinder or high-powered blender, such as a Vitamix. Green cardamom is expensive, so I reserve the pods for making chai or for spicing my café au lait.

This is a morning or afternoon cake, best served with a strong cup of coffee. The recipe is easily doubled.

1 cup minus 1 tablespoon / 190 grams granulated sugar

2 large eggs, at room temperature

1½ teaspoons freshly ground cardamom seeds from green cardamom pods

1¼ teaspoons baking powder

Pinch of fine sea salt

1¼ cups / 150 grams all-purpose flour

1 cup heavy cream

Preheat the oven the 350°F. Butter an 8½ x 4½-inch loaf pan and dust with flour.

In a stand mixer or large mixing bowl, combine the sugar and eggs and beat until pale.

In a small mixing bowl, combine the dry ingredients and whisk to blend.

Using a rubber spatula, alternately add the dry ingredients and the cream to the sugar-egg mixture.

Pour the batter into the prepared pan and bake for 50 minutes, or until a knife inserted in the center comes out clean.

APPLE, PEAR, BERRY, STONE FRUIT

and

CITRUS CAKES

Les Gâteaux aux Fruits

Gâteau aux Pommes Classique

———— Apple Cake—The Classic ————

This is the classic. A moist apple and raisin-studded loaf, scented with rum and glazed twice. Normandy is the land of apples in France. But come autumn, some variation on this cake is served throughout the country, with each region using its own liqueur. In Normandy, that would be Calvados. In Cognac, it would, of course, be Cognac. And in Armagnac, Armagnac. It is (*entre nous*) delicious made with bourbon. If you happen to be in Paris during apple season, go early one Sunday morning to the Marché Raspail, an organic farmers market that fills with an astonishing array of apple varieties, far too extensive to list. Some will hold their shape when baked, and that is the object here. In the States, I tend to use Fuji, Honeycrisp or Golden Delicious. But Jonagold, Winesap, Mutsu, Pink Lady, Granny Smith and Braeburn are all terrific baking apples. Simply take note of how sweet a variety you prefer and always make sure the apples you buy are firm to the touch and don't yield when pressed with your thumb.

For dinner *en famille*, simply brush the cake with warm apricot jam, perhaps with a bit of rum stirred in. For something a bit fancier, drizzle on the second glaze just before serving.

When pears come into season, omit the raisins, use three firm pears instead of the two apples and consider replacing the rum with Poire Williams. Beurré d'Anjou, a buttery pear variety originating in the Loire Valley, and known in the U.S. as simply Anjou pears, are ideal here. If using Bartlett or Comice pears, choose ones that are still quite firm and just short of ripe, or they will lose their shape.

CAKE

1¼ cups raisins

2 tablespoons dark rum

2 apples, such as Golden, Honeycrisp or Fuji

8½ tablespoons unsalted butter, at room temperature

1 cup / 112 grams confectioners' sugar

3 large eggs, at room temperature

1 cup plus 3 tablespoons / 143 grams all-purpose flour

¼ teaspoon fine sea salt

½ teaspoon baking powder

5 tablespoons apricot jam

GLAZE

1 tablespoon dark rum

⅓ cup / 38 grams confectioners' sugar

CAKE

Preheat the oven to 350°F. Line an 8½ x 4½-inch loaf pan with parchment. Use enough parchment to create a 3-inch overhang so that the cake can be lifted out of the pan once baked.

Place the raisins in a small heatproof bowl. Cover with boiling water, let sit a minute or two, then drain.

Bring the rum to a simmer and pour over the raisins. Set aside to macerate while you prepare the batter.

Peel and core the apples. Cut them into ⅓- to ½-inch pieces.

In a stand mixer or using electric beaters, whip the butter until smooth. Pour in the confectioners' sugar, a bit at a time, and continue to beat until the mixture is pale and creamy. One by one, add the eggs, beating after each addition. The mixture should be homogenous.

Place a sieve over the mixing bowl and sift in the flour, salt and baking powder. Using a rubber spatula, gently, but decisively, fold the flour mixture into the egg mixture. Fold in the raisins and their rum and then the apples.

Bake the cake for 50–60 minutes, or until a knife inserted in the center comes out clean. Remove the cake from the oven and set on a cooling rack, but do not remove the cake from its pan.

Warm the apricot jam. Strain it, pushing down on the solids. Brush the top of the cake with the warm strained apricot jam. Set aside to come to room temperature.

GLAZE

Just before serving, remove the cake from the pan using the parchment overhang. Discard the parchment. Warm the rum for about 20 seconds in a microwave if it is on the cold side. Combine the rum and confectioners' sugar and stir until smooth. Drizzle the glaze over the cake and serve with a dollop of crème fraiche or scoop of vanilla ice cream.

Gâteau Normand aux Pommes et au Calvados

Apple and Calvados Cake from Normandy

A few years ago, I wrote a book called *The London Cookbook*. The city was—and still is—in the midst of a culinary transformation. Once known for its soggy vegetables and tough mutton, it had, seemingly overnight, become a dazzling restaurant city. At the forefront of this delicious little revolution was Fergus Henderson, chef-proprietor of St. John Bread and Wine and the beloved paterfamilias of nose-to-tail cooking. Fergus's food is a brilliant mix of French and British, with the former thankfully tipping the scales. Case in point, this terrific apple and Calvados cake recipe, which he sent to me with this simple enticement: "A very fine cake. What is not fine with a little Calvados!" And how right he is. The Calvados in this big, rustic cake, seems to ambulate in the background, like a haunting. The chopped apples and walnuts provide texture. The cinnamon offers comfort, the clove intrigue. The oil will keep this cake moist for days, but it will be gone within hours if left unguarded. Created by a Londoner, it couldn't be more Parisian. A true gâteau. Crème fraîche is de rigueur.

3 large eggs, at room temperature

2 cups / 400 grams granulated sugar

1½ cups vegetable oil

¼ cup Calvados

3¼ cups / 390 grams all-purpose flour

1 teaspoon baking soda

2 teaspoons ground cinnamon

Pinch of salt

Pinch of ground cloves

1 cup walnuts, coarsely chopped

3–4 baking apples, preferably Granny Smith, peeled and coarsely chopped

Preheat the oven to 350°F. Butter a 9-inch springform or a 10-inch cake pan.

Whisk the eggs and sugar together either by hand, in a stand mixer or with electric beaters. Add the oil as you would to make mayonnaise: in a thin stream as you continue to whisk.

Add the Calvados while continuing to whisk.

Add the dry ingredients and whisk to incorporate.

Fold in the walnuts and apples.

Pour into the prepared pan and bake for 85–90 minutes, or until a knife inserted in the center comes out clean.

Gâteau aux Baies

—— *Berry Cake* ——

Everyone loves this cake. It is just light enough, just rich enough and dotted with raspberries, blackberries or a mixture of the two. If you've got some blueberries in the fridge, toss those in, too. And by all means, if you can source marionberries, huckleberries or boysenberries, in they go! In Paris, come June, you will see this cake made with fraises des bois, the tiny wild berries found in forests. These jewels are intensely flavored and celebrated during their short season. They are sold in little origami-like cartons and covered in tissue paper and, like white asparagus, morel mushrooms and truffles, cost their weight in gold. But their flavor is so pronounced that a mere cup would perfume this nine-inch cake.

Serve this cake with generous clouds of whipped cream and berries tossed in crème de cassis.

2 cups / 250 grams all-purpose or cake flour

2 teaspoons baking powder

½ teaspoon fine sea salt

¾ cup unsalted butter, at room temperature

1 cup / 200 grams granulated sugar

1 cup minus 1 tablespoon / 112 grams light brown sugar

3 large eggs, at room temperature

1 tablespoon limoncello

The grated zest of 1 large lemon

¾ cup plus 1 tablespoon crème fraîche

1½ cups raspberries or blackberries or a combination of both, fresh or frozen

Preheat the oven to 350°F. Butter a 9-inch springform pan and line the bottom with a round of parchment.

In a small bowl, combine the flour, baking powder and sea salt. Using a fork, whisk a bit to integrate. Set aside.

In a stand mixer at medium speed or using handheld electric beaters, cream the butter, granulated sugar and brown sugar together until pale and fluffy. Reduce the speed to medium-low and, with the mixer running, add the eggs, one at a time, then the limoncello and, finally, the lemon zest.

Using a rubber spatula, fold in half the dry ingredients, then the crème fraîche, then the remaining dry ingredients.

Pour half the batter into the pan. Dot with half the raspberries. Add the remaining batter, then dot the surface with the remaining berries. Bake for 55–65 minutes, or until a knife inserted in the center comes out clean. Let sit 10 minutes on a cooling rack before transferring the cake to a plate. Serve still a tad warm or at room temperature. This cake takes well to being refrigerated, but its crumb is best the first day.

STONE FRUIT VARIATION!: To make this an apricot cake, use an equal measure of sliced apricots. Use 2 teaspoons vanilla extract instead of the limoncello. Or use ¼ teaspoon almond extract or 1 tablespoon amaretto and 1 tablespoon, if you have it, Abricot de Roussillon. For a peach cake, switch the liqueur to crème de pèche.

Gâteau Tropical à l'Ananas Caramélisé

Caramelized Pineapple Tropical Loaf

This cake tastes like a Caribbean vacation, but it comes from two French pastry chefs in Brooklyn, New York. Noémie Videau-Zagar and Christine Herelle-Lewis met at École Grégoire-Ferrandi, the great culinary school in Paris, and both found themselves in New York married to locals. Together, they opened a catering pâtisserie called Pistache, after their favorite nut. This weekend cake is studded with caramelized pineapples and toasted coconut flakes and perfumed with lime and rum.

PINEAPPLE

2 tablespoons unsalted butter

2 tablespoons granulated, raw or light brown sugar

1 cup pineapple, diced

The grated zest of 2 limes

1 tablespoon dark rum or 1 teaspoon vanilla extract

CAKE

8½ tablespoons unsalted butter

1 cup / 130 grams confectioners' sugar

1 tablespoon honey

¼ cup / 50 grams granulated sugar

3 large eggs, at room temperature

1 tablespoon heavy cream

1 tablespoon milk

1½ cups / 200 grams cake or all-purpose flour

2 teaspoons baking powder

Pinch of fine sea salt

1 cup dried, flaked coconut, toasted (see Notes), or ⅔ cup dried, shredded coconut

Preheat the oven to 335°F. Butter a 9 x 5-inch loaf pan and dust it with flour or line it with parchment.

PINEAPPLE

In a good-sized skillet, melt the butter over medium heat and stir in the granulated sugar. Add the pineapple and toss to coat. Sauté the fruit until the sugar starts to turn golden and the edges of pineapple take on a darker hue, about 5–7 minutes. Remove from heat. Stir in the lime zest and rum.

CAKE

In a stand mixer or using handheld electric beaters, cream the butter and confectioners' sugar together until smooth and fluffy. With the mixer still running, add the honey, then the granulated sugar, then, one by one, the eggs, heavy cream and milk and beat until smooth. Fold in the flour, baking powder and salt. Fold in the caramelized pineapple and its sugar-butter mixture. Fold in the toasted coconut.

Pour the batter into the prepared pan and bake for 50 minutes, or until a knife inserted in the center comes out clean. Let cool to room temperature.

Notes: Using toasted coconut flakes adds a little crispy-crunch, while shredded coconut seems to merge harmoniously with the batter. Consider doubling the caramelized pineapple and saving half to stir into morning yogurt.

To toast the coconut, spread it out on a baking sheet and toast in the preheated oven for 5 minutes. Set aside for 5 minutes to cool before using.

Gâteau au Citron et à la Menthe

———— Lemon Mint Cake ————

I remember sitting in a little Moroccan restaurant in Montmartre and breathing in the sudden smell of fresh mint. It came as something of a wake-up call after a long feast. The waiter was soon pouring steaming mint tea from a daunting height into our tiny teacups with, thankfully, a practiced hand. This tradition is supposedly not meant to instill fear or awe—it does—but rather to tease the senses. Laced with mint, this cake is an ode to that moment. Far more common in Paris are cakes scented with verbena, laurel, lemon thyme and rosemary. But the marriage of lemon and mint is a bright, lively one. Any mint is fine here, but lemon balm, grapefruit mint, mojito mint and orange mint, also known as bergamot mint, are all a bit less boldly sharp than spearmint and peppermint and carry a citrusy aroma that highlights the generous dose of lemon in both the batter and the icing. You can easily substitute the zest of one orange for the zest of two lemons and add a few spoonfuls of orange blossom water instead of lemon juice to the icing. Lightly shower the finished cake with zest or thin slivers of mint right before serving.

CAKE

1 cup unsalted butter, at room temperature

1 cup / 120 grams light brown sugar

4 large eggs, at room temperature

1½ cups / 180 grams all-purpose flour

⅔ cup / 60 grams almond flour

2 teaspoons baking powder

¼ teaspoons fine sea salt

½ cup whole milk

The grated zest of 2 lemons

1 cup fresh mint leaves, finely chopped

ICING

½ cup unsalted butter, at room temperature

2 cups / 227 grams confectioners' sugar, sifted

2 tablespoons lemon juice or limoncello

CAKE

Preheat the oven to 375°F. Line a 9-inch cake pan with a round of parchment and butter the sides of the pan.

In a stand mixer or using electric beaters, cream the butter and brown sugar together until the color is light and the texture is fluffy. Add the eggs one at a time, beating well after each addition.

In a separate bowl, combine the all-purpose flour, almond flour, baking powder and salt. Add this to the butter mixture in three batches, alternating with the milk and beating after each addition to combine. Stir in the zest and the mint.

Pour the batter into the prepared pan and bake for 45–60 minutes, or until a knife inserted in the center comes out clean. Allow the cake to come to room temperature before icing it.

ICING

Cream the butter on low speed in a stand mixer or using electric beaters. Keeping the mixer running, slowly add the confectioners' sugar. Once combined, increase the speed to medium and beat until the mixture is light and fluffy. Sprinkle with the lemon juice and beat for another minute to incorporate. Spread the icing with an offset spatula over the surface of the cake.

Gâteau de Semoule, à l'Huile d'Olive, Yaourt et Mandarine

——— Semolina, Olive Oil, Yogurt and Tangerine Cake ———

In 2001, the celebrated Parisian chef Alain Passard turned his restaurant L'Arpège into an haute cuisine ode to the vegetable. Tired of cooking meat and fish, he wanted to focus his considerable talents on roots and leaves and other both humble and rarified produce. He kept his three Michelin stars, which he has maintained for an astonishing twenty-six years. But, more important, he created a culinary *frisson* in Paris, becoming a hero to the city's small but growing population of vegetarians. He was, of course, ahead of his time by at least a decade, if not two. And while Passard's seminal move away from meat wasn't in the name of health, diet or nutrition, it did spark a profound shift in how many Parisians thought about food, eventually giving rise to more nutritious recipes, such as this simple but wholesome semolina cake.

Semolina, as pasta lovers may know, is a flour made from durum wheat—or, to be precise, the ground endosperm of durum wheat. I mention this only as it's not for the gluten-intolerant. In fact, it's high in gluten, which is why it's often paired, when baking, with olive oil and yogurt. But it's also high in protein, iron, the B vitamins and selenium. Some cakes, such as a revani (see page 214) are made with coarse semolina, which gives an almost cornmeal-like texture. This cake is made with fine semolina, which is as smooth as flour. I like it paired with the assertiveness of tangerines, mandarins or blood oranges. Sometimes, I add a teaspoon of minced fresh rosemary to the batter, sometimes a pinch of ground coriander or white pepper.

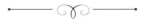

CAKE

The grated zest of 2 organic tangerines, mandarins or blood oranges

½ cup / 100 grams granulated sugar

1 cup / 163 grams fine semolina flour

½ teaspoon baking soda

1 teaspoon baking powder

¼ teaspoon fine sea salt

3 large eggs, at room temperature

½ cup mild extra-virgin olive oil

1½ cups whole yogurt, preferably creamline

1 teaspoon vanilla extract

GLAZE

1½ cups / 172 grams confectioners' sugar

3 tablespoons freshly squeezed tangerine, mandarin or blood orange juice

CAKE

Preheat the oven to 350°F. Butter a 9-inch springform pan and place a round of parchment on the bottom.

Combine the tangerine zest and granulated sugar in a small mixing bowl. Using your fingertips, rub them together to distribute the citrus oils through the sugar.

In another small mixing bowl, whisk the dry ingredients together.

In a stand mixer or using handheld electric beaters, beat the zesty sugar and eggs until light and fluffy. Add the olive oil, yogurt and vanilla and mix until homogenous. Reduce the speed to low and incorporate the dry ingredients. Mix until no streaks of flour remain.

Pour the batter into the prepared pan and bake for 45–55 minutes, or until a knife inserted in the center comes out clean. Set aside until it is warm, but no longer hot to the touch, about 20 minutes. Undo the sides of the pan and slide the cake onto a cake plate.

GLAZE

Whisk together the confectioners' sugar and tangerine juice until perfectly smooth. Drizzle the glaze over the cake's surface or, for a neater appearance, brush it on. Serve at room temperature with a dollop of crème fraîche. Thanks to the olive oil, this cake keeps well overnight at room temperature, wrapped or in a cake dome.

Gâteau aux Figues sans Farine

⸺ *Gluten-Free Fig Cake* ⸺

This fig cake is rich-rustic. Forgive me if this sounds like the name of a new furniture collection. But make it and you may agree. It's a simple, unassuming cake in appearance—the kind you cut directly from the baking dish on a Sunday night. But it is filled with mascarpone, figs and ground almonds. Mascarpone is readily available in Paris and is often used in cakes the way we use cream cheese. Did I mention it was rich? And moist, too. This is a cake to eat warm, either straight from the oven or within an hour or so. Crème fraîche is essential, here. Not because a third cream is needed—yes, the recipe includes heavy cream in addition to mascarpone—but because the tang of the crème fraîche proves a perfect foil to the baked figs.

Sadly, this cake gets a bit dense and soggy if kept overnight. Don't get me wrong. I wouldn't say no to a little piece scooped into a bowl and topped with yogurt for breakfast. But the texture of this cake is truly magic when just baked—soft enough to be only a few degrees more structured than a pudding and yet still very much a gâteau. Don't try to unmold it. It's meant to be scooped out of its baking dish with a big spoon. When fig season is over, switch to peeled, cored and halved pears. If you can find the very little Forelle pears, simply peel them and stand them upright in the batter.

¼ cup heavy cream

1 cup mascarpone

1½ cups / 170 grams confectioners' sugar

4 large eggs, at room temperature

3 cups / 300 grams almond flour

¼ cup / 30 grams cornstarch

¼ teaspoon fine sea salt

The grated zest of 1 large, organic orange

A dozen black figs that are ripe but not yet bursting open

Preheat the oven to 350°F. Butter the sides of a 10-inch springform pan or cast-iron skillet and lay a round of parchment on the bottom. Or line a 9 x 13-inch baking dish with parchment.

In a stand mixer or using electric beaters, beat the cream and mascarpone together. Add the sugar and beat to integrate. Add the eggs, one at a time, beating after each addition, then beat in the zest.

Using a rubber spatula, fold in the dry ingredients.

Cut the figs into quarters, remove and discard the tough stem, and arrange them skin side down in the prepared pan. Pour the batter over the figs and bake for 30–40 minutes, or until a knife inserted in the center of the cake comes out clean. Serve while still warm and pass a bowl of crème fraîche or a pint of vanilla ice cream.

Un Grand Gâteau à l'Orange

—— *A Great Big Orange Cake* ——

This is a big cake—bursting with orange, tangy with crème fraîche, comfortingly familiar and beloved by young and old. It is tall, has a tender crumb and will remain impeccable for three days. Ideal for family gatherings and Sunday lunches or suppers, it can also be dressed up last minute with a dark chocolate ganache for a forgotten birthday or spur-of-the-moment celebration. No surprise, it likes a glass of Champagne. A large Bundt pan, while not exactly French, fits its sunny, generous disposition. Chantilly, not needed. It is sometimes called Le Petit Prince, for the classic children's book by Antoine de Saint-Exupéry.

CAKE

1 cup unsalted butter, at room temperature

2½ cups / 500 grams granulated sugar

6 eggs, at room temperature

The grated zest of 3 organic oranges

1 cup crème fraîche

1 tablespoon Grand Marnier

3 cups / 390 grams all-purpose flour

1½ teaspoons baking powder

½ teaspoon fine sea salt

SYRUP

The juice of 2 super juicy or 3 organic oranges

2 tablespoons lemon juice

½ cup / 100 grams granulated sugar

1 tablespoon Grand Marnier

CAKE

Preheat the oven to 350°F. Generously butter a 12- to 15-cup Bundt pan, such as the Anniversary Bundt from NordicWare. Anything smaller, and the batter will spill over.

In a stand mixer or using electric beaters, cream the butter and sugar until truly pale and fluffy. Keeping the mixer running, add the eggs, one or two at a time. Continue whisking until the mixture is perfectly smooth. Add the zest and the crème fraîche and whisk until incorporated. Add the Grand Marnier and combine. Turn the mixer to low and add the flour, baking powder and salt in two batches. Beat until no streaks of flour are visible.

Pour the batter into the prepared pan and bake for 60–70 minutes, or until a knife inserted into the cake comes out clean. Allow to cool for five minutes.

SYRUP

Combine the orange and lemon juice with the sugar in a small saucepan and warm over low heat until the sugar has dissolved. Off heat, stir in the Grand Marnier.

Give the cake a dozen or so pricks with the tip of a sharp knife. Pour the syrup over the cake and set aside to absorb for 20 minutes. Invert onto a cake plate. If the cake doesn't easily unmold, simply let it sit upside down on the plate for another 5 minutes or so.

Allow the cake to come fully to room temperature, then cover with a cake dome or plastic wrap if not serving right away. Serve plain, at room temperature.

Gâteau Polenta à l'Orange Sanguine et au Romarin

Blood Orange Rosemary Polenta Cake

This is a winter cake, infused with rosemary and blood orange and lightly textured with polenta. It's barely sweet. The sugar plays a supporting role, leaving the herb and citrus duo to star. Serve it with a compote of dried fruits and a little crème fraîche after dinner. Save a slice for the morning to top with yogurt and a drizzle of the reduced blood orange juice.

If blood oranges are not in season, use the zest of regular oranges and two tablespoons of Solerno, a Sicilian blood orange liqueur, in place of the juice.

The grated zest and juice of 2 blood oranges

1¼ cups / 150 grams all-purpose flour

¾ cup / 120 grams polenta or cornmeal (see Note)

2 teaspoons baking powder

¾ teaspoon fine sea salt

½ cup unsalted butter, at room temperature

¾ cup / 150 grams granulated sugar

3 large eggs, at room temperature

1 tablespoon minced rosemary

2 tablespoons extra-virgin olive oil

½ cup whole milk

Preheat the oven to 350°F. Line a 9-inch springform pan with a round of parchment and butter the sides.

Bring the juice of the blood oranges to a simmer and cook until reduced by half. Pour into a heatproof container and set aside to come to room temperature. You will need ¼ cup of reduced juice. (Save the rest for a cocktail or to pour onto yogurt.)

Whisk the flour, polenta, baking powder and salt together in a mixing bowl.

In the bowl of a stand mixer or in a large mixing bowl and using electric beaters, beat the butter, sugar and zest together for 4 minutes, or until pale and fluffy. Add the eggs, one at a time, then the rosemary, juice and olive oil. Beat until thoroughly integrated.

Reduce the speed to low. Alternating between the two, add the dry ingredients and the milk in three additions. Using a rubber spatula, scrape the sides of the bowl and give the batter one last mix before pouring it into the prepared pan. Bake the cake for 30 minutes, or until a knife inserted in the center comes out clean.

Serve the cake at room temperature either alone, as a snacking cake, or with poached or stewed winter fruit and crème fraîche for dessert.

Note: *Choose a medium-grain polenta or cornmeal. Fine will offer no texture and coarse will offer too much for most people's taste.*

Gâteau Renversé à l'Orange Sanguine, à la Semoule et aux Amandes

—— *Blood Orange, Semolina and Almond Upside-Down Cake* ——

For centuries, the sun-drenched city of Nice bounced back and forth between Italian and French rule. "Bounced" isn't really the right word, as much fighting was involved, and, of course, where there is fighting, there is always tragedy. The far happier story is that the inhabitants of Nice married the two great cuisines of its rival rulers, picking and choosing from each with intimate knowledge. This cake is that history in a pan. The semolina, blood oranges and almonds conjure southern Italy. The butter, Grand Marnier and crème fraîche are, needless to say, profoundly French. The tradition of drizzling a cake with syrup is one that is found all over the Mediterranean. Here it intensifies the citrus flavor of the cake and makes it deliciously moist. This is a cake that will not dry up on you overnight.

The semolina in this cake moves it a few steps toward a delicate cornbread in texture and away from the fluffiness we think of when we think of cake. But it is not dense, simply moist, syrupy with a textured crumb and the colors of a sunset.

2 organic lemons

3 organic oranges, preferably blood oranges

2 cups / 320 grams semolina flour

2 teaspoons baking powder

2 cups / 200 grams almond flour

1¼ cups unsalted butter, at room temperature

2⅓ cups / 466 grams granulated sugar

5 large eggs, at room temperature

1 teaspoon vanilla extract

2 tablespoons water

1 tablespoon Grand Marnier or orange or pomegranate juice

Preheat the oven to 350°F. Butter then line a 9-inch springform pan with a round of parchment.

Grate the zest of 1 lemon and 2 oranges and set aside. Peel all the oranges and remove any remaining pith. Cut them into ¼-inch-thick slices and arrange the slices in the bottom of the pan. They should touch but not overlap.

Combine the semolina flour, baking powder and almond flour in a bowl and whisk to combine.

Use an electric mixer to cream butter with 1⅓ cups of sugar until pale and fluffy, 6–7 minutes. Add the eggs, one at a time, beating well after each addition. Add the vanilla and reserved citrus zest and beat well to fully combine. Fold in the flour mixture and beat until no streaks remain.

Pour the batter over the oranges and bake in the middle of the oven for 1 hour, or until a knife inserted in the center comes out clean.

While the cake bakes, prepare the syrup. Place the remaining sugar in a small saucepan with the water. Zest and juice the remaining lemon and orange and add both to the sugar water. Bring to a simmer to dissolve the sugar and continue to cook, stirring, until the liquid has reduced by half. Add the Grand Marnier and bring the syrup just back to a simmer. Turn off the stove, but leave the saucepan on the burner to keep it warm.

When the cake is done, transfer it to a cooling rack but let it remain in its pan. Use the tip of a sharp knife to pierce its surface about 20 times. Drizzle with half the warm syrup and set aside for 10 minutes. Invert the cake onto a platter and drizzle with the remaining syrup. Serve warm or at room temperature.

Gâteau aux Bananes Moelleuses

—————— *Moist Banana Bread* ——————

Parisians have taken to banana bread with the same excited, slightly bemused delight previously reserved only for *les brownies New Yorkais* and *les cookies* (chocolate chip cookies). While bananas are nearly as common in Paris as they are in the U.S., they are still considered a tropical fruit, rather than merely that ubiquitous, common thing we slice onto cereal, squeeze into the sides of lunch boxes, and turn into quick bread if left on the counter too long. In other words, they are more likely to be paired with other tropical fruits, such as coconut, lime, pineapple and mango, than with walnuts and chocolate chips. In this recipe, a good dose of lime balances the richness of coconut milk, resulting in a very moist cake. You can barely taste the coconut, but after trying this recipe once, I'd be hard pressed to return to recipes using oil. This is a dense, wet loaf, but not a heavy one. If you'd like more of a coconut taste, simply fold in a cup of shredded coconut or coconut flakes or a quarter teaspoon of coconut extract. Another discovery too good not to share: Banane du Brésil by Giffard. This banana liqueur seems to capture the pure essence of banana and can be used instead of rum.

4 very ripe bananas

½ cup whole coconut milk from a can

2 teaspoons grated lime zest

1 tablespoon lime juice

1¾ cups plus 1 tablespoon / 220 grams all-purpose flour

1 teaspoon baking powder

1 teaspoon baking soda

½ cup butter, at room temperature

1 cup / 200 grams granulated sugar

1 large egg, at room temperature

2 teaspoons dark rum

¼ teaspoon coconut extract, optional

½ cup chopped macadamia nuts, optional

Preheat the oven to 350°F. Butter a 9 x 5-inch loaf pan and place a rectangle of parchment on the bottom.

Pureé the bananas in a food processor. You will need 1¼ cups for this recipe.

Shake the can of coconut milk to combine the creamy part with the watery part.

In a small mixing bowl, whisk the banana puree with the coconut milk, lime zest and juice until well combined.

In another mixing bowl, whisk the flour, baking powder and baking soda until well combined.

In a third, larger mixing bowl, beat the butter and sugar until light and fluffy. Add the egg and beat again to combine. Add the rum and the coconut extract, if using, and, again, beat to combine.

Fold in the dry ingredients and the wet ingredients until no streaks of flour remain. Fold in the macadamia nuts, if using. Pour the batter into the prepared pan and bake for 1 hour, or until a knife inserted in the center of the cake comes out clean.

Let the cake cool for 10 minutes before unmolding it. If you can, wait an hour before serving it to allow the flavors to bloom. This cake keeps well at room temperature, wrapped in a clean tea towel, or in the fridge, wrapped in plastic.

Gâteau Ispahan de Dorie et Pierre

—— *Dorie and Pierre's Ispahan Cake* ——

I first met Dorie Greenspan at the French Consulate in New York. I don't remember the reason for the event or anything that was said in the very many and, most certainly, very serious speeches that were given that day by, I'm sure, very notable people. All I remember is catching sight of Dorie across the room. Dressed in her customary French sailor's blue and sporting a chic scarf tied neatly around her neck, she was radiant. Lit from within. Dorie's charisma stems from an infectious enthusiasm, from a spirit of unlimited generosity and from what can only be described as energetic curiosity. It's impossible not to adore her. And adore her, I do. We sat next to each other that day, and a friendship was born. When I decided to write this book, I emailed Dorie, aware that Paris and baking are very much her territory. I didn't want to encroach and was prepared to back right off. But she emailed in response that very night, adamant that I must write it. With "must" underlined. She had given me her blessing, and I burst into tears.

This recipe comes courtesy of Dorie, who, in turn, credits the extraordinary pâtissier Pierre Hermé with the inspiration. In other words, you are now in the hands of not one, but two brilliant bakers. I've already mentioned the Parisian fervor over Hermé's rose water confections, in particular the rose, raspberry and lychee macaron that led to an entire collection of Ispahan creations—Ispahan being the name of a highly fragrant Persian rose. But I've never met a Parisian who would consider making macarons at home. Thankfully, Dorie has captured the essence of Ispahan in this exceptionally lovely and simple cake.

Dorie writes with a particular mix of warmth and precision. When you read and cook from her books, you know you have a guide who won't let you slip or trip or miss even the most minute step. She is all about clarity and makes even the most novice of bakers feel safe. I've kept this recipe mostly in her words for all of these good reasons.

3 tablespoons rose syrup

2 tablespoons whole milk

2 cups / 200 grams almond flour

1 cup / 114 grams confectioners' sugar

3 large eggs, separated, plus 1 large egg, at room temperature

2½ tablespoons granulated sugar

¾ cup unsalted butter, at room temperature

¼ teaspoon rose extract

½ cup plus 1 tablespoon / 68 grams all-purpose flour

1 pint raspberries

Preheat the oven to 350°F. Generously butter a 9 x 5-inch loaf pan and lightly dust it with flour.

In a small bowl, combine the rose syrup and milk.

Set a sieve over a medium-sized mixing bowl and sift in the almond flour and confectioners' sugar. Whisk to combine.

Using a large mixing bowl and electric beaters or a stand mixer, beat the egg whites until they just start to hold their shape, then gradually add the granulated sugar, beating until the whites hold firm, glossy peaks. (If you need the mixer bowl, gently slide the whites into another bowl. There's no need to wash the bowl.)

Combine the butter and almond flour mixture in the now-empty mixer bowl or another large mixing bowl and beat at medium speed for 3 minutes, or until very smooth. Leaving the beater on medium, add the egg yolks, one at a time, beating for 1 minute after each addition. Add the rose-flavored milk and the extract and beat for 1 minute more.

Stir one-quarter of the egg whites into the batter to lighten it. Then, using a rubber spatula and a light but quick touch, alternately fold the remaining whites and the all-purpose flour into the batter.

Pour one-third of the batter into the prepared loaf pan and spread to even it. Make three rows of berries down the length of the pan—don't let the berries touch the side of the pan—then cover with another third of batter. Make three more rows of berries, then carefully cover these with the last of the batter.

Reduce the oven temperature to 300°F and bake the cake for 55–65 minutes, or until a knife inserted in the center comes out clean. The top of the cake will be a lovely brown and feel springy to the touch, and the cake will have started to pull away from the sides of the pan. Transfer the cake to a cooling rack for about 3 minutes, then unmold it, invert it and let it cool to room temperature on the rack.

A note on ingredients: Rose syrup—not rose water!—and rose extract are both needed. Once you've got an open bottle of rose syrup in your fridge, however, you'll find yourself pouring it into lemonade, onto strawberries, over ice cream and maybe adding a small shot to a glass of sparkling wine.

REGIONAL CLASSICS

Les Classiques de Nos Régions

Gâteau Breton

—————— *Breton Butter Cake* ——————

Butter is no simple affair in France. No, no. Consider it a passion born in infancy and lovingly nurtured with precision, devotion and abundance throughout one's life, outlasting all manner of exotic ingredients. And while it is easy to run to the corner shop for a rather good stick of butter in a pinch, Parisians are far more likely to buy butter at their local fromagerie or laiterie. Here, you might find a selection of more than a dozen varieties of butter, from beurre pâtissier, with a fat content of no less than 99.8 percent, to butters holding their own AOC (Appellation d'Origine Contrôlée), to the lovingly named beurre tendre, a butter that is whipped to tender perfection. Choosing a butter is a ritual no less considered than choosing a bottle of wine for dinner. It should be paired to its use and served chilled, but not cold. This is true throughout France, but particularly so in Normandy and Brittany, where the cream is as rich as the land is fertile.

This cake, as you've no doubt guessed by now, is all about the butter. In fact, for it to be called a true gâteau Breton, twenty percent of its batter must be butter. Anything less, and the knights charged with preserving culinary tradition will descend upon your kitchen in a storm of fury. (Yes, such knights really do exist.) But fear not, it is among the simplest cakes to make and, in truth, any good European-style butter with a high fat content will do. I use Plugrá, Kerrygold or Lurpak. Traditionally, a gâteau Breton is made with only four ingredients—butter, flour, sugar and eggs. But a few spoonfuls of dark rum give it a little depth and cut its richness, and a teaspoon of baking powder ensures it isn't too flat for modern-day tastes. This is a simple cake with a texture somewhere between a shortbread and a pound cake. It is slightly on the dry side and meant to be served with a generous dollop of crème fraîche. Often you'll find a thin layer of jam baked into the middle. This might be cherry, raspberry, plum or apricot. But I find the extra steps aren't worth the trouble, when a spoonful of jam on the plate is just as satisfying. In summer, I like to serve this with fresh fruit, macerated for a few hours in sugar. It is a rich cake, if not overly sweet. Small slices should do the trick. The Bretons like to age this cake, waiting twenty-four hours before eating it. True to its humble roots, it is a practical cake that way. Made with pantry ingredients, it is easily transportable and stores well at room temperature over several days.

- 1 cup unsalted European butter, at room temperature
- 1 cup / 200 grams granulated sugar
- 5 large egg yolks, at room temperature
- 2 tablespoons dark rum or orange flower water
- 1 cup / 120 grams all-purpose flour
- 1 cup / 120 grams cake flour
- 1 teaspoon baking powder
- ½ teaspoon salt
- 1 large egg
- 1 tablespoon milk

Line an 8-inch springform pan or 9-inch fluted tart pan with a round of parchment.

In a large mixing bowl, cream the butter and sugar together using handheld electric beaters for roughly 4 minutes, until pale but not fluffy. The idea isn't to incorporate large amounts of air into the cake as it is meant to be dense and decadent. One by one, beat in the five egg yolks until all are fully incorporated. Add the rum and beat to combine.

Place a sieve over the mixing bowl and sift in the all-purpose flour, cake flour, baking powder and salt. Give the mixture a quick fold with a rubber spatula, then beat briefly on low until no streaks of flour remain.

Transfer the batter—it will be thick and tacky—to the baking pan. Cover with plastic wrap. Use the palm of your hand to lightly smooth the top. Refrigerate for 30 minutes. Preheat the oven to 350°F.

Lightly whisk the whole egg with the milk. Remove the pan from the fridge, discard the plastic wrap and, using a pastry brush, brush the top of the cake with the egg wash. Drag the tines of a fork across the surface in a crisscrossing diamond pattern. Give the cake another light brushing of egg wash. Bake for 20 minutes, then reduce the heat to 325°F and bake for another 15–20 minutes, or until the cake is a rich golden brown and the edges have started to pull away from the sides of the pan.

Allow the cake to cool in the pan for 5 minutes before moving it to a cake plate. Your slices will be neater if you slice the cake while still warm. The cake can be eaten warm or at room temperature. Serve with a generous dollop of crème fraîche.

JAM VARIATION: If you'd like to try this with a layer of jam, fill the prepared tart pan with half the batter, freeze for 10 minutes, add ¾ cup of jam, freeze for another 10 minutes and add the final layer of batter. It will need 45 minutes total baking time.

Gâteau Breton aux Amandes

Breton Butter Almond Cake

While the previous recipe is the classic, this variation has a nearly undiscernible amount of almond flour, which gives it a very faint frangipane taste and appealing texture. Like the classic, it ripens and deepens and is, arguably, at its best on day two or three, by which time it will have taken on the consistency of shortbread. But unlike the classic, which almost tastes too much like butter—is that even possible?—just out of the oven, this version, thanks perhaps to the almond flour, is decadently buttery when still warm. Still no escaping the facts—this is a very, very rich snacking cake. The bitterness of a dark-roast coffee or a breakfast tea or the decisiveness of a Cognac or Armagnac will cut this richness while, para-doxically, showcasing it. The point of a snacking cake, I'm told, is that it keeps for several days. One can have a small slice when hunger strikes, be it morning, noon or night. This cake keeps well for a week. If you can manage to reserve a slice that long, my hat goes off to you. And, chances are, you are French. Perhaps it is because good food in France is never in question, never a rarity, that the French are able to restrain themselves with such ease. And temptation, oddly, is particularly easy to navigate in Paris. You can walk past a pâtisserie or fromagerie with the certainty that you will pass several more that day. Or that the same delicacies will be available, as they always have been, except in wartime. Superb food is no less appreciated—it might even be more so, as it isn't devoured as if it were endangered. Food is eaten mindfully, with a satisfying focus. These are, of course, generalizations. But whenever I make this cake, I am reminded that it is, in fact, meant to last a week. There's nearly as much pleasure in knowing it will be there tomorrow as there is in eating it today.

A fair warning. This does not resemble any American cake I know. It's a celebration of good butter, and its texture is rich, dense and somewhere between a shortbread cookie and a dense pound cake. Use the very best European-style butter you can find and relish the perfect simplicity of this beloved cake.

1¼ cups / 284 grams unsalted European
   butter

¾ cup / 150 grams superfine sugar

4 large egg yolks, at room temperature

½ cup / 50 grams almond flour

2 tablespoons dark rum

1 teaspoon vanilla extract

2 tablespoons whole milk

1 cup / 120 grams cake flour

¼ teaspoon fine sea salt

1 cup / 120 grams all-purpose flour

1 whole egg, lightly beaten

Preheat the oven to 325°F. Butter a 9- or 9½-inch fluted tart pan with a removable bottom.

In a stand mixer or using handheld electric beaters, cream the butter and sugar at medium speed until pale and smooth. With the mixer still running, add the egg yolks, one at a time, until incorporated. Add the almond flour, rum, vanilla and 1 tablespoon of the milk and continue to beat until homogenous, about a minute.

Turn the mixer speed to low and add half the cake flour and the salt, mix to combine, then add the remaining cake flour. Remove the bowl from the stand and, using a rubber spatula, fold in the all-purpose flour in two steps, until no streaks of flour are visible. Fold in the remaining tablespoon of milk.

Pour the batter into the prepared tart pan and refrigerate for 5 minutes.

Using a pastry brush, lightly paint the cake with the beaten egg. Using the tines of a fork, draw a crisscross pattern over the surface of the cake.

Bake for 35–45 minutes, or until the cake is a rich golden brown. Transfer to a cooling rack for 15 minutes before removing the cake from the pan. Allow to come to room temperature. If not serving right away, cover with a cake dome and keep at room temperature. A small dollop of crème fraîche adds a cool tang.

Far Breton

—— *Breton Flan* ——

Eating this is a sensual experience. It's a bit like crème brûlée in that you should really close your eyes for the first bite and give yourself over to the exquisite pleasure of the soft silken creamy lush slippery richness. But a far Breton has a bit more substance and, in this recipe, a boozy undercurrent. Prunes may have a bad rap in the United States, but in France, they're the stuff of legend. *Les pruneaux d'Agen*, the most rarefied, date back to the Crusades, when thirteenth-century monks in l'Abbaye de Clairac, in the southwest of France, crossbred a Syrian plum tree from Damascus with a local variety from the Lot-et-Garonne, producing a fruit that has a sweet depth of flavor that is almost date-like in its intensity. These prunes are protected by the French government with both their own *appellation* and *Indication Géographique Protégée*, or IGP. It is Agen prunes, for example, that you steep in Armagnac and serve in small Limoges bowls on special occasions. If you're still not convinced, call them dried plums.

Of course, regional specialties stay regional until you get to the capital. While Bretons make this ancient recipe using a local prune and dark rum, in Paris, Armagnac or Cognac elevate this humble flan into the realm of the extraordinary. If convenience or purse strings dictate rum, I tend to make this with raisins, not prunes, as the rum-raisin match reminds me of my father's favorite ice cream flavor. But only do this if you can find truly large, plump raisins, the sort you get in farmers markets in California or online, not the shriveled, hard pebbles in red boxes meant for lunch boxes. A little luxury is required here.

This recipe serves six. It can be eaten warm or at room temperature and must be served directly from its gratin dish. The sweet spot, in my opinion, is about thirty to forty minutes after removing it from the oven. Don't wait more than a few hours. And don't try to refrigerate it or keep it overnight. It will lose its ephemeral quality.

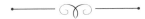

14 pitted prunes

⅓ cup Armagnac, Cognac or rum

1 cup / 120 grams cake flour

½ cup / 100 grams superfine sugar

¼ teaspoon fine sea salt

3 large eggs, at room temperature

2 cups whole milk

⅓ cup / 5½ tablespoons unsalted butter, melted and cooled to room temperature

1 tablespoon Demerara or raw sugar

In a covered nonreactive bowl, such as glass or porcelain, steep the prunes in the Armagnac for 24 hours at room temperature.

Preheat the oven to 400°F. Butter a shallow 6-cup gratin dish.

Sift the flour, superfine sugar and salt into a large mixing bowl. With the back of a spoon, lightly nudge these ingredients to the side of the bowl to make a well in the center.

In a small bowl, whisk the eggs to break them up and create a homogenous mixture, then pour this into the well. Pour about a third of the milk onto the eggs and whisk to combine. Add another third and, this time, start lightly whisking in the dry ingredients to form a batter. Add the remaining milk and integrate all the dry ingredients. Pour in the melted butter and whisk into a smooth batter. Set aside for 10 minutes.

Scatter the prunes in the baking dish. Pour any remaining Armagnac into the batter. Once the batter has rested ten minutes, whisk to recombine and pour over the prunes. Bake for 30–40 minutes. Sprinkle with Demerara sugar and let sit for half an hour before serving still warm from the baking dish.

Note: If using raisins instead of prunes, use ¾ cup raisins and ¼ cup rum. You will only need to steep them for 4–6 hours.

Gâteau de ton Enfance

—— *Childhood Cake* ——

W hen the Michelin-starred, super sexy, massively lauded Parisian chef Jean-François Piège made public his recipe for a *gâteau à l'orange* on his son's birthday, Paris swooned. Not because he looked so adorable whipping up this one-bowl cake that bakes for only a *vingtaine de minutes* (twenty or so minutes) in a video on the magazine *Le Point*'s website, but because the cake itself stirred up memories of so many Parisians' own *gâteau de ton Enfance*.

This is a moist, slightly springy, slightly sticky cake that is indeed reminiscent of childhood, even if you never had such a cake in childhood. It conjures the flavors of a creamsicle, but with none of that artificial orange or saccharine sweetness. It is comfort at its core. No wonder its popularity surged during the Covid-19 quarantine. Like yogurt cake and quatre-quarts, this is an after-school treat or dessert for the family. Don't ice, glaze or brush it with syrup. It will be too moist if you do. Rather, embrace its humble, sunny appearance.

Piège whips up this cake in under three minutes once his *mise en place* is set and, no doubt, because he whisks like a pro. The recipe follows the basic ratio of equal weights of butter, sugar, flour and eggs. But there are a few pointers. Not all eggs weigh the same. I sometimes need to whisk three eggs and pour off a bit to get to one hundred twenty grams if I'm using farmers market eggs rather than large supermarket eggs. You might think that a full tablespoon of baking powder would lead to a towering cake, but it doesn't. This is largely because you aren't whipping air into egg whites. Once this cake is baked, cool it in the pan for ten minutes, but not longer, or it will stick to the sides. Now, the hard part. Wait ten minutes to eat it. It needs absolutely nothing on the side.

PAN

1 tablespoon butter

2 tablespoons granulated or raw sugar, plus more if needed

BATTER

½ cup plus 1 tablespoon / 9 tablespoons unsalted butter, at room temperature

½ cup plus 2 tablespoons / 125 grams superfine sugar

2 large / 120 grams eggs, at room temperature

1 large and juicy organic juicing orange

1 cup / 120 grams cake flour

1 tablespoon baking powder

¼ teaspoon fine sea salt

Preheat the oven to 350°F. Very generously slather a 9-inch cake pan with the 1 tablespoon butter. Then sprinkle it with the 2 tablespoons granulated sugar, trying to cover as much of the bottom and sides as possible. If you need more, use it.

In a good-sized mixing bowl, cream the butter and superfine sugar. Piège does this with a whisk. If I'm feeling lazy, I'll use electric beaters, at medium speed. Once pale and fluffy, add the eggs and whisk until you see no streaks of yolk.

Zest the orange directly into the batter, then cut the orange in half and juice it into a measuring cup. You will need ½ cup juice. Add this to the batter and stir until homogenous.

Place a sieve over the mixing bowl and sift in the flour, baking powder and salt. Give the batter a quick but determined whisking to thoroughly integrate all the ingredients. Pour into the prepared pan and bake for 20–30 minutes, until the cake starts to pull away from the sides of the pan and a knife inserted in the center comes out clean. The cake should be a golden brown.

Set it on a rack to cool for 10 minutes, then invert onto a serving plate. Serve at room temperature.

Gâteau à l'Huile d'Olive

—— *Olive Oil Cake* ——

While the world prizes Italian olive oil for its herbaceous complexity, Parisians merely nod politely and keep their lush, delicate Niçoise olive oil a well-guarded secret, preferring not to export their limited supply. The only notable make I've seen in the United States is that of Nicolas Alziari, and it is delicious, if also pricey. For this classic Mediterranean cake, the olive oil need not be from Nice, but it must be on the buttery or fruity, well-rounded, sweeter side. Avoid the strong, grassy, green-hued olive oils, best kept for dipping bread.

This cake is one I make more, perhaps, than any other cake. It is, I realize, as close to perfection as anything I'll ever serve. And it is ridiculously easy, made with ingredients that I most often have on hand. The only substitution I'll sometimes make is to use one teaspoon of grated Meyer lemon zest and one teaspoon orange zest if I'm running low on oranges, and yuzu juice is a revelation, here. Many people serve olive oil cake with whipped cream and macerated fruit, but this truly needs nothing. I serve it in big, fabulous plain slices. If it's not all gone by the end of dinner, I'll save a slice to have with an espresso in the morning.

2 cups / 240 grams all-purpose flour

1 tablespoon baking powder

¼ teaspoon fine sea salt

1¼ cups / 250 grams granulated sugar

3 large eggs, at room temperature

¾ cup extra-virgin olive oil

¾ cup whole milk

2 teaspoons grated orange zest and
   1 teaspoon grated lemon zest

Juice of 1 juicy orange

Preheat the oven to 350°F. Butter a 9-inch springform pan and line it with a round of parchment. Butter and flour the sides of the pan.

Stir together the flour, baking powder and salt in a small bowl.

In a stand mixer or using electric beaters at medium speed, beat the sugar and eggs until fluffy and pale yellow. One by one, with the mixer on low, add the olive oil, milk, orange and lemon zests and the juice, raise the speed to medium and beat for another minute or two, until homogenous. Fold in the flour mixture with a rubber spatula until just blended.

Pour the batter into the prepared pan and bake for 45 minutes, or until golden brown and a knife inserted in the center comes out clean. The cake is delicious both warm and at room temperature. Thanks to the oil, it will keep well overnight.

Clafoutis aux Framboises

—— *Raspberry Clafoutis* ——

My first memories of clafoutis are of the chilled, leaden squares that were served in the cafeteria at my school in Paris. They were rubbery and tasteless and nearly turned me off this classic forever. Roughly two decades later, I was at a friend's for dinner, happily chatting away, when I smelled something wonderful wafting in from her kitchen—a bit like a pancake, a bit like a flan, it had notes of vanilla and cooked cream and filled the room with a soft cloud of comfort. Moments later, I was tasting a soft, pudding-like clafoutis. By the second bite, I was a convert. But not entirely so. What I came to realize is that I don't love the classic choice of cherries in the batter. I prefer either a berry with just enough suggestion of tartness to cut through the richness of the milk and cream, or the tenderness of a stone fruit, ripe and sliced, or autumn apples or winter pears with a little liqueur tossed in for good measure. No doubt, I simply can't get past those early memories. But you are free, so cherry away!

This recipe is rich and unctuous, but never heavy. It makes as perfect a clafoutis as I've ever had. Sometimes, I grate in the zest of an orange. Sometimes, I use two teaspoons of rum instead of one teaspoon of vanilla. I rarely add spice because the joy of clafoutis is in its simplicity. The use of almond flour may be surprising, but it is not uncommon. It allows for a bit of structure without relying on more flour, which would weigh the custard down.

1 cup / 200 grams granulated sugar	1 cup whole milk
5 large eggs, at room temperature	1 cup heavy cream
¾ cup / 75 grams almond flour	1 teaspoon vanilla extract
½ teaspoon sea salt	1⅓ cups fresh or frozen raspberries
¾ cup / 90 grams all-purpose flour	Confectioners' sugar, for dusting

Preheat the oven to 375°F. Butter a 10-inch round gratin dish and dust it with 1 teaspoon of the granulated sugar.

In a large mixing bowl, beat the remaining granulated sugar and the eggs at medium-low speed for three minutes. Add the almond flour and salt and beat to combine. Place a sieve over the bowl and sift the all-purpose flour into the batter, then fold it in. Add the milk, cream and vanilla and beat until the mixture is smooth, about 3 minutes. Let the batter rest for 10 minutes, then give it a quick whisking to draw it all back together again.

Pour the batter into the prepared gratin dish. If using fresh raspberries, scatter them over the top. If using frozen raspberries, make sure to break up any that have stuck together, then scatter them over the top. Include any little broken bits, as they add taste and color.

Bake for 35–45 minutes, or until the center of the clafoutis is set. Allow to cool a few minutes, dust with the confectioners' sugar, and serve.

Clafoutis is best eaten right away, while it is still pudding-like. If refrigerated, it will become dense. Delicious, of course, for breakfast, but not optimal for serving.

VARIATIONS

Try blackberries or loganberries and add the zest of 1 orange.

Try apricots or peaches and add 1 tablespoon amaretto or ¼ teaspoon almond extract.

Note: You do not want a watery fruit. This means that if using stone fruit, opt for just ripe or just short of peak. Somewhere between firm and soft. Not the ripe that drips juice down your T-shirt when you bite into it.

Clafoutis aux Pommes à la Normande
— *Norman Apple Clafoutis* —

This is true rustic, one-pan cooking. It will, however, surprise in its delicacy. If you've grown up in the United States, chances are your memory of baked apples is entwined with the fragrance of cinnamon and vanilla. And for good reason. Each note draws out the inherent sweet complexity of the other. But the French are more inclined to express the apple in its purest beauty. Here, it is caramelized in only a bit of butter and sugar. Calvados wakes the palate and lemon zest cuts through the richness of the cream. For those who prefer a fresh apple taste, simply slice the apples thinly and don't sauté them. They will have brightness but will be a touch less supple.

Normandy has long been a favored weekend spot for Parisians. In the summer, the beaches beckon. In fall, the scent of apples fills the air. Nearly every farmer with an orchard seems to make his or her own Calvados, or Calva, as it's called for short. The homemade ones can taste as raw and fiery as moonshine, but a well-made aged Calvados can rival the best Armagnacs and Cognacs. Needless to say, it is used in most every Norman dish, both savory and sweet, as is the region's prized butter and cream. This clafoutis brings them all to the party.

When I was a young girl, we rented a house in a small hamlet called Barneville-la-Bertran, about ten minutes' drive from the harbor town of Honfleur. Weekends, we would drive up from Paris and stop, late Friday, at a local farmer's for milk, butter, crème fraîche, eggs and just-picked apples. He'd offer my parents a glass of his homemade Calva and, the moment he opened the bottle, a heady rush of alcohol and apples would fill the room. No wonder, then, that the smell of this clafoutis baking arouses deep nostalgia in me. But, memories aside, what's not to love? Apples, butter, cream . . . if any combination could conjure childhood, it is surely this one. And if you want to add cinnamon, go ahead. But try it once without and you may find yourself surprised by the sheer appley pleasure it affords.

Come Sunday, we'd drive home to Paris, with a tote of fresh apples in the back of the station wagon. When the traffic slowed, I'd look into the other cars on the highway and see other families with bags of apples. No doubt, they, too, would be having a clafoutis aux pommes Monday night. Most likely with a dollop of Norman crème fraîche.

3 apples, such as golden delicious (see Notes)

3 tablespoons unsalted butter

2 tablespoons light brown sugar

4 large eggs, at room temperature

⅓ cup / 66 grams granulated sugar

1½ cups heavy cream

The grated zest of 1 large lemon

½ teaspoon sea salt

3 tablespoons Calvados or apple brandy

7 tablespoons / 53 grams all-purpose flour

Confectioners' sugar, for dusting

Crème fraîche, for serving

Preheat the oven to 375°F.

Peel, quarter and core the apples. Slice them, depending on the size of the apples, into six or eight pieces.

Heat the butter in a 10-inch ovenproof skillet over medium heat. Once the butter starts to foam, add the apples and gently toss to coat in the butter. Sauté the apples for 1 minute, flip them and sprinkle with half of the brown sugar. Sauté them for another minute, flip and sprinkle with the remaining brown sugar. Remove from heat. The apples should give off a delicious caramelized buttery appley smell, but still retain their shape.

In stand mixer or using handheld electric beaters, whisk the eggs and granulated sugar at medium speed until pale and fluffy, about 4 minutes. With the mixer still running, add the cream, lemon zest, salt and Calvados and beat until integrated. Reduce the speed to low. Sprinkle in the flour and mix until just smooth. Set aside to rest for 15 minutes.

Fanning them out from the center, arrange the apple slices in one layer in the skillet. Pour the batter over the apples and bake until the center of the clafoutis is set, 35–45 minutes. Let sit for 5 minutes, then serve with cool crème fraîche.

APRICOT CLAFOUTIS: Replace the apples with apricots and the Calvados with Sauternes, and sprinkle with a layer of sliced almonds before baking. Dust with confectioners' sugar just before bringing it to the table.

Notes: *Choose an apple variety that retains its shape when baked and is neither too sweet, nor too tart. My preference is for golden apples or for a mixture of two or three.*

Clafoutis is best served straight from the oven with a dollop of crème fraîche on the side. If you refrigerate leftovers, bring them to room temperature before eating them. The clafoutis will have lost its lovely texture, but not its flavor.

Clafoutis aux Poires et au Chocolat

———— Chocolate and Pear Clafoutis ————

Here, I've taken the most comforting of all French desserts—the clafoutis—and replaced the usual summer cherries found in this flan-like dish with winter pears and dark chocolate. It is rich. Let me repeat myself. It is rich. This is a distinctly Parisian dessert, as it dares to rethink a classic. Outside the city, it is still surprisingly rare to see tradition upturned. When I make this clafoutis, I'm instantly back in my mother's kitchen. She's always added Poire Williams to Julia Child's recipe for chocolate mousse. I'd stir the melting chocolate for her, breathing it in, waiting to lick the spoon, and then suddenly I'd get a heady whiff of the liqueur as she opened the bottle. Her instinct was spot-on. The coupling of pears and chocolate has always been one of tender deference. Neither seeks to upstage the other, offering instead a subtle, delicate boost of flavor and mood. Bring a little Poire Williams into the mix and things may get suggestive, but never overpowering. Comice pears, that variety distinctive for a wash of pink blush on one side and a rounded, sweet, almost perfumed flavor, have a short season, but are unparalleled in taste. In Paris, you'll often find them wrapped individually in tissue paper as they bruise easily when ripe. They are perfect simply peeled and sliced, but they also give this clafoutis the barest hint of a floral note, which lightens the intensity of the dark chocolate. A scattering of toasted sliced almonds and a dusting of cocoa and confectioners' sugar will dress this dessert up, but I never bother. The intoxicating smell of the baking clafoutis will have already teased everyone in the house into a state of high anticipation.

1 tablespoon unsalted butter, at room temperature

⅓ cup plus 1 tablespoon / 79 grams granulated sugar

170 grams dark chocolate, 64%–70% cacao

2 tablespoons Poire Williams or another pear brandy

3 extra-large eggs, at room temperature

6 tablespoons / 45 grams all-purpose flour

1½ cups heavy cream

¼ teaspoon fleur de sel

3 firm but ripe pears, ideally Comice, peeled and sliced

Preheat the oven to 375°F. With the tablespoon of butter, grease a 10-inch round baking dish (ideally ceramic) and sprinkle the bottom and sides with 1 tablespoon of the sugar.

Melt the chocolate in a double boiler and then allow to cool slightly. Stir in the Poire Williams.

Beat the eggs and the ⅓ cup of sugar in the bowl of an electric mixer fitted with the paddle attachment or with a handheld beater on medium speed until light and fluffy. Lower the speed and mix in the flour, cream, salt and melted chocolate. Set aside for 10 minutes. Then give it a quick whisk to draw it all back together again.

Arrange the pear slices in a single layer, slightly fanned out, in the prepared baking dish. Pour the batter over the pears and bake until the top is golden brown and the custard is firm, about 35 minutes. Remove from the oven. Let the clafoutis sit for 5 minutes, then serve with a dollop of crème fraîche still cool from the fridge.

Les Nonnettes

—— *Honey Spice Cakes* ——

I confess I hesitated to include these little muffin-shaped rye-and-honey-spiced cakes. Not that they aren't good—they are terrific. Moist, deeply flavored, with a surprise burst of jam inside and a lemony glaze on top. But they are an acquired taste. Far more assertive and far less immediately and sweetly accessible than our pumpkin spice, *les épices à pain d'épices* is the traditional mix of spices used in French holiday spice breads and in these *nonnettes*. It's earthier and given a bit of a licorice astringency from star anise and anise seeds. The trick is in the balance. Mine tilts toward ginger and includes nutmeg to soften and ground the flavors. These little cakes have a spoonful of jam in their interior. Marmalade is the norm, but cherry, raspberry, ginger, plum, blackberry and black currant are my preference. And if you can make or find it, a clementine or tangerine marmalade is fabulous.

This is a medieval recipe. Or, at least, it would be if I didn't beat my eggs in a stand mixer, use a silicone muffin mold and bake in an electric oven! This is, rather, my loose adaptation of a recipe I found on L'Academie du Goût, a site founded by, among others, Alain Ducasse. But it is equally true that nonnettes date back to the city of Dijon in the Middle Ages, when the local nuns—*les nonnes*, hence the name—would bake these in their convent, no doubt because they last several days and appear somewhat austere. Of course, I ice them, as austerity is not exactly in my repertoire. In the nineteenth century, as trains were beginning to crisscross the country, nonnettes were the favored snack. And they do indeed travel well and are eaten out of hand. If I were hiking, I'd carry these in my pack. Try them on picnics and late weekend breakfasts. And they are a must in the autumn, when that first craving sounds for something deep and hearty with a long-echoing flavor.

SPICE MIX

4 cloves

1½ teaspoons ground ginger

1 star anise

½ teaspoon anise seeds

⅛ teaspoon freshly grated nutmeg

2 teaspoons ground cinnamon

¼ teaspoon fine sea salt

A few grindings of pepper

NONNETTES

4 tablespoons unsalted butter

⅞ cup whole milk

¾ cup / 250 grams honey, preferably wild-flower or another medium-dark variety

¼ cup / 50 grams granulated sugar

2 large eggs, at room temperature

1⅔ cups / 200 grams all-purpose flour

7½ tablespoons / 50 grams fine dark rye flour

2 teaspoons baking powder

½ cup jam or marmalade of your choice

GLAZE

4–5 teaspoons lemon juice

1 cup confectioners' sugar

SPICE MIX

In a clean coffee grinder, spice grinder or Vitamix, combine the cloves, ginger, star anise, anise seeds, nutmeg, cinnamon, salt and pepper. Grind to a powder. (I include the ground spices with the whole ones to create a fully integrated mixture.) Set aside.

NONNETTES

Preheat the oven to 350°F. Butter the cups of a muffin pan or line with parchment cups.

Melt the butter and set aside.

In a small saucepan over low heat, warm the milk, honey and sugar together, stirring until the sugar and honey have dissolved into the milk. Do not bring to a simmer. Remove from heat and set aside.

In a stand mixer or using handheld electric beaters, beat the eggs until pale. Keeping the mixer running, slowly pour in the lukewarm sweetened milk. Add the ground spices and continue to beat. Add the all-purpose flour, rye flour and baking powder and beat just until integrated. Beat in the melted butter.

Pour the batter into the prepared muffin pan, filling the cups only a third full. Spoon a teaspoon or so of jam onto the center of each, then fill with the remaining batter. Bake for 25–30 minutes, or until a knife inserted in the center comes out clean. Set aside to cool for 10 minutes before popping them out of their pan.

GLAZE

Combine the lemon juice and confectioners' sugar. Stir until smooth. Ice the tops of the muffins. Eat warm or at room temperature.

Gâteau de Savoie

———— Savoy Cake ————

Serve this delicate beauty with some fruit in syrup and a bit of crème Chantilly. I like it, in winter, with sliced Cara Cara oranges doused in a little extra orange blossom water and, in the summer, with apricots that have been poached in sweet wine or with sliced berries that have been macerating for a bit in sugar and have given up some of their juice. This cake is not dry, but it does like a little liquid. To play up the orange blossom water, I'll add just a little to the crème Chantilly and perhaps sweeten it with a spoonful or two of orange blossom honey instead of sugar. This recipe, popular again thanks to Alain Ducasse, dates back to the fourteenth century.

The Savoy is one of the more fascinating regions of France, as it borders both Switzerland and Italy and is home to the French Alps. Its location gave it great political import but also meant that the region frequently found itself caught in a tug-of-war between French and Italian rulers. And, as it happens, the House of Savoy became one of the ruling dynasties of Italy in the second half of the nineteenth century. None of this geographical friction seems to have rubbed off on this recipe, however, as this cake couldn't be more classically French in technique, taste and texture. The orange blossom water is my addition, and it can easily be omitted or replaced with two teaspoons of vanilla extract.

1 tablespoon unsalted butter, at room temperature

¼ cup / 30 grams light brown sugar

5 large egg whites / 150 grams, at room temperature

¼ teaspoon fine sea salt

5 large egg yolks / 100 grams, at room temperature

¾ cup plus 1 tablespoon / 165 grams superfine sugar

Scant ½ cup / 60 grams cake flour

½ cup / 60 grams cornstarch

1 tablespoon orange blossom water, optional

Confectioners' sugar, for dusting

Preheat the oven to 335°F. Butter a 9-inch cake pan lavishly, using the full tablespoon of softened butter. Pour in the light brown sugar and shake the pan to distribute the sugar across the bottom, then on the sides. Turn the pan over to discard any excess sugar, but don't tap it. The sugar will caramelize, which is part of what makes this cake so good. Place the pan in the fridge while making the batter.

In a stand mixer or using handheld electric beaters, whisk the egg whites to nearly stiff peaks, or, as the French say, until they form the beak of a bird. They should hold their shape but not be dry. Sprinkle on the salt and beat until integrated. Transfer to a clean bowl and set aside.

Combine the egg yolks and superfine sugar in the now-empty bowl of the stand mixer (no need to wash it first) and whisk at medium-high speed until pale yellow. The mixture should leave ribbons in its wake. Place a sieve over the bowl and sift in the cake flour and cornstarch. Using a rubber spatula, fold these into the yolk mixture. Add the orange blossom water, if using it, and fold to combine.

Gently but decisively, fold a third of the whites into the batter until smooth, then another third, then the last third. No streaks of white should remain, but the mixture should still be voluminous.

Pour the batter into the prepared pan and bake for 20 minutes, then reduce the heat to 300°F and bake for another 10 minutes, or until a knife inserted in the center comes out clean.

Remove from the oven and set on a cooling rack. After only 2 minutes, flip the cake onto a cake plate. Allow to come to room temperature. Before serving, dust with confectioners' sugar. Do not refrigerate this cake! It should be eaten the day it is made.

Gâteau de Nantes

— *Almond Rum Cake* —

This boozy beauty hails from Nantes and dates back to the early eighteenth century. Once the capital of Brittany and home to its illustrious dukes, Nantes remains one of France's busiest ports. It lies, most enviably, on the Loire River not more than thirty miles inland from the Atlantic Ocean. But if sea trade is not your business, you are more likely to visit Nantes for the medieval Château des Ducs de Bretagne, for its ravishing cathedral, and for a slice of this exceptional cake.

Circa 1820, when the recipe, featuring cane sugar, Bourbon vanilla and dark rum, was created by a local pastry chef named Rouleau, it was instantly seen as the tastiest way to show off the town's prosperous trade with the West Indies. Two hundred years later, it remains a somewhat fancy cake that just happens to be very simple to make, nearly impossible to make badly, and eminently practical as it is even better on day two. It does, however, fall squarely in the dinner party category due to three heady pours of rum—one in the batter, one in the soaking syrup, and one in the glaze. All to say, this is the cake for late, grown-up dinners that are perhaps a bit dressy and maybe celebratory. You know the kind: the kids are asleep, the wine is flowing, the candles are lit, and the conversation hasn't paused in three hours. Elegant in its sheen of white glaze, it is a rich, moist and refined cake. Sleek and assured, it prefers to stand alone, without dollops of cream or sugared berries crowding its presentation.

Now, stay with me, as I take you from Nantes to Paris to Boston or, more specifically, to 177 Milk Street, home to Chris Kimball's food magazine, television show, cooking school and podcast. For years, I had been using a terrific recipe for a gâteau Nantais—"Nantais" refers to those born in Nantes—when I came across one in Kimball's magazine. The addition of peppercorns and allspice berries to the soaking syrup struck me as a brilliant way to add intrigue to the rum. Add them only if you like a slightly peppery kick. I've included both the traditional rum glaze and a lemon glaze. The lemon glaze makes the cake less boozy, more zesty. Both are terrific.

CAKE

6 large eggs, at room temperature

1 cup butter, at room temperature

1½ cups / 300 grams granulated sugar

The grated zest of 4 lemons

2½ cups / 250 grams almond flour

½ teaspoon fine sea salt

⅔ cup / 80 grams all-purpose flour

6 tablespoons dark rum

SOAKING SYRUP

3 tablespoons granulated sugar

⅓ cup water

1 tablespoon whole allspice, optional

1 teaspoon black peppercorns, optional

½ cup dark rum

TRADITIONAL RUM GLAZE

¼ cup dark rum

1½ cups / 172 grams confectioners' sugar, sifted

NONTRADITIONAL LEMON GLAZE

¼ cup lemon juice

1½ cups / 172 grams confectioners' sugar, sifted

¼ teaspoon sea salt

CAKE

Preheat the oven to 350°F. Butter a 9-inch cake pan.

In a small bowl, beat the eggs with a fork, then set aside.

In a large mixing bowl or in a stand mixer at medium speed, beat the butter, granulated sugar and zest until pale and fluffy. Add the almond flour and salt and beat until incorporated. With the mixer running, add the beaten eggs, a little at a time. Increase the speed to medium-high and continue beating until the mixture is pale and voluminous. Switch to a rubber spatula and fold in the all-purpose flour. Turning the mixer to low, beat in the rum until just integrated.

Pour into the buttered pan and bake until golden, 50–55 minutes, or until a knife inserted in the center comes out clean.

Continued

SOAKING SYRUP

In a high-sided saucepan, combine the granulated sugar, water and allspice and peppercorns, if using. Bring to a boil, stirring to dissolve the sugar. Continue to boil for another 5 minutes to reduce the liquid. Remove the pan from the heat. Stir in the rum. Return the pan to the heat and simmer over medium heat for 2 minutes, being careful not to ignite the rum. (If the rum accidentally ignites, simply cover the saucepan with the base of a skillet until the lack of oxygen has extinguished the flames.) Leave the syrup on the warm burner. When ready to use, strain it through a fine sieve and discard the solids or reserve for another use.

Let the cake cool in the pan for 5 minutes on a wire rack. Invert onto a platter. No need to re-invert, as the bottom of the cake will better absorb the syrup. With the tip of a knife, make several small shallow slashes in the cake. Brush the syrup on the cake. You may want to do this in two batches, letting the first absorb before using the last of syrup. Set the cake aside, uncovered, to cool to room temperature, about 90 minutes, before glazing it.

GLAZE

For the traditional rum glaze, whisk together the rum and confectioners' sugar until smooth.

For the nontraditional lemon glaze, whisk together the lemon juice, confectioners' sugar and salt until smooth.

Pour the glaze onto the center of the cake in a steady stream, letting it spread naturally over the entire surface and over the sides. Allow the glaze to set, about 1 hour, uncovered, at room temperature.

Serve at room temperature.

Note: *This cake has a lovely moist crumb due to the ample rum, the oil in the almonds and plenty of butter. It is best to leave it at room temperature, uncovered, for at least the first several hours. If keeping it overnight, use a cake dome or tent it with foil. Wrapping it in plastic, sealing or doming it before it is truly down to a cool room temperature will make the crumb a little too wet and will make the glaze sticky. The cake is delicious on day one and even better on day two.*

Gâteau Basque

———— *Basque Cake* ————

This custardy extravaganza hails from the northern Basque region of France, near the Pyrénées mountains. Filled with pastry cream, it is a sensual affair. A layer of drunken cherries or cherry jam merely adds to the seduction. A gâteau Basque is technically not a gâteau, in that dough encases a flan-like custard. It's also not something you can whip up in ten minutes, and sadly there are no shortcuts. The dough needs time to chill in the fridge, though it can be made in advance and frozen. Traditionally, cherry jam is spread over the bottom layer of dough before spooning on the custard. But a gâteau Basque can also be made without the cherries, as is done across the border in the Basque region of Spain. I tend to add brandied cherries directly to the custard. Pick your fancy. The cherries need only macerate in brandy or kirsch for a few hours, but they are even better if given a full day.

Continued

DOUGH

- 9 tablespoons unsalted butter, at room temperature
- 1 cup / 200 grams granulated sugar
- The grated zest of 1 lemon
- 2 large egg yolks, at room temperature
- 1 large egg, at room temperature

- 1½ cups plus 2 tablespoons / 210 grams all-purpose flour
- ½ cup plus 2 tablespoons / 62 grams almond flour
- ¾ tablespoon baking powder
- ¾ teaspoon fine sea salt

PASTRY CREAM

- 6 large egg yolks, at room temperature
- 2 large eggs, at room temperature
- ½ cup / 65 grams cornstarch
- ½ cup / 100 grams granulated sugar

- 3 tablespoons all-purpose flour
- 2¼ cups whole milk
- 1 vanilla bean, split and seeds scraped

ASSEMBLY

- 1 cup brandied cherries, drained

- 1 egg, beaten with 1 tablespoon milk to make an egg wash

DOUGH

In the bowl of a stand mixer fitted with the paddle attachment, beat the butter, sugar and lemon zest at medium speed until fluffy, 3–4 minutes, stopping to scrape the sides of the bowl. Add the egg yolks and whole egg, one at a time, beating well after each addition.

In a medium bowl, whisk together the all-purpose flour, almond flour, baking powder and salt. Reduce the speed to low. Gradually add the flour mixture to the butter mixture, beating just until combined. Turn out the dough and shape into 2 disks. Wrap each disk in plastic and refrigerate for at least 1 hour.

PASTRY CREAM

Combine the egg yolks and whole eggs in a medium bowl and set aside.

Combine the cornstarch, sugar and all-purpose flour in a separate bowl.

In a medium saucepan, bring the milk and vanilla seeds to a simmer over moderate heat. Pour the hot milk into the flour mixture, whisking constantly. Then return to the pot and cook, stirring until thick and bubbling, about 5 minutes.

Very slowly pour in the eggs and cook, whisking constantly, for 3 more minutes.

Scrape the pastry cream into a clean bowl, press plastic wrap on the surface and let cool to room temperature, about 30 minutes.

ASSEMBLY

Butter a 9-inch springform pan and dust it with flour.

On a lightly floured surface, roll 1 disk of dough into a 12-inch circle. Transfer to the prepared pan, pressing into the bottom and up the sides. Refrigerate for at least 30 minutes.

Pour the pastry cream filling into the prepared crust along with the brandied cherries, distributing them evenly. Refrigerate for at least 30 minutes.

Roll the remaining dough into a 12-inch circle. Place it over the filling, crimp the edges and trim the excess dough. Refrigerate for at least 30 minutes.

Preheat the oven to 400°F.

Brush the surface with the egg wash. Bake for 25 minutes. Reduce the oven temperature to 350°F and bake for 25 minutes more, or until the center feels set and the crust is a deep golden brown. Set aside to come to room temperature.

NUT CAKES

and

TORTES

Les Gâteaux aux Noix

Pain de Gênes

—— *Genovese Almond Cake* ——

This *pain* is really a *gâteau*, and it is named for the city of Genoa, but it is really French. It looks plain, but it is moist and tastes of marzipan. Pain de Gênes, as it happens, dates back to the 1840s, when the Parisian pastry chef Fauvel created it to commemorate the French siege of the Italian city of Genoa in 1800. Under their brilliant commander, André Masséna, the French force held off an Austrian force some ten times larger than their own for nearly sixty days, allowing Napoleon the chance to cross the harrowing Great St. Bernard Pass and surprise and finally defeat the Austrians at Marengo. To this day, Masséna's tactics remain among the most brilliant in military history. As to the cake at hand? During the siege, almonds, native to the region, saved the French soldiers from certain starvation.

The recipe has changed very little over the years, incorporating a little baking powder and vanilla extract, but still giving center stage to the flavor of almonds. I add a touch of lemon zest to cut the sweetness, and sometimes I'll forgo the vanilla in favor of orange blossom water, kirsch, dark rum, Cointreau or Grand Marnier. It remains a beloved recipe, for good reason. Pain de Gênes calls for almond paste, which is far more common in Europe than it is in the U.S., and it is an absolute staple in Denmark and Sweden. Here's why it belongs in your pantry, too: as it is sealed, it usually lasts about a year. But don't decide to use the one that's been buried in the back of your cupboard for three years. It needs to be soft and moist and unopened. I find that almond flour loses its flavor after a few months. It's still functional at that point, but its flavor is muted. Almond paste is, therefore, a baker's little helper. It's almond flour and sugar, integrated and ready to go. What it doesn't offer is control over the ratio of nut to sugar. It's sweet, so use it only in a recipe that calls for little if any additional sugar. I use a brand called Odense. Make a note to buy their almond paste and not their marzipan, as both come in similar tubes. Marzipan is basically candy and far too sweet for baking. By the way, one inch of an Odense tube roughly equals one ounce. Wrap leftovers tightly in plastic to store. Or add nuggets of it to your next cookie, crisp or crumble. It will surprise you with little pockets of almondy sweetness.

This cake lasts well overnight if you brush it with a light syrup made with orange blossom water or orange zest and sugar syrup. Store well wrapped, at room temperature. For a slightly more imaginative appearance, press sliced almonds into the butter after you butter the cake pan. You'll need about half a cup of blanched almond slices. Crème fraîche is the way to go here, and fruit—berries or stone fruit, fresh or poached. The Swedes make a similar almond cake, which they serve with lingonberry jam. Lingonberries are slightly tart, somewhere between a raspberry and a currant in taste. Pain de Gênes loves a glass of Sauternes or a pot of Earl Grey tea.

2 large egg whites, at room temperature

2 tablespoons granulated sugar

¼ teaspoon fine sea salt

2 large eggs, at room temperature

The grated zest of ½ lemon

1 teaspoon vanilla extract

9 ounces / 255 grams almond paste, such as Odense , cut into ½-inch-thick slices

3½ tablespoons cornstarch

1¼ teaspoons baking powder

6 tablespoons butter, melted, at room temperature

Preheat the oven to 350°F. Butter the sides of an 8-inch cake pan and line the bottom with a round of parchment.

In a clean metal mixing bowl or a stand mixer, beat the egg whites until frothy and white. Add the sugar and salt and beat until stiff peaks form. Set aside.

In a second mixing bowl or stand mixer, beat the eggs, lemon zest, vanilla and almond paste until smooth, pale and thick. There should be no lumps of paste. If there are, continue until smooth. Sift the cornstarch and baking powder directly into the bowl. Beat to integrate. Add the melted butter and beat until thoroughly combined. Gently, but thoroughly, fold the egg whites into the batter using a rubber spatula until no white streaks remain.

Pour into the prepared pan and bake for 30 minutes, or until a knife inserted in the center comes out clean. The cake will be a pale brown and will not jiggle. It is best eaten at room temperature.

PAIN DE GÊNES AU CHOCOLAT

Entirely untraditional, but terrific, is the possible addition of chocolate. To make this a *pain de Gênes au chocolat*, simply fold in 125 grams of room-temperature melted chocolate after beating the eggs and almond paste. Replace the lemon zest with orange zest.

Gâteau Simple aux Noix

—— *Simple Walnut Cake* ——

I love this cake. It is moist and not too sweet and filled with ground walnuts, which are rich in omegas. It likes an afternoon espresso, and it is sublime with an after-dinner Armagnac. Easily put together in ten minutes with nothing but pantry staples, it is one of those recipes that will save you a hundred times over. Add the zest of half an orange or the slightest hint of nutmeg or cloves if you'd like, but this cake really wants to be a pure ode to the walnut.

11½ tablespoons unsalted butter

1½ cups / 150 grams walnut halves

2 cups / 227 grams confectioners' sugar

6 large egg whites

⅔ cup / 80 grams all-purpose flour

½ teaspoon fine sea salt

3 tablespoons honey

Preheat the oven to 325°F. Line a 9-inch springform pan with parchment and butter the sides.

Make a beurre noisette by melting the butter in a skillet over medium heat, then continuing to cook it until it turns a rich golden color and smells like hazelnuts. Immediately remove from heat. Set aside somewhere warm.

In a food processor, grind the walnuts with the confectioners' sugar until the mixture has the consistency of flour.

In a mixing bowl or the bowl of a stand mixer, beat the egg whites until frothy, about 1 minute. Add the walnut-sugar powder and beat until homogenous and smooth. Add the flour and salt and beat just to combine.

Stir the honey into the warm beurre noisette, then pour this into the batter. Whisk well to combine.

Pour the batter into the prepared pan and bake for 30–40 minutes, or until a knife inserted in the center of the cake comes out clean and the top of the cake is a deep gold.

Serve at room temperature any time of day or night.

Gâteau aux Noix et au Café

—— *Walnut Espresso Cake* ——

This cake drives civilized, well-mannered people to distraction. The cake itself is good, but the icing is truly irresistible. At least, if you are a coffee drinker. As it is all about the icing, I've made it into a layer cake so as to have two layers of icing in each bite, but for a casual supper, simply make one larger single-layer cake and frost it generously. Do try to use European or high-fat butter for this recipe. This is the birthday cake for that friend who painstakingly hand-grinds her own beans, even at six in the morning with a hangover.

CAKE

3 large eggs, at room temperature

¾ cup plus 1 tablespoon unsalted
    European butter, at room
    temperature

¾ cup plus 2 tablespoons / 175 grams
    light brown sugar

2 teaspoons vanilla extract

1½ cups / 180 grams cake flour

2½ teaspoons baking powder

½ teaspoon fine sea salt

1 tablespoon espresso powder,
    preferably from King Arthur Flour,
    or 1½ teaspoons coffee extract

BUTTERCREAM

1 cup butter, at room temperature

3½ cups / 400 grams confectioners'
    sugar

¼ cup espresso

1-2 teaspoons dark rum

DECORATION

40 walnut halves

Continued

CAKE

Preheat the oven to 350°F. Line the bottom of two 8-inch springform pans with rounds of parchment and butter the sides. (You may also make this a one-layer cake, using a 10-inch springform pan.)

In a small pitcher or measuring cup with a spout, whisk the eggs with a fork to break up the yolks.

Using a stand mixer or handheld beaters, cream the butter and sugar together until very pale and fluffy. Truly, until it is almost as pale as milk. Add about a third of the eggs while continuing to beat. When the egg has been incorporated, add another third. Then the final third. Add the vanilla and mix to incorporate.

Set a sieve over the mixing bowl and sift the dry ingredients directly onto the batter. Using a rubber spatula, gently fold these dry ingredients in, just until no streaks of flour remain.

Divide the batter between the two prepared cake pans and smooth the tops with a tender touch. Bake for 20–25 minutes. Remove to a cooling rack. After about 10 minutes, invert the cakes onto the rack to finish cooling. Allow to come to room temperature before icing the cakes.

BUTTERCREAM

While the cakes are cooling, make the buttercream. Using a stand mixer or handheld electric beaters, cream the butter for 1 minute. Add the confectioners' sugar and beat until creamy and smooth. Add the espresso and rum and beat to combine. If you are not icing the cake right away, refrigerate the icing in a covered container. Bring it to room temperature before icing the cake.

ASSEMBLY

When icing a cake, you always want to ice the bottom side, as it is more porous. If the cake is domed in shaped, slice a thin layer off the top to make it even and level. If you do this, either side is fine for icing.

Ice one layer with half the buttercream. Nestle about 20 walnut halves in the buttercream. Cover with the second layer of cake. Ice the second layer with the remaining buttercream. Very lightly press the remaining walnut halves in a pretty pattern of concentric circles into the buttercream. You can leave the sides of the cake bare or ice them. Not using all of this icing is a crime, however, so put those last spoonfuls on top, in the middle, or on the sides.

If making this as a larger, one-layer cake, simply cover the top with all the icing and all the walnuts. It will look excessive but taste fabulous.

This cake is best within a few hours of icing. If you are making it in the morning and serving it at dinner, wrap the cake layers in plastic once they've come entirely to room temperature. Alternatively, place them in an airtight container or under a cake dome. Close to serving time, ice the cakes.

Serving this with coffee is an exercise in redundancy, but serving it with tea is practically sacrilegious. And whipped cream would only get in the way of the coffee rush. Serve it plain or with a glass of dessert wine.

Gâteau aux Noisettes sans Farine

Flourless Brown Butter Hazelnut Torte

This gluten-free beauty can be made up to three days in advance thanks to the high oil content in hazelnuts. This also means that it's almost impossible to overcook. The recipe is a logical one. *Noisette* is the French word for hazelnut. Beurre noisette—browned butter—is so named because it takes on the hue and nutty flavor of hazelnuts as it cooks. Here, the two come together to produce a torte with an exceptionally nutty depth and dimension. The recipe falls squarely in the financier, *friande* and *visitandine* family of cakes made with egg whites and nuts, but it is more clearly a dessert cake than a snack. Don't get me wrong—you will snack on this, too, if every last crumb doesn't disappear after dinner. A torte, by the way, is a cake that is made with nuts or breadcrumbs instead of flour.

1 cup plus 1 tablespoon unsalted butter	5 large egg whites
1¼ cups shelled and skinned hazelnuts	3 tablespoons turbinado sugar
1⅓ cups / 152 grams confectioners' sugar	1 teaspoon vanilla extract
⅓ cup / 33 grams almond flour	2 teaspoons Frangelico
½ teaspoon fine sea salt	Crème fraîche, for serving

Preheat the oven to 350°F.

Butter a 9- or 10-inch springform pan and line the bottom with a round of parchment.

To make the beurre noisette, melt the butter in a skillet set over medium-low heat. Once the butter melts, raise the heat and watch carefully. Continue to cook until the butter turns a deep golden brown and smells like hazelnuts. Immediately, remove it from heat and set it aside.

Blitz the hazelnuts and confectioners' sugar in a food processor to form a fine powder. Add the almond flour and salt and pulse a few times to combine.

In a stand mixer or large mixing bowl, whisk the egg whites at medium-low speed until frothy, then add the turbinado sugar and beat at medium-high speed to form stiff peaks. Gently fold the whipped egg whites into the dry ingredients with a rubber spatula. Thoroughly but gently, fold in the beurre noisette, vanilla extract and Frangelico.

Pour the batter into prepared pan and bake for approximately 45 minutes, or until a knife inserted in the center of the cake comes out perfectly clean. Don't be tempted to under-bake this torte as this will make it dense.

Serve the cake still slightly warm or at room temperature with big dollops of slightly whipped crème fraîche. To dress it up, dust it lightly with confectioners' sugar. But I like the simplicity of its rich brown color. It's a bit like a good cashmere sweater, that way. Skip the jewelry and let the luxury speak for itself.

Note: Do yourself a favor and buy hazelnuts that have been both shelled and skinned rather than commit yourself to being overly industrious.

Gâteau au Gianduja

— *Gianduja Torte* —

Gianduja is that absurdly sexy coupling of chocolate and hazelnuts. First a confection, it originated in the Piedmont region of Italy, an area known for its abundance of hazelnuts, but it quickly became one of the most popular flavors of gelato throughout Italy and, in fact, much of the gelato-eating world. I call this torte by its Italian name, but I've only ever had it in Paris. Except when I make it in New York, which I do often because it is the ideal dinner party cake. Gluten-free, as moist on days two and three as it is on day one, and rich, rich, rich. Even the thinnest of slices feels indulgent, which means this torte can accommodate the sudden arrival of extra guests. A dollop of crème fraîche is de rigueur, as it offsets the decadence. Yes, you know you're in trouble when you're turning to crème fraîche as a foil for even richer foods. Let's just say it's all in the cool tang of it, and leave it at that.

To truly taste the hazelnuts, I do recommend the additional step of lightly toasting peeled ones and grinding them to a flour once cool. To do this, I buy already peeled and blanched hazelnuts, as I really hate skinning them. Then I chill them in the fridge. I also put my food processor blade in the freezer. When I grind the nuts, I add a tablespoon or two of the sugar and pulse if the nuts start to clump. If you're in a rush and buy hazelnut flour, don't worry. The chocolate will simply be the more predominant flavor, but when is that ever a problem? I also add a tablespoon of the Italian hazelnut liqueur Frangelico. If you are avoiding alcohol, add a quarter teaspoon of hazelnut extract.

Don't even think about a ganache or icing. It will be too intense. A dusting of confectioners' sugar is a pretty touch, but an unadorned chocolate torte has its own confident elegance.

14 tablespoons unsalted butter

200 grams dark chocolate, 66%–75% cacao, preferably Valrhona Guanaja

6 large eggs, separated, at room temperature

1 cup / 200 grams granulated sugar

2 cups / 200 grams almond flour

100 grams hazelnuts, peeled, toasted and ground to a flour

1 tablespoon unsweetened cocoa powder

1 tablespoon Frangelico liqueur

¼ teaspoon fine sea salt

Preheat the oven to 325°F. Butter the sides of a 9-inch springform pan and line the bottom with a round of parchment.

In a bain-marie, melt the butter and chocolate together, stir to combine and set aside, off heat.

In a stand mixer or using handheld electric beaters, beat the egg yolks and sugar until pale and fluffy. Add the almond flour and the ground hazelnuts and mix well to thoroughly combine. Add the cocoa powder and mix again. Repeat with the Frangelico.

Beat the egg whites with the salt until they form nearly stiff peaks. Stir a quarter of the egg whites into the batter to lighten it, then gently, with a rubber spatula, fold in the rest.

Pour the batter into the prepared pan and bake for 40–50 minutes, or until a knife inserted in the center comes out clean.

Set on a cooling rack for 15 minutes, then transfer to a cake plate. Serve at room temperature. This torte keeps well overnight, wrapped in aluminum foil and kept at room temperature. To store it for 2 days, wrap it and refrigerate it, but make sure to bring it to room temperature before serving it.

Gâteau à la Noix de Coco sans Farine

——— Flourless Coconut Cake ———

Soft, squidgy, textured with coconut flakes, sticky with butter, this is almost candy-like on the day it is baked, particularly when warm. By day two, it will have become less of a confection and more of a proper cake. It's a moist cake, and whipped cream is somewhat beside the point. Did I just say that? Whipped cream is never beside the point, but I don't feel this cake asks for its company.

14 tablespoons unsalted butter, at room temperature

1⅓ cups / 270 grams granulated sugar

½ teaspoon coconut extract

½ teaspoon vanilla paste or extract

4 large eggs, at room temperature

1⅔ cups / 180 grams almond flour

1½ cups / 70 grams unsweetened coconut flakes

Preheat the oven to 330°F. Butter the sides of a 9-inch springform pan and line with a round of parchment.

In the bowl of a stand mixer or using handheld electric beaters, cream the butter and sugar together until light and fluffy. Add the coconut extract and vanilla paste and whisk to combine. One by one, with the mixer running, add the eggs, beating well after each addition until the mixture is smooth. Add the almond flour and beat until thoroughly integrated. Fold in the coconut flakes.

Pour the batter into the prepared pan and bake for 40–50 minutes, or until the surface is golden and a knife inserted in the center of the cake comes out clean.

Allow the cake to come fully to room temperature before removing it from the pan. Serve at room temperature. Avoid refrigerating this cake. There's no need, and it would only make it dense. If keeping it overnight, simply wrap it up and leave it on the counter.

Note: *Please use coconut flakes, not shredded coconut. The texture of the flakes is what we're after.*

Gâteau à la Pistache

— *Pistachio Cake* —

Pistachios abound in Paris—look in most any pâtisserie window, and you'll see impossibly delicate pistachio macarons, glazed pistachio petit fours, pistachio financiers and chocolate truffles filled with unctuous pistachio fondant. Order a chocolate terrine at a well-heeled restaurant, and it will surely come atop a silken bed of pistachio cream. Stop by the venerable food boutique Fauchon, and you will find Iranian pistachios, deservedly considered the best in the world, selling for a pretty fortune. Pop into a *glacier* (ice cream and sorbet shop), and the pistachio flavor will be half-gone by afternoon. If well-made, none of these will be the crazy green we associate with pistachios, as only food dye creates such a color. More likely, they'll be a pale pastel green. Parisians share this mad love of pistachios with much of the Middle East and have adopted many of their desserts, often putting a French spin on them, as is the case in this fabulous recipe.

It is hard to describe just how good this cake is. It is moist but not wet, almost pudding-like when warm but still decidedly a proper cake, rich beyond imagination yet light as a feather to eat. The pistachio plays its chords subtly, part of a well-balanced ensemble. Parisians like their cakes just sweet enough, never sugary. They do, as you can see here, like their cream and their kirsch and a little fine sea salt to discreetly draw out the essence of each ingredient. For pure comfort, eat this cake about fifteen to thirty minutes out of the oven, while still warm. Or wait until it is room temperature, when its flavors will have bloomed—it will still be every bit as tender, so go ahead and make it in the morning to serve at dinner. Don't even think of serving this with more cream—it would be too much. A fork is all that's needed.

In the States, I order my pistachios and pistachio paste directly from Fiddyment Farms in California to ensure that they are fresh. I buy them in bulk and store them in the freezer. Do make sure to buy raw and unsalted nuts for this recipe.

½ cup / 70 grams shelled, raw pistachios

1½ cups minus 1 tablespoon / 175 grams
    all-purpose flour

½ teaspoon fine sea salt

2 teaspoons baking powder

3 large eggs

1¼ cups granulated sugar

1 tablespoon kirsch

2 cups heavy cream

Preheat the oven to 350°F. Butter a 9-inch springform pan.

Pulse the pistachios in a food processor until they are coarsely chopped—they should be around the size of uncooked basmati rice kernels or fennel seeds. Set them aside.

In a small mixing bowl, whisk the flour, salt and baking powder with a fork to combine.

In a stand mixer or using handheld electric beaters, whisk the eggs and the sugar until quite light and fluffy. Add the kirsch and beat to combine. Fold in the dry ingredients, then the pistachios.

In another large mixing bowl or using a stand mixer, whip the heavy cream until it forms stiff peaks. Fold the batter into the whipped cream with a light but thorough touch.

Pour into the prepared pan and bake for 50 minutes, or until a knife inserted in the center comes out clean. Allow the cake to cool for 10 or 15 minutes in the pan before transferring it to a cake plate. Serve warm or room temperature. The cake will keep covered at room temperature all day. In winter, when the kitchen is cool, I'll leave it out overnight, covered or in an airtight container. In summer, however, it needs to go in the fridge overnight. This will change its consistency, but it will still be good for snacking.

Gâteau aux Marrons /
Gâteau Purée de Châtaignes

—— Chestnut Cake ——

This is a sweet, moist cake and can easily be made a day in advance. Almond flour offers texture and offsets the density of the chestnut purée while keeping matters squarely within the nut family. It is gluten-free but quite decadent. Chestnut purée is so common in Paris—it's truly a pantry staple, often spread directly from tubes onto a morning tartine. The one I use is from Clément Faugier, and it is easily found online. It is sweetened and has a hint of vanilla. In cakes and pastries, chestnut purée is often minimally altered. A Mont Blanc, for example, showcases its slightly sticky, candied attraction with only a little whipped cream and meringue to temper it. It is popular as a bûche de Noël flavor and, generally, makes appearances at Christmas and New Year's celebrations, when candied chestnuts are passed round with an endearing mix of seriousness and joy. In cake, chestnut is usually paired with chocolate and often mousse-like in form. But, here, it plays the starring role in a simple one-layer, unadorned cake that can tilt rustic or, with a dusting of confectioners' sugar, fancy. It's best at room temperature and can be stored overnight wrapped or covered by a cake dome. Chilling it will change the texture and is not necessary to preserve it.

200 grams sweetened chestnut purée, preferably from Clément Faugier

1 cup plus 1 tablespoon / 150 grams confectioners' sugar

7 tablespoons / 100 grams unsalted butter, at room temperature

3 extra-large eggs

1 tablespoon rum, Cognac or Armagnac, or 1 teaspoon vanilla extract

1⅓ cups / 150 grams almond flour

½ teaspoon baking powder

¼ teaspoon fine sea salt

4 extra-large egg whites

Preheat the oven to 350°F. Generously butter and flour the sides of an 8-inch cake pan and line the bottom with a round of parchment.

In a stand mixer or using handheld electric beaters, whisk the chestnut purée, confectioners' sugar, butter, eggs and rum at medium-high speed for about 5 minutes, or until pale and smooth. Add the almond flour, baking powder and salt and beat to combine.

In a clean mixing bowl using clean beaters, beat the egg whites until nearly stiff. Mix a quarter into the chestnut batter to lighten it, then fold in the remaining egg whites.

Pour into the prepared pan and bake for 50 minutes, or until a knife inserted in the center comes out clean. Allow the cake to come to room temperature on a cooling rack before unmolding it onto a cake plate. Serve at room temperature with a dollop of crème fraîche Chantilly.

Gâteau Weekend aux Pignons de Pin

Pine Nut Weekend Cake

A friend of my mother's used to make this cake as gifts every Christmas and leave one outside our door. When she moved out of town, I wrote her requesting the recipe. She was quick to tell me the recipe had been given to her from someone who had, in turn, gotten it from someone else . . . and so forth. Always a good sign, although I wish I could give credit where credit is due, as this is truly a special recipe. In Paris, pignoli—Europeans tend to call pine nuts by their Italian name—usually come vacuum packed for freshness. In the States, I keep them in an airtight container in the fridge. Technically, they are seeds, not nuts. Here, they give a gentle crunch and tender sweetness. To dress this cake up, serve it with cherries, pitted and tossed with a little kirsch or Amaretto Disaronno and a dollop of crème fraîche, lightened with a touch of cream and whisked a bit with a fork. If cherries aren't in season, big spoonfuls of Luxardo maraschino cherries will make people smile, and inevitably the jar gets passed around for seconds. As I like a straight shot down memory lane, I eat it plain.

CAKE

- 3 cups / 360 grams all-purpose flour
- 1 tablespoon plus 1 teaspoon baking powder
- ½ teaspoon fine sea salt
- 2 cups heavy cream

- 2 teaspoons vanilla extract
- ½ teaspoon almond extract
- 2 cups / 400 grams granulated sugar
- 4 large eggs, at room temperature
- 1 cup pignoli nuts

SOAKING SYRUP

- ⅔ cup kirsch
- ⅓ cup / 66 grams granulated sugar

CAKE

Preheat the oven to 350°F. Butter two 9 x 5-inch loaf pans.

Sift together the flour, baking powder and salt and set aside.

In a stand mixer or using handheld electric beaters, whip the cream at medium-high speed until it holds its shape. Add the vanilla and almond extracts and sugar. Beat in the eggs one at a time. The mixture will have an appealing fluffy volume, like that of a duvet that's just been shaken.

Fold in the dry ingredients until well mixed and no streaks of flour remain.

Pour about a quarter of the batter into each pan. Sprinkle each with ¼ cup of the pignoli. Cover evenly with the remaining batter. Smooth the tops and sprinkle with the remaining pignoli. Bake for 50–60 minutes, or until a knife inserted in the center of a cake comes out clean.

SOAKING SYRUP

While the cakes are baking, boil the kirsch until reduced to ⅓ cup and, off heat, add the sugar and stir to dissolve. Or if you prefer a grown-up version, simply warm ⅓ cup kirsch with the sugar, but do not bring to a boil and evaporate the alcohol.

Remove the cakes from the oven and, while still warm, brush them with the syrup. Let the cakes cool in the pans for about 15 minutes before moving them to a wire cooling rack.

These cakes will keep well for a day, if tightly wrapped in plastic once they've come to room temperature. On the third day, toast slices of the cake for breakfast.

CHOCOLATE CAKES

Les Gâteaux au Chocolat

Gâteau au Chocolat Mi-Cuit
de Pierre Hermé

When Pierre Hermé posted the barest details of this chocolate loaf cake he makes at home, his followers, the world over, entered *une vraie folie*. It was in the early months of the pandemic, and people were baking their way to some semblance of calm. But when one of the greatest pastry chefs the world has known simply says to combine the ingredients in a bowl, mix and bake, we do need to stop and consider what level of expertise he thinks we're bringing to the table. Let's just say, there's more to this recipe than could fit on his post, and yet it is remarkably quick and stunningly good. So here's a version with some instruction and a few useful tips.

The butter needs to truly be at room temperature. Leave it out a full day. The eggs should also be at room temperature. Hermé calls this cake *mi-cuit*, which means half-baked. The center will be molten, which means you won't be able to do a knife test to see if it is fully baked. The best solution is to use an oven thermometer and bake it for exactly thirty-five minutes. As it is molten, it needs to cool in its pan before being transferred to a plate. If you plan to carry it anywhere, refrigerate it first, then allow it to come to room temperature before serving it. Hermé bakes this in a long French loaf pan, which I recommend. As it is narrower than our loaf pans, it allows for faster cooking—meaning that the exterior will still be moist when the interior is just beginning to set. These pans run roughly eleven by four inches. But here's the beauty of this cake: follow these small points and, in forty minutes start to finish, you will have an extraordinary cake worthy of the great Pierre Hermé.

250 grams bittersweet chocolate, ideally Valrhona Guanaja 70% cacao

1 cup plus 2 tablespoons truly room temperature butter

1 cup minus 2 tablespoons / 180 grams granulated sugar

4 large eggs, at room temperature

½ cup plus 1 tablespoon / 70 grams cake flour

Preheat the oven to 350°F. Butter a long French loaf pan or a standard American 9 x 5-inch loaf pan, and dust with cocoa powder.

Melt the chocolate in a double boiler and set aside.

Beat the butter and sugar in a mixing bowl with electric beaters until pale. Add the eggs one by one, beating after each addition to integrate them into the batter. Place a sieve over the mixing bowl and sift in the flour. With the mixer on low, quickly blend it in. Pour in the melted chocolate with the mixer running and beat only until no streaks remain.

Pour the batter into the prepared loaf pan and bake for exactly 35 minutes if your oven is accurate; otherwise check after 30 minutes. The edges should be set, but the center will remain molten. The surface will no longer be shiny. A knife inserted in the center of the cake will *not* come out clean, but it shouldn't be goopy, either.

Set the cake on a cooling rack. Do not unmold until it is truly at room temperature. I usually place it in the fridge for 15 minutes before unmolding it, as the unset center makes this cake a bit fragile.

Serve at room temperature.

Bouchons au Chocolat
—— *Chocolate Corks* ——

A *bouchon* is a cork. But this bouchon is *à goûter*—to snack on—and is everything a cork is not, except in size and shape. It is chocolate and moist and deep in flavor. Lighter and more delicate than a brownie, it nonetheless provides the antidote to even the most urgent of chocolate cravings. Parisians are masters of moderation. This virtue sadly didn't rub off on me during my years in the city. But the ritual of a small-chocolate-a-day most definitely engraved itself in my imagination. Nearly every Parisian I know religiously treats herself to a small square of dark chocolate a day, often taken with an espresso in the late afternoon. On weekends, a bouchon might step in, or perhaps a chocolate macaron, such as the famed ones of Ladurée, but hardly a day goes by without that small but exquisite treat. Abstinence and depravation are simply not in the French culinary vocabulary, because moderation is. My takeaway is that every day must involve a treat, and that said treat needs to be so fabulous that it satisfies completely. Enter the chocolate bouchon. Ideally these are made in little cork-shaped molds, but a mini muffin pan will do, as will one of those bite-sized square brownie molds or even a madeleine pan. I recommend silicon molds, as they release the bouchons easily and cool quickly. The lightest dusting of confectioners' sugar is all that's needed. A small note to travelers. In Bordeaux, if you ask for a bouchon at a pâtisserie, you may instead be handed a bouchon de Bordeaux. Also in the shape of a cork, these regional confections are made with almond paste and studded with raisins that have soaked in liqueur or eau-de-vie. They will delight but not appease the chocolate hunter looking for an afternoon quickie.

2 tablespoons hot espresso

2 tablespoons unsweetened cocoa
powder, such as Valrhona

1 tablespoon dark rum

115 grams bittersweet chocolate, around
70% cacao

6 tablespoons unsalted butter

1 large egg, at room temperature

3 tablespoons light brown sugar

¼ cup / 50 grams granulated sugar

⅓ cup / 40 grams cake flour

½ teaspoon baking powder

¼ teaspoon fine sea salt

45 grams mini bittersweet chocolate
chips or chopped bittersweet
chocolate

1 tablespoon confectioners' sugar

Preheat the oven to 325°F. If using metal molds, butter them. If silicone, simply place on a baking sheet. (Most molds make a dozen. If using a 24-mold pan, double the recipe.)

Pour the hot espresso over the cocoa powder and stir to dissolve. Add the rum and stir to combine. Set aside.

In a double boiler, melt the chocolate and butter together. Remove from heat.

In a stand mixer or using handheld electric beaters, whisk the egg to break it up. Add the light brown and granulated sugars and whisk until homogenous. Add the espresso-coffee mixture and the butter-chocolate mixture and whisk until smooth.

Place a sieve over the mixing bowl and sift in the flour, baking powder and salt. Fold these dry ingredients into the batter with a rubber spatula. Fold in the mini chocolate chips.

Spoon the batter into the bouchon molds. Bake for 20–22 minutes, or until a knife inserted in the center of a bouchon comes out with only a few crumbs. Transfer to a cooling rack.

After about 20 minutes, unmold the bouchons. Serve them top side up, lightly dusted with the confectioners' sugar.

Continued

VARIATIONS

These are delicate and, despite being rich, quite light. I, therefore, don't recommend adding nuts. If you do add candied orange or ginger, chop it finely. Chocolate is the star here and shouldn't be upstaged.

ORANGE: Replace the espresso with boiling water and the rum with Cointreau. Add the grated zest of half a small organic orange when whisking the light brown and granulated sugars into the egg. Alternatively, replace the espresso with boiling water, the rum with 1 teaspoon vanilla extract, and the mini chips with finely chopped candied orange.

RASPBERRY: Replace the espresso with boiling water and the rum with crème de framboise. Fill each bouchon mold halfway, place a raspberry in the center, and fill with the remaining batter.

GINGER: Replace the espresso with boiling water and the mini chocolate chips with finely chopped crystallized ginger.

CARDAMOM: Add ¼ teaspoon freshly ground cardamom seeds from green cardamom pods to the dry ingredients.

CINNAMON: Replace the rum with 1 teaspoon vanilla extract. Add 1 teaspoon ground cinnamon to the dry ingredients.

GIANDUJA: Replace the rum with Frangelico.

CHILE: Add ¼ teaspoon ground Aleppo pepper to the dry ingredients.

Les Cupcakes

———— Franco-American Chocolate Cupcakes ————

David Lebovitz's books take pride of place in my bookshelves. I've been a devoted fan of his since Amanda Hesser first served me a slice of his ginger cake after dinner one night some twenty years ago. And we've both been making this cake ever since. But it was when David moved to Paris that I truly began to read him and to watch him become both more French and more American, because that is what happens when living abroad. We naturally choose the elements of each of our countries' cultural and culinary mores and particularities that speak to us and, in so doing, become more firmly, more definitively, true citizens of each.

And these little cupcakes of David's? When he sent me the recipe, he was celebrating having just flown to Paris from New York—to his French husband, French kitchen and well-traveled American muffin tray.

200 grams bittersweet or semisweet chocolate, coarsely chopped

½ cup vegetable or other neutral oil

½ cup plain whole-milk yogurt

1 cup / 200 grams granulated sugar

3 large eggs, at room temperature

1 teaspoon vanilla extract

½ teaspoon almond extract

1½ cups / 180 grams all-purpose flour

1½ teaspoons baking powder

¼ teaspoon fine sea salt

Preheat the oven to 350°F. Line a 12-cup muffin pan with parchment cupcake liners, or butter each cup.

In a double boiler, melt the chocolate with ¼ cup of the vegetable oil. Once melted and smooth, remove from heat and set aside.

In a small mixing bowl, combine the remaining ¼ cup of oil with the yogurt, sugar, eggs and vanilla and almond extracts.

In a large mixing bowl, whisk together the flour, baking powder and salt. Make a well in the center and add the yogurt mixture. Stir lightly a couple of times with a rubber spatula, then add the melted chocolate and stir until just smooth.

Pour the batter into the muffin cups and bake for 25 minutes, or until they feel barely set in the middle. Set on a cooling rack and serve warm, but not hot, or at room temperature.

The cupcakes may be stored in an airtight container at room temperature for up to 4 days.

Gâteau Marbré au Chocolat et à l'Orange

— *Chocolate Orange Marble Cake* —

I was skeptical of marbled cakes until making this one. Instead of seeing them as the best of two options, I saw them as a weaker version of each, as if the baker were merely indecisive. But Parisians love marbled cakes—they buy them, make them, gift them. Part of the pleasure is in not seeing the mysterious patterns you've created until you slice it. But here the real pleasure is to be found in how the citrus notes mingle in each bite with the deep, dark chocolate. Try making this with Valrhona Manjari. The lively brightness of this rich chocolate is a perfect partner for the orange and Cointreau. In fact, it is a miraculous chocolate that seems to have a playful depth to it. And that is what this cake is all about.

CAKE

100 grams dark chocolate, 64%–66% cacao, broken up

1¼ cups / 285 grams unsalted butter, at room temperature

1 cup / 200 grams granulated sugar

3 tablespoons crème fraîche

2 tablespoons Cointreau or orange juice

1 tablespoon honey

½ teaspoon vanilla extract

The grated zest of 4 organic oranges

2 cups / 240 grams cake flour

2 teaspoons baking powder

½ teaspoon fine sea salt

4 large or extra-large eggs

SOAKING SYRUP

½ cup / 100 grams granulated sugar

½ cup water

3 tablespoons orange juice

2 teaspoons lemon juice

1 tablespoon Cointreau, or an additional tablespoon of orange juice

CAKE

Preheat the oven to 350°F. Line a 9 x 5-inch loaf pan with parchment paper by cutting one rectangle to cover the pan lengthwise and another to cover its width. Leave a few inches overhang, as it makes lifting the cake out of the pan easy.

In a double boiler, melt the chocolate and set aside to cool to warm room temperature.

In a stand mixer or using handheld electric beaters, cream the butter and sugar together for 2 minutes at medium speed. Add the crème fraîche, Cointreau, honey, vanilla and zest. Mix for another minute or two, until thoroughly combined.

Place a sieve over the mixing bowl and sift in the flour, baking powder and salt, alternating with the eggs, beating thoroughly after every addition at low speed.

Thoroughly stir one-third of the batter into the melted chocolate.

Pour the plain batter into the prepared loaf pan. On top of this, pour on the chocolate batter. Marble the batters by dipping a soup spoon in, twisting and lifting it out—do this several times down the length of the cake. Bake for 60–70 minutes, or until a knife inserted in the center of the cake comes out clean.

SOAKING SYRUP

While the cake is baking, make the syrup by heating the sugar and water to a boil in a small saucepan. Stir to dissolve the sugar. Allow to thicken for a minute. Remove from heat and stir in the orange and lemon juices and Cointreau. Set aside while the cake finishes baking.

Remove the cake from the oven and set it on a cooling rack. After 5 minutes, slowly pour the syrup over the cake, allowing it to be absorbed as you go. Let the cake sit for 20 minutes before removing it from the pan.

Serve at room temperature or store at room temperature, well wrapped. (There's a lot of moisture in this cake, so don't wrap or cover it until it has really and truly cooled to room temperature.) Wrapped, the cake will keep at room temperature for 3 days or in the freezer for a month.

Gâteau Suzy

———— Suzy's Cake ————

Suzy may not be the first name that springs to mind when thinking gâteau au chocolat, but it is, to many a Parisian, synonymous with one of the city's best. Google "Suzy" + "gâteau au chocolat" + "recette" and you'll find thousands of sites, but only a few have the one true recipe. So, a bit of a lesson in lore. Pierre Hermé, Parisian master of all things chocolate, had a friend named Suzy Palatin, who was both a fashion model and a cookbook author. She created a recipe for chocolate cake that was so very, very good that she passed it along to Pierre. Now, to give Pierre Hermé a recipe for chocolate cake is akin to offering Roger Federer a tennis lesson. But Suzy knew she had a winner, and sure enough, the recipe became a favorite of Pierre's. According to the hundreds of media outlets that have featured Suzy and her cake, Pierre declared it the *"meilleur gâteau au chocolat du monde."* High praise indeed from the oracle himself, and I'd have to agree with his opinion, as would most of Paris. Around town, this cake is known simply as Gâteau Suzy.

250 grams dark chocolate, such as Valrhona Guanaja 70% cacao

1 cup plus 2 tablespoons / 255 grams unsalted butter, at room temperature

1 cup plus 2 tablespoons / 225 grams granulated sugar

4 large eggs, at room temperature

¼ teaspoon fine sea salt

½ cup plus 1 tablespoon / 68 grams cake flour

Preheat the oven to 350°F. Butter a 9-inch cake pan and dust with cocoa. Lay a round of parchment on the bottom.

Melt the chocolate in a double boiler, remove from heat and set aside to cool a bit. It should be warm and still pourable, but not hot, when used.

In a stand mixer or using handheld electric beaters at medium-high speed, cream the butter and sugar together until pale and fluffy. One by one, with the mixer still running, add the eggs, then the salt. Reduce the speed to low and add the melted chocolate. Using a rubber spatula, fold in the cake flour until no streaks of white remain.

Pour the batter into the prepared pan and bake for 25–28 minutes. The cake is done when the surface is matte and the sides have started to shrink away from the pan. A knife inserted in the center of the cake will come out with a few wet streaks of batter. In other words, you are purposefully undercooking this cake.

Transfer to a cooling rack. Once at room temperature, cover loosely with aluminum foil and refrigerate for at least an hour. Invert onto a cake plate and allow to come to room temperature and serve with a dollop of crème fraîche.

If not eating this cake the day it is made, wrap it in plastic once it is cool and keep refrigerated for up to 72 hours. Return it to room temperature before serving.

VARIATIONS

ORANGE CONFIT OR CRYSTALLIZED GINGER: Fold in ½ cup finely chopped candied orange or crystallized ginger tossed in 1 teaspoon flour as a last step.

CARDAMOM ROSE: Add 1 teaspoon freshly ground cardamom seeds from green cardamom pods when adding the flour. Cover the cake in edible red rose petals.

SPICED: Add 1 teaspoon ground Saigon cinnamon, ½ teaspoon ground dried chipotle chiles and the zest of an orange when adding the flour. Serve with a shot of tequila or mezcal.

Note: For a slightly lighter cake, the egg whites may be beaten and folded in. But this cake isn't about lightness. Its cracked surface belies a luxurious richness and a ganache would be too much of a good thing.

Gâteau Tout Simple au Chocolat Amer et au Café

— *Bittersweet Chocolate Espresso Cake* —

I've never met a Parisian who liked fudge or fudge cakes. They find them too sticky, too sweet, too explicit. Instead, the chocolate cake of choice at dinner parties is a single, unfrosted layer of cake that manages to hover in the balance between dense and delicate. This is that cake. It is for the bittersweet chocolate lovers amongst us. Dark, moist, with a scant touch of flour to give the barest of structure, this cake has a deep, satisfying finish. It is surely the little black cocktail dress of cakes. This is not unlike the Gâteau Suzy (page 132), but it is a little smaller and thicker. A touch of coffee accentuates the chocolate flavor without reading as mocha. And a little rum gives it a faint edge, without detracting from the chocolate.

200 grams bittersweet chocolate, preferably Valrhona Guanaja 70% cacao

4 large eggs, separated, at room temperature

⅛ teaspoon fine sea salt

11 tablespoons unsalted butter, at room temperature

⅔ cup / 150 grams granulated sugar

⅓ cup / 50 grams all-purpose flour

1 teaspoon espresso powder, 2 teaspoons instant espresso or ¼ teaspoon coffee extract

2 teaspoons dark rum

Preheat the oven to 350°F. Butter an 8-inch cake pan or 8-inch springform pan and line with a round of parchment.

Melt the chocolate in a double boiler, remove from heat and set aside to cool slightly.

Beat the egg whites in a stand mixer or with electric beaters until soft peaks form. Add the salt and continue to beat until the peaks are just short of stiff.

In another mixing bowl, cream the butter and sugar together until pale and voluminous. Continuing to beat, add the egg yolks, one at a time. Switching to a rubber spatula, fold in the flour. Stir the espresso powder into the rum, and add this to the batter. Stir in one-fourth of the egg whites to lighten the mixture, then fold in the remaining egg whites with a swift, decisive, gentle motion until no streaks remain.

Pour into the prepared cake pan. Turn the oven down to 300°F and bake for 30 minutes. Allow to cool in the pan for 15 minutes, then carefully transfer to a cake plate. If you wait until the cake is at room temperature, it will be harder to transfer.

Eat the same day or refrigerate and bring to room temperature. This cake likes a billowy Chantilly.

Gâteau au Chocolat Moelleux
—— *Molten Chocolate Cakes* ——

Jean-Georges Vongerichten lays claim to this recipe. No doubt his story is true, and he did take a cake out of the oven too soon, thereby discovering the unadulterated pleasure of a molten chocolate interior, but such cakes are not at all new to France. They are called *gâteau au chocolat moelleux* and are sometimes made in cake pans, sometimes in cups, sometimes in ramekins. At restaurants, a waiter might poke a hole in the center of the cake, tableside, and spoon in a pistachio crème Anglaise, but, at home, a little whipped cream, crème fraîche or ice cream adds that sexy hot-cold, swirly dance on your tongue. No wonder this is the cake of Valentine's Day and marriage proposals. Add a touch of spice—ginger, cinnamon, chile—or go pure chocolate. These are perfect dinner party fare, as they can be prepared and refrigerated in advance, then baked to order.

1 tablespoon unsweetened cocoa powder

120 grams bittersweet chocolate, preferably Valrhona Guanaja 70% cacao

½ cup unsalted butter

2 large eggs, at room temperature

2 additional egg yolks, at room temperature

¼ cup / 50 grams granulated sugar

⅛ teaspoon fine sea salt

2 tablespoons all-purpose flour

Preheat the oven to 450°F. Generously butter four 6-ounce ramekins. Dust with the cocoa powder, then flip and tap out any excess. Place the ramekins in the fridge while preparing the batter.

In a double boiler, melt the chocolate and butter, stirring occasionally, until melted and smooth. Remove from heat.

In a stand mixer or using handheld electric beaters, whisk the eggs, egg yolks, sugar and salt until pale. Give the chocolate a stir to recombine. Working with a decisive, quick but gentle movement, fold the melted chocolate mixture into the beaten egg mixture. Then fold in the flour just until no streaks remain. Pour the batter into the ramekins.

(The batter can be poured into the ramekins and refrigerated, covered, for several hours. But bring to room temperature before baking.)

Set the ramekins on a baking sheet and bake for 12–13 minutes. The sides should be firm but the center still soft and a little wobbly. Serve immediately, in their ramekins.

Note: *If you don't have ramekins, you may bake these in oven-safe teacups.*

Marquise au Chocolat

—— Chocolate Marquise ——

For those of us who like our chocolate dark, rich and sensual, enter the marquise au chocolat. This is a dessert I cannot resist. A thick, cool slice of marquise, often served atop a pistachio crème Anglaise or raspberry coulis. It is a paradox. Dense, but light. When you first taste it, you sense you will need to bite it, and then suddenly it transforms into an ethereal cloud of pure chocolate. It's a mousse, it's a cake, it's a semifreddo, it's a chilled chocolate custard, it's a slab of the good stuff. It's impossible to categorize. It doesn't even need baking. I spike my marquise with Poire Williams. The pear perfume hovers gently, adding a little mysterious levity that also seems to draw out the sweetness of dark chocolate. Coffee or a stronger liqueur seems too pronounced here, but a little crème de framboise would give it a faint berry fruitiness.

1 tablespoon vegetable or other neutral
   oil

450 grams chocolate, preferably
   Valrhona Guanaja 70% cacao, broken
   into pieces

1 cup unsalted butter, cut into chunks

3 tablespoons granulated sugar

1 tablespoon Poire Williams

8 large eggs, separated, at room
   temperature

Pinch of fleur de sel (optional)

Lightly oil the sides of an 8½ x 4½-inch loaf pan or decorative mold.

Melt the chocolate and butter in a double boiler and stir to combine. Stir in the sugar and stir to dissolve. Remove from heat and let cool to room temperature before stirring in the Poire Williams.

Meanwhile, in a stand mixer or using handheld electric beaters at medium-high, beat the egg whites until they form firm, but not dry, peaks. Set aside.

Stir the egg yolks, one at a time, into the chocolate mixture. Stir in the fleur de sel, if using. Stir in one-fourth of the egg whites to lighten it. Gently fold the remaining whites into the chocolate mixture until no streaks remain.

Pour into the prepared loaf pan and cover with plastic wrap. Refrigerate for at least 8 hours and up to 24 or freeze for about 2 hours, until set.

To serve, dip a sharp knife in hot water then wipe dry and use to cut the cold marquise into 6 portions. Leave it to warm a touch—about 10 minutes if refrigerated and 30 if frozen.

Gâteau aux Poires et au Chocolat

—— *Chocolate and Pear Cake* ——

Quick to the pan, quick to the plate, this cake has a rustic look but a refined taste. Ever in favor of shortcuts, Parisians tend to use jarred pears in syrup when making this cake. Before I continue, let me state that French jarred fruit is an entirely different species from American canned fruit. Think intact, perfect peeled little pears in a clear glass jar suspended in a simple sugar syrup. Pretty enough to display. Did I mention how much I love food shopping in Paris? These always go in my shopping cart. But I started experimenting and discovered that this cake is even more appealing when made with fresh pears and a heady dose of Poire Williams to accentuate their delicate flavor. But, by all means, poach your pears. Perhaps in a fruity red wine or port or with ginger or cardamom. And if you do poach them, save the poaching liquid and reduce it to a syrup. Cooled to room temperature, it will be delicious spooned over a bowl of yogurt.

A dusting of confectioners' sugar will dress this cake up for dinner. A dollop of whipped crème fraîche will complete the picture.

200 grams dark chocolate, 64%–70% cacao

11 tablespoons unsalted butter

½ cup / 100 grams granulated sugar

3 large eggs, separated, at room temperature

1 cup / 120 grams cake flour

2 teaspoons baking powder

2 large, 3 medium or 4 small pears, peeled

3 tablespoons Poire Williams

Preheat the oven to 350°F. Butter the sides of an 8-inch cake pan and line the bottom with a round of parchment.

In a double boiler, melt the chocolate and butter together and stir to combine. Add the sugar and stir to integrate. Add the egg yolks, break them up with a fork, then stir well to integrate. Stir in the flour and baking powder until fully incorporated and no streaks of white remain. You should now have a smooth, homogenous batter.

Beat the egg whites to snowy peaks. Stir roughly a quarter into the chocolate mixture to lighten it, then fold in the rest. As the batter is heavy, you will need to fold vigorously. Chop the pears into half-inch chunks and toss with the Poire Williams. Fold into the batter.

Pour into the prepared pan and bake for 35 minutes, or until a knife inserted in the center of the cake comes out clean. Serve at room temperature.

VARIATIONS

POACHED PEAR: If poaching pears to make this cake, reduce the poaching liquid to a syrup and use only 2 tablespoons of the Poire Williams, as you don't want to overpower the pears or the chocolate.

RASPBERRY: Substitute 1½ cups raspberries for the pears and 2 tablespoons crème de framboise for the Poire Williams.

PRUNE ARMAGNAC: Substitute 1 cup prunes that have soaked in 3 tablespoons warm Armagnac for the pears and Poire Williams.

BRANDIED CHERRY: Substitute 1 cup pitted cherries in liqueur (brandy or kirsch) for the pears and Poire Williams. (These sometimes go by the name of brandied cherries.) Another possibility is 1 cup Luxardo maraschino cherries, also with their liqueur.

BANANAS FOSTER: For a totally fabulously American take on this French classic, consider 1½ cups bananas, sliced, in place of the pears, and a dark rum in place of the Poire Williams. If going this route, serve the cake still a little warm, with vanilla ice cream.

Note: *Choose pears that are ripe but not overly so. Anjou are perhaps the best and most widely available option in the States. Bosc and little Forelle pears will also do well in this cake. My favorite pear is the Comice, but it is a fragile thing of beauty and can only stand up to baking if just short of ripe.*

Moelleux Chocolat Framboise

—— *Molten Chocolate Raspberry Cake* ——

I'm a screenwriter, and one of the things you learn to do in the movie business is describe what you're pitching by appropriating very successful movies and linking them. Supposedly it's shorthand, but we all know it is to make executives see dollar signs. Hello *Stars Wars* meets *The Lion King*. Or would you prefer *Titanic* meets *Casablanca*? To use Hollywood jargon, this is gratin meets molten meets self-saucing meets soufflé.

This is indeed a molten chocolate cake baked large in a soufflé dish. The molten interior makes it self-saucing, and, as it covers fresh fruit, it is something, too, of a gratin. It is deliciously sloppy, oozing lava-like streams of chocolate—yes, serve in a bowl with a spoon. One thing to know: timing is important. In a shallow baking dish, it might bake in as little as twenty minutes. In a small, high-sided one, it might take closer to half an hour. What's key is that the interior remain molten. The center should tremble when the cake is moved. The center should be piping hot and show a bit of structure but still be saucy underneath. Feel free to substitute little wild strawberries, blueberries or currants for the raspberries. This recipe produces six cups of batter, which lends itself to being baked in a shallow eight- to ten-cup gratin dish or cake pan. Don't try to unmold this—it must be served immediately with a big serving spoon directly from the hot baking dish with plenty of crème fraîche, Chantilly or ice cream.

200 grams dark chocolate, such as
    Valrhona Manjari 64% cacao

1 cup unsalted butter, at room
    temperature

7 large eggs, at room temperature

1 tablespoon crème de framboise

¾ cup plus 1 tablespoon / 105 grams cake
    or all-purpose flour

¼ teaspoon fine sea salt

1 half-pint raspberries

Preheat the oven to 400°F. Butter a shallow 8-cup gratin dish or a 9-inch cake pan. An 11 x 7-inch baking pan will work as well.

In a double boiler, melt the chocolate. Pour into the bowl of a stand mixer and set to medium. With the mixer running, add the butter in pieces. It should melt, while also reducing the temperature of the chocolate. One by one, with the mixer still running, add the eggs, then the crème de framboise. Reduce the speed to low and add the flour and salt. Mix until no streaks of flour remain. Pour the batter into the prepared gratin dish and dot with the raspberries, letting them sink or gently pushing them down until nearly covered.

Reduce the oven temperature to 350°F and bake for 25–40 minutes, depending on the size of the pan. (Baked in an 11 x 7-inch pan, it may take only 30 minutes, while in a 9-inch cake pan, it may take closer to 40. And if your oven runs hot, it may be cooked in only 25.) It is done when the sides are set but the center remains molten and jiggles a little when the dish is moved.

Gâteau au Chocolat et aux Framboises

—— *Chocolate Raspberry Cake* ——

Remember when every chocolate cake was served with raspberries or had raspberries in the batter? It became so ubiquitous that it ceased to be chic. In fact, it was widely derided by food snobs. But, in truth, the combination of chocolate and raspberries is a classic and deserves revisiting. Here, a rich chocolate batter accented with crème de framboise or Chambord is poured over berries. Serve this with a little crème fraîche Chantilly.

This batter is dark and deep enough for chocolate connoisseurs but has just enough flour and structure to be a called a cake, rather than a chocolate confection. It should be a touch undercooked, but not molten, as is the previous recipe. It is, instead, a nine-inch round of *savoir faire* with a slightly rustic cracked surface, a decadent interior, and a long finish. All that is necessary to achieve perfection is excellent chocolate. I use Valrhona Alpaco 66% cacao in this recipe. Alpaco appeals equally to those in the bittersweet camp and those hoping for a bit more sweet creaminess and familiarity but who have moved past the milk chocolate years of their childhood.

Serve with crème fraîche or Chantilly. A dusting of confectioners' sugar will dress it up, but chocolate in the nude is pretty beautiful and the raspberries will surprise.

200 grams dark chocolate, such as Valrhona Alpaco 66% or Guanaja 70% cacao

14 tablespoons unsalted butter, at room temperature, cut into large pieces

4 large eggs, separated, at room temperature

1 cup / 200 grams granulated sugar

2 tablespoons crème de framboise or Chambord

¼ teaspoon fine sea salt

¾ cup / 90 grams cake flour

1–2 cups raspberries

Preheat the oven to 350°F. Butter the sides of a 9-inch springform pan, dust with cocoa and lay a round of parchment on the bottom.

Melt the chocolate and butter in a double boiler and stir to combine. Remove from heat and set aside to cool slightly. It should be warm and pourable, but not hot, when used.

In a stand mixer or using handheld electric beaters, beat the egg yolks and sugar together for 4–5 minutes at medium speed until very pale. Pour in the chocolate-butter mixture and the crème de framboise and continue to beat until thoroughly integrated, about 30 seconds more.

Using clean beaters, whisk the egg whites with the salt until they hold large, soft peaks. Stir one-fourth of these into the chocolate batter to lighten it, then, using a rubber spatula, fold the remaining egg whites into the batter using a swift but delicate motion. Fold in the flour.

Line the base of the cake pan with a single layer of raspberries. Pour the batter over the berries.

Bake for 25 minutes, or until the top is a bit cracked and a knife inserted in the center of the cake comes out with a few wet streaks of batter. Place on a cooling rack for 5 minutes before transferring it to a cake plate.

This cake is best eaten at room temperature the day it is baked. To keep it overnight, wrap it well and refrigerate it. Let it come back to room temperature before serving. On the second day, its texture will be denser, but its flavor will be just as decadent.

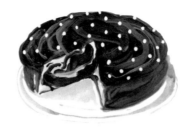

Gâteau au Chocolat Marbré

—————— Chocolate Ganache Marbled Chocolate Cake ——————

Oh, this cake . . . chocolate on chocolate. Literally. You make chocolate batter. You make ganache. You pour the ganache on top of the batter and swirl it in, just enough to slightly marble the two together. Each bite contains rich cake and even richer, slightly molten ganache. It is the brainchild of Pascal Rigo. Born in Bordeaux, Rigo cut his teeth cooking in Paris restaurants before moving to San Francisco and opening La Boulange. Before long, he had twenty-three locations. In 2013, Starbucks bought La Boulange for $100 million, only to shutter it two years later. Thankfully, this recipe comes to you for the mere price of a book, but it is, indeed, worth far more. I depart slightly from Rigo in the ganache, as I prefer mine made with only dark chocolate, and he mixes semi and bittersweet. But, then again, Starbucks hasn't knocked on my door. This cake begs to be served with Chantilly. It is neatest when sliced cold, but tastes best when warmed very briefly in a microwave or oven.

GANACHE

½ cup plus 1 tablespoon heavy cream

4 ounces bittersweet chocolate

1½ teaspoons honey, Lyle's Golden Syrup or light corn syrup

CAKE

4 large or extra-large eggs, separated, at room temperature

340 grams bittersweet chocolate, roughly chopped.

½ cup unsalted butter

2 tablespoons unsweetened cocoa powder

2 additional egg whites

½ teaspoon fine sea salt

½ cup/ 100 grams granulated sugar

GANACHE

Bring the heavy cream to a simmer and immediately pour it over the chocolate. Stir to melt the chocolate, then stir in the honey. You will need ½ cup of the ganache for the recipe and it should be used warm, not hot.

CAKE

Preheat the oven to 325°F. Butter the sides of a 10-inch springform pan and dust with cocoa powder. Place a round of parchment on the bottom.

In a small bowl, whisk the egg yolks until you have a uniform yellow mixture.

Melt the chocolate and butter in the top of a double boiler, stirring until homogenous. Remove from heat and stir in the cocoa. Whisk in the egg yolks.

In a stand mixer or large mixing bowl, beat the 6 egg whites and salt on medium speed until foamy. Increase the speed to high and slowly pour in the sugar. Continue beating until the whites begin to form stiff peaks but still droop a little when you lift up the whisk.

Now, I know this is counterintuitive, but trust me. Pour in the chocolate mixture while keeping the mixer running. Continue beating until there are no streaks of white visible.

Pour the batter into the prepared pan and smooth it evenly across the pan. Pour ½ cup of the warm ganache on top of the batter. Using the flat edge of a dinner knife or the back of a soup spoon, marble the ganache into the batter. Just a little swirling will do.

Bake for 35–40 minutes, or until the center of the cake no longer looks shiny. The cake will be puffed up and wobbly in the center, but the edges will be set. The cake will become firmer as it cools.

Set the cake on a cooling rack and allow it to cool for 20 or so minutes before removing the sides of the pan. Don't try to invert this cake onto a platter. Refrigerate it, then slide it onto a cake plate. The cake keeps well, refrigerated, for up to 3 days, making it an ideal make-ahead dessert. To serve, bring it to room temperature and, just before serving it, warm the cake in a low oven or slice by slice in a microwave very briefly. You are not trying to truly heat it, but rather to warm it enough that the ganache is a bit molten. Big dollops of crème Chantilly are essential.

Gâteau au Chocolat au Vin Rouge sans Farine

—— *Flourless Chocolate and Red Wine Cake* ——

Ethereal. A mysterious note hovering in the background. Not quite fruity, not quite earthy, it has the rounded quality of a fine wine . . . and wine it is. This flourless, deeply chocolatey, mousse-like cake has a full glass of red wine in it. We all know that moment when we peer at last night's bottle, wondering at how little remains. It's hardly a stretch imagining how a certain French cook thought to add that last precious pour into their other treasure of the day—a saucepan of melted dark chocolate. Et voila, *le gâteau au chocolat au vin rouge*. Most recipes I've seen for this cake add wine the way one might espresso or rum, as an accent, albeit a lush one. The particular technique I use here is thanks to Eric Treuillé. Eric was born in the Cahors wine country of the South West and moved to London as a chef and stayed to run the city's best cookbook shop, Books for Cooks. He makes a simple syrup by combining the wine and sugar and bringing it nearly to a simmer. Half he pours into the melted chocolate, while the other half is beaten with the eggs. The resulting cake has the lightness of a mousse and the intensity of a flourless chocolate confection. Don't worry if the middle caves as the cake cools. What it lacks in appearance, it more than makes up for in taste.

¾ cup red wine

¾ cup / 150 grams granulated sugar

300 grams dark chocolate, around
   66%–70% cacao

11 tablespoons unsalted butter

5 large eggs, at room temperature

Preheat the oven to 350°F. Butter the sides of a 9-inch springform pan and line the bottom with a round of parchment.

Combine the wine and sugar in a small saucepan over very low heat. Stir as the mixture warms to dissolve the sugar. Continue to cook only until the syrup begins to tremble and remove it from heat before it comes to a simmer. Set aside to cool for a few minutes.

In a second saucepan, heat the chocolate, butter and half the syrup in a double boiler until the chocolate has melted. Remove from heat and stir until smooth.

Using a stand mixer or electric beaters, whisk the eggs and remaining syrup until very thick, pale and mousse-like. The eggs should hold a ribbon trail when the whisk is lifted. Be patient, this will take at least 9 or 10 minutes and it is essential to the cake's structure.

Stir a big spoonful of the egg mousse into the melted chocolate, then pour the chocolate into the eggs and fold until there are almost no streaks remaining.

Pour the batter into the prepared pan and bake for 20–25 minutes, or until the cake appears set but is still wobbly and moussey in the very center. It will continue to set as it cools. Remove from the oven and leave on a cooling rack until truly at room temperature before unmolding and serving it.

A little cloud of whipped cream will balance the richness of this cake. Speaking of richness, serve small portions. It's nearly impossible to slice this cake neatly, and so I tend to serve it in small, shallow bowls or even on pretty saucers.

Gâteau au Chocolat et au Whiskey

—— *Chocolate Whiskey Cake* ——

This boozy, indulgent cake was inspired by a recipe attributed to a Madame Frederic Chartier that I found in an old hand-bound collection. It caught my eye, and I made it for New Year's Eve. It's definitely that sort of late-night, hedonistic cake, incredibly rich with an intoxicating mouthful of whiskey in each bite. A small band of us had taken Covid tests so we could bid 2020 goodbye together and usher in what we hoped would be a year of physical, emotional and political healing. In a year in which we'd been apart from our friends for months at a time, being together took on an added dimension, aware, as we were, that we'd no doubt be isolated again before long. And so we feasted, a feast to tide us over, and a hopeful promise made to gather again in a year's time and indulge in this deliriously decadent cake.

Madame Chartier calls for granulated sugar in the ganache frosting, but I found it hard to dissolve the sugar without overheating the chocolate. A spoonful of strong, hot coffee did do the trick, but confectioners' sugar is the obvious solution. It simply makes a thicker ganache, better suited to frosting than pouring. Next year—note the optimism—I will use superfine sugar and coffee, as I love the marriage of chocolate, coffee and whiskey. Cut this very grown-up, but fudgy cake in small slices. Unsweetened whipped cream is essential.

CAKE

¼ cup good whiskey

½ cup raisins

170 grams chocolate, around 60%–70% cacao

½ cup unsalted butter

3 large eggs, separated, at room temperature

⅔ cup / 130 grams granulated sugar

5 tablespoons potato starch

⅔ cup / 66 grams almond flour

GANACHE

85 grams dark chocolate

3 tablespoons unsalted butter

1 tablespoon hot espresso

3 tablespoons granulated or confectioners' sugar

CAKE

Preheat the oven to 350°F. Place a round of parchment in the bottom of an 8-inch springform pan and butter the sides.

Warm the whiskey and pour it over the raisins. Set aside.

In a double boiler, melt the chocolate and butter. Stir until smooth and remove from heat.

Beat the egg yolks and sugar in a large mixing bowl using electric beaters for a good 5 minutes, or until pale and voluminous. Keep the mixer running and pour in the chocolate in a slow steady stream. Add the potato starch and the almond flour and beat until smooth. Fold in the raisins and whiskey.

In a clean mixing bowl and using clean beaters, whip the egg whites at medium-high speed until firm. Stir a fourth into the chocolate batter to lighten it, then gently but decisively fold in the rest until no streaks of white remain.

Pour the batter into the prepared pan and bake for 23–26 minutes. Don't overbake! The cake should be soft in the middle. A knife inserted in the cake should come out still moist and with a smudge of chocolatey batter.

Set aside to come to room temperature. After about five minutes, remove the sides of the springform pan. Once at room temperature, frost with the ganache.

GANACHE

Melt the chocolate and butter in a double boiler with the espresso. Stir until smooth. Sprinkle in the granulated sugar and stir until perfectly smooth.

Refrigerate the cake for half an hour or until about an hour before serving it.

Cake Chocolat Orange

Chocolate and Candied-Orange Loaf

Dark chocolate and candied orange give this cake an almost confection-like flavor, but it is not too sweet and, thanks to its sturdiness, can travel for *le weekend*. Serve for dessert with a dollop of crème fraîche or all day, in thick slices, with coffee or, at midnight, with a snifter of Cognac. On the third day, try it toasted and blanketed in marmalade. In fact, a marmalade glaze will add a sweet pucker. Either warm a jar of marmalade until liquefied, strain and pour over the cake, or make a proper glaze by straining, then adding in a little confectioners' sugar. About the almond paste. I use Odense. This recipe requires five ounces, which is most, but not all, of one tube. I simply chop up the remaining two ounces and add it with the chocolate chunks. Ideally, the paste should be quite fresh. If stale, you may need to break it up in a food processor.

13 tablespoons unsalted butter, preferably European

1½ cups / 180 grams all-purpose flour

⅓ cup plus 1 tablespoon / 40 grams unsweetened cocoa powder, preferably Valrhona

½ teaspoon baking powder

¼ teaspoon fine sea salt

5 ounces / 140 grams almond paste, such as Odense

¾ cup plus 1 tablespoon / 165 grams granulated sugar

4 large eggs, at room temperature

⅔ cup whole milk, at room temperature

1 tablespoon Cointreau or Grand Marnier

½ teaspoon vanilla extract

80 grams dark chocolate, broken into chunks or ¾ cup chocolate chips

½ cup candied orange, roughly chopped into ½-inch pieces

Preheat the oven to 340°F. Butter a 9 x 5-inch loaf pan and place it on a baking sheet.

Melt the butter over low heat and set aside to cool until warm but not hot.

Sift the flour, cocoa powder, baking powder and salt and whisk to combine. Set aside.

In a stand mixer or using handheld electric beaters, beat the almond paste and sugar until sandy in texture. One at a time, at medium speed, add the eggs. Increase the speed to high and whisk for a solid 10 minutes until the mixture forms pale ribbons in its wake. Decrease the speed to low and add the milk, Cointreau and vanilla and whisk until integrated. Add the dry ingredients and continue to whisk at low speed to fully integrate them.

Using a rubber spatula, fold in the chocolate and candied orange. Then, finally, the melted butter.

Pour the batter into the prepared pan and bake for 55–65 minutes. A knife inserted in the center should come out nearly, but not completely, clean. If it comes out wet with chocolate, you may have simply hit a chunk or chip. In that case, test again rather than risk overbaking the cake. Allow to cool for 5 minutes, then unmold and allow to cool to room temperature.

If storing this cake overnight, wrap it well, once fully cooled to room temperature, in plastic. Leave it at room temperature and it will remain moist for 2 to 3 days, if kept wrapped. If freezing it, place the wrapped cake in a freezer bag and eat within a month or so.

Fondant Baulois

—— *Baulois Chocolate Cake* ——

In the early 1980s, a certain Monsieur Denis began selling a chocolate cake in his little shop in the coastal town of La Baule. It quickly became a sensation, and countless people, pastry chefs and home cooks alike, have tried to reproduce his celebrated fondant. (A fondant is something between a pudding and a molten cake.) The recipe remains a well-guarded family secret, but I believe pastry chef and author Christophe Adam may have come close. And if he hasn't, well, no matter. He's created something delicious. The Fondant Baulois, as it has come to be known, is a dense chocolate cake made with light brown sugar and very little flour. Adam bakes his at a low temperature and refrigerates it overnight. The overnight chill helps it set, allowing you to remove it from the oven before it has fully baked. Trust your sense of smell. When the kitchen smells of chocolate, the cake is done. Its center should still tremble a bit, and a knife inserted won't come out clean. But the surface of the cake will be dry. I'm afraid you really do need a seven-inch springform for this recipe.

- 115 grams bittersweet chocolate, around 70%–74% cacao
- 10 tablespoons unsalted butter
- 3 large eggs, at room temperature
- ¾ cup plus 1 tablespoon / 100 grams light brown sugar
- ¼ teaspoon fine sea salt
- 3 tablespoons / 20 grams cake flour

Preheat the oven to 250°F. Butter the sides of a 7-inch springform pan and line the bottom with a round of parchment.

Melt the chocolate and butter in a bain-marie over a low simmer. Remove from heat and set aside.

In a stand mixer or using handheld electric beaters, whisk the eggs, brown sugar and salt together at medium-high speed for 5 minutes, or until the mixture is pale and voluminous. Add the flour and whisk to combine. Add the melted chocolate-butter mixture and whisk until the mixture is homogenous.

Pour the batter into the prepared pan and bake for 25–30 minutes. The center will be underbaked and still a bit wobbly, but the surface will be dry. Err on the side of undercooked, if not certain.

Allow to come to room temperature, then cover tightly with plastic wrap or aluminum foil and refrigerate overnight. Bring to room temperature and serve with a dollop of crème fraîche.

Le Fondant Baulois au Caramel Beurre Salé

—— *Salted-Caramel Baulois* ——

Parisian and, in fact, all French desserts tend to strike an intentional balance between sweet and flavor. By this, I mean that rarely will sugar be the dominant taste in even the richest desserts. It's always the dance between sugar and, say, chocolate or apples or spice. And so the satisfaction in baking lies not merely in satisfying a sweet tooth or sugar craving, but in delivering something nuanced. This is even true in les gâteaux de Mamie—the French expression for those cakes mothers and grandmothers baked for their kids. But the salted-caramel craze tossed all restraint, all claims to sophisticated palates, to the wind, on both sides of the Atlantic. This is the sweetest cake in this book, even balanced with a shower of Maldon sea salt. But it is *good*. Make it when an unexpected posse of teenagers or twentysomethings shows up, or simply when the mood calls for full-frontal chocolate salted caramel.

As with all gâteaux fondants, keeping a Baluois at room temperature is ideal. But two hours in the fridge will help set it, allowing you to undercook it, which really is the point here. It should be served at a cool room temperature, but if you like fudge, then you'll like it dense and cold. And a small heads-up: the oven temperature starts high, then is lowered, so don't put it in the oven to bake and disappear! This calls for a Chantilly made with one-third cup of crème fraîche and two-thirds cup heavy cream.

- 100 grams bittersweet chocolate, such as Valrhona Manjari
- 100 grams milk chocolate, such as Valrhona Bahibé
- 14 tablespoons unsalted butter
- 2 heaping tablespoons salted caramel
- 5 large eggs, at room temperature
- 1½ cups / 180 grams light brown sugar
- 1 teaspoon vanilla extract
- ¼ teaspoon fine sea salt
- 3 tablespoons / 22 grams all-purpose flour
- 1 teaspoon Maldon sea salt

Preheat the oven to 410°F. Butter the sides of a 9-inch cake pan and lay a round of parchment inside.

In a double boiler, melt the bittersweet and milk chocolates and the butter together, stirring until smooth. Remove from heat. Add the salted caramel and stir to combine. Set aside.

In a stand mixer or using handheld electric beaters, beat the eggs and sugar together until they have tripled in volume. Add the vanilla and fine sea salt. With the mixer still running, pour in the chocolate-caramel mixture in a slow steady stream. Stop once fully integrated. Using a rubber spatula, fold in the flour just until no streaks remain.

Pour the batter into the prepared pan and bake for 5 minutes. Reduce the oven temperature to 250°F and continue to bake for an additional 40 minutes.

Place on a cooling rack to come to room temperature, then refrigerate, loosely tented with aluminum foil, for 2 hours before unmolding. Serve at cool room temperature, sprinkled with the Maldon sea salt and with a billowy cloud of Chantilly on the side.

Fondant Caramel Brûlé Chocolat

——— Burnt Caramel Chocolate Cake ———

This is an improbable success. Improbable because caramel solidifies when it touches something cold or even cool, such as batter. The trick is to use eggs that are really and truly at room temperature, as you don't want the hot caramel to be shocked solid by cold eggs. This is a small cake, but it is intensely rich. A little goes a long way. It begs for barely sweetened or unsweetened Chantilly, made with one part crème fraîche to two parts heavy cream.

3 large eggs, at room temperature

5 teaspoons all-purpose flour

¼ teaspoon fine sea salt

125 grams bittersweet chocolate, around 70% cacao, such as Valrhona

1 cup / 250 grams sugar, ideally superfine

⅓ cup water

The juice of ½ lemon

10½ tablespoons unsalted butter, at room temperature

2 teaspoons rum, bourbon, Cognac or Armagnac

Preheat the oven to 320°F. Butter an 8-inch cake pan and line the bottom with a round of parchment.

In a stand mixer or using handheld electric beaters, whisk the eggs for a full 6 minutes, or until they have doubled in size. Add the flour and salt and mix for another 2 minutes. Set aside.

Melt the chocolate in a double boiler and set aside.

Make a caramel by combining the sugar and water in a heavy-bottomed and high-sided pot over medium-high heat. Stir briefly to help dissolve the sugar, then add the lemon juice and stir to combine. Stop stirring and bring the mixture to a boil. Continue cooking, occasionally—with oven mitts—swirling the pan. When the mixture is a dark amber, immediately remove it from heat. Using great caution—this will sputter—add the butter, a chunk at a time, stirring well after each addition. Then add the rum and stir. Pour into a pitcher or measuring cup with a spout. Set the mixer at medium-low and pour the caramel in a slow, steady stream into the egg mixture, then add the chocolate and mix only until no streaks remain.

Pour the batter into the prepared pan and bake for 45 minutes, or until a knife inserted in the center comes out moist but clean. Set on a cooling rack to bring to room temperature, then refrigerate for 4–24 hours. Remove from the fridge 30 minutes before serving it.

CAKES
to
LAYER

Les Génoises

LES GÉNOISES

A génoise is a French sponge cake. It also happens to be *the* building block of pâtisserie, appearing in everything from tiny petit fours to towering wedding cakes. While slightly more intricate than a simple quatre-quarts, weekend cake or yogurt cake, a génoise is similarly that back-pocket recipe that lends itself to last-minute improvisation at home. It's not difficult to make—it simply requires many minutes in a stand mixer. It is an ingenious thing. Thanks to its strong structure, it can be flavored and built into almost any imaginable layer cake or kept as a single-layer cake.

What's important to understand is that a génoise is only a foundation. A slice of plain génoise will leave you unsatisfied. It is not exactly dry, but nor is it moist. This is on purpose, as it is meant to absorb—like a sponge—abundant syrup and retain its structure without getting the least bit soggy. And this it does beautifully. Brush it with liqueur and suddenly it makes sense. Or drizzle it with a simple syrup made with coffee and rum, then glaze it with a chocolate ganache, and you have something spectacular.

I'm including two different recipes in this chapter. (You will also see sheet-pan versions in the Holiday Cakes chapter, page 259, as the génoise is also the foundation of bûches de Noël and most any *rouleau*, or rolled cake.) The first recipe is the classic. The second recipe includes butter and does not require heating the eggs and sugar in a bain-marie. Both are excellent. And you'll find some ideas here to get you dreaming. Here, you'll find some of the most fabulous layer cakes imaginable. When sold in a pâtisserie, these might be multi-layered confections with elaborate decorations and fillings, but, when made at home and without any fuss, they can easily hit the same sweet spot.

TRICKS OF THE TRADE

Take out your scale, at least for measuring the flour. If you use superfine sugar, use the same weight as granulated sugar, not the same cup measurement.

If you've run out of parchment paper, put your buttered and floured cake pan in the fridge while preparing the batter. This helps keep the surface nonstick.

Traditionally, eggs, rather than a leavening agent, provide lift and structure, and they must, therefore, be whipped until they have tripled and very nearly quadrupled in size. This will take a solid eight minutes in a mixer.

Sifting. It matters here. Use a fine sieve.

Folding. Fold until no streaks of flour are visible, but use a light touch so as not to deflate the eggs.

Bake the moment your batter is ready. Don't let it sit.

A rising heat makes for a rising cake. Skip the convection fan.

A génoise bakes quickly. Don't overbake, particularly if using a sheet pan and hoping to roll the cake into a rouleau. If baked too long, it will get stiff and not roll as easily.

Unmold the génoise right after you remove it from the oven, by flipping it onto a cooling rack. Or, if using a sheet pan, by pulling it with the parchment off the pan and onto a rack or countertop.

If storing the génoise overnight, wait until it is really and truly at room temperature before covering it with a cake dome, wrapping it in plastic or putting it in an airtight container. It should be stored at room temperature and will easily last forty-eight hours.

Use a long, serrated knife—longer than the diameter of the cake—to cut the génoise into two or three layers. A long knife makes for one even cut.

Brush the inside layers as well as the outside layers with syrup.

Bake two and freeze one.

Continued

ASSEMBLING

At home, a génoise is either served as a single-layer cake or it is cut horizontally into two or three layers. Either way, the layers are brushed liberally with soaking syrup and filled with anything from jam to buttercream, from ganache to mousse, from fresh berries to poached stone fruit. Chantilly is almost always a given here, and makes for a quick frosting and even a quick filling.

IDEAS

Brush with a syrup of coffee and rum and frost with a simple dark chocolate ganache.

Brush with a rose syrup and serve with fresh strawberries and whipped cream.

Brush with orange blossom water and serve with crème fraîche and poached apricots.

Brush with an amaretto syrup, cover with toasted almond slices and serve with crème fraîche and poached apricots.

Brush with lemon syrup and fill with lemon curd. A lemon or limoncello glaze will complete it. Replace the lemon with any other citrus, such as orange, blood orange, lime, grapefruit or Meyer lemon. Serve with whipped crème fraîche.

Brush with a syrup of saffron, rose and cardamom and serve with crème fraîche.

Brush with Grand Marnier or Cointreau and serve with slices of oranges sprinkled with sparkling wine and the seeds of a vanilla bean.

Brush with Grand Marnier or Cointreau and spread with a layer of marmalade.

Brush with a Chambord syrup and fill with raspberry jam.

Brush with crème de framboise and serve with raspberries tossed, of course, in more crème de framboise and add a huge dollop of crème Chantilly. A layer of raspberry jam wouldn't be remiss.

Brush with a Poire Williams syrup and serve with poached pears.

Brush with crème de pêche and serve with perfectly ripe, peeled peaches and whipped cream.

Brush with crème de cassis and fill with Chantilly into which black currant jam has been folded.

Give the top a final brushing with warm strained apricot jam or warm, strained marmalade.

Give the top a dusting of confectioners' sugar and set in a 400°F oven for two minutes. The heat will make the sugar shiny. Or dust at the last minute, and the sugar will look like just-fallen snow.

Génoise Classique

—— Classic Génoise ——

Please don't take classic to mean old-fashioned. This is the génoise Parisians make most often, as the recipe has only three ingredients and the amounts are a ratio, making it easy to memorize and increase or decrease as needed. The rule of thumb is 30 grams of sugar and 30 grams of cake flour for every extra-large egg. The recipe below uses four eggs, 120 grams sugar and 120 grams cake flour and is sized for a nine-inch round cake pan or a nine-inch square cake pan. You may also use these quantities to bake a thinner génoise in a sheet pan—to then be rolled or sliced for layers.

Citrus zest, spice, vanilla seeds, even espresso powder all may be added. I add ¼ teaspoon fine sea salt. Add spice, salt and powder with the flour, while zest and vanilla seeds are best added with the eggs.

Whisking by hand will take up to fifteen minutes, depending upon your vigor and strength and whatever mental demons you are trying to exorcise, or merely until the mixture has at least tripled in size. Stand mixer, I thank you.

4 extra-large eggs (see Note), at room temperature

½ cup / 120 grams superfine sugar

1 cup / 120 grams cake flour

Preheat the oven to 350°F. Butter a 9-inch cake pan, dust it with flour and line it with a round of parchment.

Bring the water in a bain-marie to a simmer. Reduce the heat and maintain the water just below a simmer.

If using a stand mixer: Set the mixing bowl with the eggs and sugar over the bain-marie and vigorously whisk for 2 minutes to warm the mixture. Remove from heat and immediately lock the bowl into place in the stand mixer and set the whisk speed to medium-high. It should take around 8 minutes for the eggs to triple and very nearly quadruple in size and become quite pale. If you are adding salt or vanilla seeds, do so around the midpoint.

If using handheld beaters: Set a mixing bowl with the eggs and sugar over the bain-marie and beat over medium speed for 2 minutes. Remove the bowl from the heat and continue to beat for another 10 minutes, or until the mixture has tripled and very nearly quadrupled in volume and is quite pale.

Place a sieve over the mixing bowl and sift in a third of the flour. Using a rubber spatula, give the mixture a few gentle but assertive folds, then sift in the next third. Repeat. Fold only until no streaks of flour remain. Try to deflate the eggs as little as possible.

Immediately pour the batter into the prepared pan and bake for 15–20 minutes. The cake will be quite pale, but a knife inserted in the center should come out clean. Mine is usually ready at 17 minutes, but the timing will depend upon your oven. Invert right away onto a cooling rack and allow to come to room temperature.

Note: *Please note that this recipe calls for extra-large eggs, not large eggs.*

Génoise Riche à la Vanille

——— *Rich Vanilla Génoise* ———

This recipe, inspired by one in *Baking with Julia*, departs from tradition in technique, but the results remain remarkably close to the classic. Instead of heating the eggs and sugar, as is the standard cooking-school method, here they are beaten at room temperature until they've tripled in volume. The addition of a touch of butter adds a welcome richness and keeps the cake slightly moist, but not too moist to absorb a generous brushing of soaking syrup.

4 large eggs, at room temperature

½ cup / 110 grams superfine sugar

1½ teaspoons vanilla extract

¼ teaspoon fine sea salt

1 cup / 120 grams cake flour

2 tablespoons unsalted butter, melted, still warm but not hot

Set a rack in the lower third of the oven and preheat to 350°F. Butter and dust an 8-inch round cake pan with flour and line the bottom with a round of parchment.

In a stand mixer or using handheld electric beaters, whisk the eggs and sugar at medium-high speed until pale, voluminous and nearly quadrupled in volume. This will take 8–10 minutes. When you lift the whisk, you should see a ribbon fall back but not sink for a good 10 seconds. Add the vanilla and salt and whisk to incorporate.

Place a sieve over the bowl and sift in half the flour. Using a rubber spatula, fold the flour into the batter. Sift in the remaining flour and, again, fold it in until no streaks of flour remain.

Vigorously stir about a cup of the batter into the melted butter. Then, using the rubber spatula, fold the melted butter mixture into the batter. Fold gently, but decisively. You do not want to deflate the eggs, but nor do you want the batter sitting atop a puddle of butter.

Immediately, pour the batter into the prepared cake pan and bake for 25 minutes, or until a knife inserted in the center comes out clean and the surface springs back when lightly pressed. You'll also notice the cake starting to shrink away from the sides of the pan.

Invert onto a cooling rack and allow to come to room temperature.

Les Classiques

·——— *The Classics* ———·

These are the greats, the timeless classics. And, while tastes and trends are ever-changing, these never go out of style. They are all made with layers of génoise—either vanilla, almond or chocolate—and frosted. They look like American birthday cakes but instead of moist, dense cake layers, these layers are light and brushed with flavorful soaking syrup, filled with buttercream and most often iced with more buttercream or ganache. When sold at a pâtisserie, the layers are thin and many. When made at home, two layers are ample. Sometimes a coating of jam is used, sometimes nuts decorate the top.

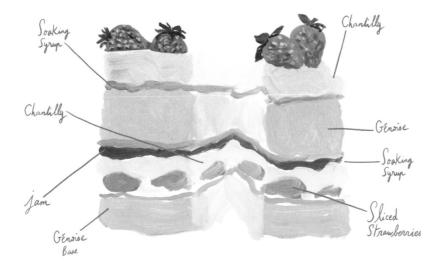

THE BASIC ASSEMBLY

These cakes are all made and assembled in much the same way, so consider these instructions your blueprint. I've left them loose, as playfulness, here, is more important than precision. Have fun with these and follow your instinct and taste on how little or how much to soak and coat these beauties. Recipes for soaking syrups, buttercreams, glazes and ganache may be found in the last chapter (page 305).

Continued

Bake a classic (page 166), rich vanilla (168) or chocolate (page 185) génoise. Let it cool to room temperature.

Cut the génoise in half horizontally.

Brush both inner sides with generous amounts—about 4 tablespoons total—of soaking syrup.

Coat the bottom half with roughly a ⅓-inch layer of buttercream, a ¼-inch layer of jam or a ½-inch layer of Chantilly.

Top with the second layer of génoise.

Brush the surface with another tablespoon or two of soaking syrup.

Frost with buttercream, ganache, glaze or Chantilly, or pile high with berries.

THE TIMING

The génoise can be made a day in advance and stored at room temperature wrapped well in plastic. The soaking syrup can be made in advance and kept in a sealed jar in the fridge for a few days. Buttercream is best made the day you are serving it.

The list of cakes is in alphabetical order. For a fraisier, see page 176.

Abricotine
  Génoise
  Kirsch soaking syrup
  Apricot jam
  Apricot jam glaze

This features two cake standbys: kirsch, which is nearly as commonly used as rum and vanilla, and apricot jam, which is often melted, as it is here, strained and used as a glaze that is both pretty and useful, in that it locks in the cake's moisture. An Abricotine is filled with apricot jam instead of with a buttercream or Chantilly. This couldn't be faster to assemble and, as it uses jam and not fresh fruit, can brighten a winter's night as easily as it can gently close a summer's dinner *en plein air*. You will sometimes see this cake called Régent à l'Abricot.

Ardéchois

Génoise

Armagnac soaking syrup

Chestnut cream (see page 227)

Chocolate glaze or ganache frosting

The Ardèche is a region in southeastern France known for its superior crop of chestnuts. My shortcut version is to replace the buttercream with chestnut Chantilly. If you don't have Armagnac on hand, use Cognac, bourbon or dark rum. This cake also goes by the names Chataigneraie and Marronier.

Caraïbe

Génoise

Curaçao, Cointreau or Grand Marnier soaking syrup

Seville orange thin-cut marmalade

Curaçao, Cointreau or Grand Marnier buttercream

Chocolate glaze or ganache frosting

Related to the Délicieux, the Caraïbe includes two thin layers of marmalade and curaçao is used in place of the Grand Marnier. I'm not a fan of bright blue liqueur, so I use Grand Marnier or Cointreau. The order is génoise, soaking syrup, marmalade, buttercream, repeat, blanket in ganache.

Côte d'Ivoire

Chocolate génoise

Rum soaking syrup

Chantilly

Unsweetened cocoa powder

Super easy. A chocolate génoise, brushed with a rum soaking syrup, is filled with Chantilly. Cocoa powder dusts the surface and Chantilly graces the sides. This cake is so named because the sides of the cake are the color of ivory.

Délicieux

Génoise

Grand Marnier soaking syrup

Grand Marnier ganache

Chocolate glaze, optional

The name says it all. The over-the-top version includes a chocolate glaze on top of the layers of ganache and a necklace of chocolate sprinkles. Take a mouthful of this cake, shut your eyes, and tell me you don't think that the orange and chocolate are deep into a feisty flirtation. While coffee accentuates the chocolatiness of chocolate, orange, in this heady dose of Grand Marnier, seems to toy with it in a playful opposites-attract sort of dance.

Forêt Noire

Chocolate génoise

Kirsch-soaked cherries

Chantilly

A beloved cake made with layers of chocolate génoise and filled with kirsch-soaked cherries and Chantilly. In pâtisseries, you may find a more complex version in which the whipped cream filling is given structure with just enough gelatin to keep it from turning back into cream, but not so much as to solidify it. When made at home, the whipped cream is simply added at the last minute.

Framboisine

Génoise

Crème de framboise or Chambord soaking syrup

Raspberry jam

Raspberry buttercream

Marzipan sheeting or fresh raspberries

As you might imagine, this one is all about raspberries. Crème de framboise or Chambord flavor the soaking syrup and the buttercream. A layer of raspberry jam brings it home. All nice and simple until, that is, you get to the traditional sheet of marzipan (often dyed pink) that blankets a framboisine. The marzipan must be rolled to a uniform height and impeccable smoothness and, quite frankly, I think such a step is best left to the pros. The trouble with marzipan sheeting is that a messy version of it looks messy, not charming. Instead, keep it fresh, color-ful and colorful and easy and decorate with fresh raspberries. Should you want the almond flavor, use an almond génoise and add ¼ teaspoon almond extract in the batter. When kirsch is used instead of crème de framboise, this cake goes by the name Marly aux Framboises.

Gâteau de Madame
Chocolate génoise

Kirsch or vanilla soaking syrup

Chantilly

Dark chocolate shavings

Here, a chocolate génoise is brushed with a kirsch or vanilla soaking syrup, filled and iced with Chantilly, and covered with an abundance of dark chocolate shavings.

Gâteau de Pâcques
Génoise

Kirsch soaking syrup

Raspberry jam

Chantilly, with cream cheese whipped in

Morello or Amarena cherries or other cherries soaked in kirsch

This is often served at Easter, or Pâcques. A génoise is brushed in kirsch soaking syrup, covered in raspberry jam, filled with a cream-cheese Chantilly and topped with cherries soaked in kirsch. For the cream, whip a Chantilly made with 1¾ cups heavy cream and 3 tablespoons confectioners' sugar. Beat in ⅓ cup cream cheese, sliced into small pieces, until integrated. Note that you will need about 45 cherries, depending on their size, to cover an 8-inch génoise.

Grenoblois
Génoise

Espresso soaking syrup

Coffee buttercream

Chopped toasted walnuts

Surrounding the city of Grenoble in the French Alps are some of the best walnut groves in France. This cake is similar to the Moka in its use of coffee buttercream and espresso soaking syrup, but it includes a layer of chopped toasted walnuts and is decorated with walnut halves. I tend to use a chocolate génoise, but either vanilla, nut or chocolate may be used.

Marguerite Cassis
    Almond génoise
    Crème de cassis soaking syrup
    Black currant preserves
    Crème de cassis buttercream

This one's a beauty. When I can't find black currant preserves, I use lingonberry preserves, which have a similar tartness. The formal version of this is decorated with a big chocolate marguerite or daisy. My shortcut is—you guessed it—crème de cassis Chantilly.

Marquis
    Génoise
    Kirsch soaking syrup
    Whipped cream
    Sliced ripe peaches

Not to be confused with a Marquise au Chocolat, this cake is made at the height of peach season. It's nothing more complicated than génoise brushed with a kirsch soaking syrup, slathered with whipped cream, covered with slices of very ripe peaches, slathered with more whipped cream and topped with the second half of the génoise, which is then also coated in whipped cream and decorated with more delicious peaches. It spells summer. I tend to gravitate toward crème de pêche or amaretto in place of the kirsch.

Moka
Vanilla génoise
Espresso soaking syrup
Coffee buttercream

This is not a mocha cake, despite the similar name, but rather a cake infused with espresso soaking syrup, filled and frosted with a coffee buttercream. The sides are often decorated with a base rim of toasted chopped almonds. It was created in Paris by pâtissier Guignard in 1857, and it caused a sensation. When coffee became all the rage in France, it was often referred to as moka, as shipments of the beans came through the port of Al Mukha on the Red Sea. Whoever first thought to mix coffee and chocolate was a culinary demigod, but that's the story of mocha, not moka.

Noisetier

> Génoise
>
> Kirsch soaking syrup
>
> Praliné buttercream
>
> Chopped toasted blanched hazelnuts

Like the Grenoblois, the Noisetier is a celebration of nuts—in this case, hazelnuts—and includes a layer of chopped nuts and is decorated with whole nuts. Traditionally made with kirsch, I prefer it with Frangelico, for a triple dose of hazelnut.

Romeo

> Génoise
>
> Rum soaking syrup
>
> Rum buttercream with rum raisins folded in

Rum raisin splendor. This is my father's favorite, and Romeo was the name of my beloved childhood Bouvier des Flandres—no wonder I'm partial to this one. If you like rum raisin ice cream, you'll like this cake. Rum-soaked raisins are folded into the buttercream, giving the cake a boozy note and little pockets of intense flavor.

Thermidor

> Chocolate génoise
>
> Dark rum soaking syrup
>
> Rum ganache

The double dose of rum and chocolate keep this cake among the most popular gâteaux in Paris.

Fraisier

— Strawberry Cake —

Consider a fraisier a strawberry shortcake that has gone to finishing school. It is a wildly popular cake because it is pretty much perfect. A properly dressed fraisier is best bought at a pâtisserie. It will have alternating layers of génoise, kirsch-spiked pastry cream and perfectly ripe strawberries. The top will be covered in a jelly-like blanket of red—that is, a strawberry glaze solidified with gelatin. Its surface will be so smooth that you just might see your reflection shining back at you upon close inspection. And you will want to inspect it. Closely. The sides will be lined with vertical strawberry slices. These always remind me of the Queen's Guard standing at attention outside Buckingham Palace in their red uniforms. Of course, most Parisians would not make such a labor-intensive confection at home. Here, then, is the home version, made with whipped cream and flaunting the delicious haphazard beauty of a shortcake.

BERRIES

3 pints fresh strawberries, hulled and sliced

¼ cup / 50 grams granulated sugar

¼ cup crème de fraise, crème de framboise or crème de cassis

Toss the sliced berries, sugar and crème de fraise together and let sit for at least 30 minutes and up to 4 hours.

SOAKING SYRUP

⅔ cup / 132 grams granulated sugar

⅔ cup water

3 tablespoons kirsch

Bring the sugar and water to a simmer and cook until all the sugar has dissolved and the liquid has reduced by half. Remove from heat and allow to come to room temperature. Stir in the kirsch.

CHANTILLY

1 cup heavy cream

½ cup crème fraîche

2 tablespoons confectioners' sugar

1 teaspoon vanilla extract

Whip the cream, crème fraîche, confectioners' sugar and vanilla until it is voluminous and can hold a peak.

ASSEMBLY

1 génoise

Using a long, serrated knife—ideally longer than the diameter of the cake—evenly slice a ¼-inch layer off the top of the génoise and discard. The surface should now be even and porous.

Slice the génoise into two horizontal layers. Brush the inner side of each layer with the soaking syrup.

Cover the bottom layer of cake with half the macerated sliced strawberries. Cover the berries with a thick layer of the Chantilly.

Continued

Place the top layer of cake over the Chantilly. Brush the surface with soaking syrup. This time, first spread with a thick layer of the Chantilly. Then top decoratively with the remaining sliced berries. Serve right away with dollops of any remaining Chantilly.

Due to the Chantilly, this cake is best served right away. But, refrigerated leftovers are good for breakfast.

VARIATIONS

Replace the sliced strawberries with whole raspberries. Replace the crème de fraise with crème de framboise.

Replace the kirsch with rose water. Or replace the kirsch soaking syrup with rose syrup. For a gorgeous finish, sprinkle with fresh rose petals.

Replace the sliced strawberries with chopped tropical fruit—mangoes, kiwi, papaya, pineapple. Replace the crème de fraise with 2 tablespoons lime juice. Replace the kirsch with rum.

Replace the sliced strawberries with sliced stone fruit—apricots, peaches, nectarines. Replace the crème de fraise with 1 tablespoon lemon juice. Replace the kirsch with amaretto or apricot liqueur.

Note: This is a cake that can be made with nearly any fruit. And, if the craving strikes in deepest winter, a good jam will do the trick.

Rouleau Fraise-Rhubarbe,
Glaçage au Citron

———— Strawberry-Rhubarb Rouleau, Lemon Buttercream ————

This is summer rolled up into a cake. A vanilla génoise is filled with either fresh strawberries tossed in crème de framboise or roasted with rhubarb and rose syrup. The fruit creates its own soaking syrup. A very lemony buttercream keeps it frisky. This can also be made as a layer cake. I find all-purpose flour gives this cake a bit of an edge when rolling, but I switch to cake flour when layering it.

VANILLA GÉNOISE

½ cup unsalted butter

1 tablespoon vanilla extract

8 large eggs, at room temperature

1 cup / 225 grams superfine sugar

1½ cups / 180 grams all-purpose flour

A few tablespoons confectioners' sugar, for assembly

Roasted Strawberry-Rhubarb Rose Compote (page 181)

Very Lemony Buttercream (page 181)

Preheat the oven to 350°F. Butter two 8-inch cake pans and line each with a round of parchment. Alternatively, butter one half sheet pan and line it with parchment.

Melt the butter in a small saucepan. Pour it through a fine sieve and discard any milk solids. Stir the vanilla into the melted butter and set aside somewhere warm.

Bring the water in a bain-marie to a simmer. Reduce the heat to maintain the barest simmer.

Combine the eggs and sugar in the bowl of your stand mixer or a mixing bowl and place it over the bain-marie. Vigorously whisk for 2–3 minutes to warm the mixture. Remove the bowl from heat and immediately lock it into place in the stand mixer and set the whisk speed to medium-high or use handheld electric beaters. Beat for about 8 minutes, or until the mixture has tripled and nearly quadrupled in size. It will be pale and mayonnaise-like and leave ribbons when you lift the whisk.

Continued

Place a sieve over the mixing bowl and sift in a third of the flour. Using a rubber spatula, give the mixture a few gentle but assertive folds, then sift in the next third. Repeat. Fold until no streaks of flour remain. Try to deflate the eggs as little as possible.

Fold a cup of the batter into the melted butter to lighten it, then fold this back into the batter.

Pour into your prepared cake pans or baking sheet. Bake for 30 minutes if using round pans or 15–17 minutes if using the sheet pan. When the cake is fully cooked, a knife inserted in the center will come out clean, the sides will have started to pull away from the pans, and the surface will spring back when lightly pressed.

ASSEMBLY

If making a layer cake, invert the round layers onto a cooling rack and let them come to room temperature. Set one aside for another day, if not using it. Cut the other one horizontally into two layers and fill with the roasted strawberry-rhubarb compote. Its liquid takes the place of a soaking syrup. Ice the entire cake with lemon buttercream and refrigerate for 15 minutes to allow the buttercream to set.

If using a sheet pan, run a knife around the edges to separate the cake from the pan. Sift a tablespoon or so of confectioners' sugar evenly over the surface of the cake, then cover with a clean tea towel and then a cooling rack. Flip the cake out of the pan so the towel is in between the cake and the rack. Peel off the parchment and sift a little more confectioners' sugar evenly over the cake.

With one of the short ends of the sponge facing toward you, roll up the still-warm cake with the tea towel inside and set it aside to come to room temperature.

When ready to assemble, unroll, remove the towel, cover the génoise with the strawberry-rhubarb compote, leaving a border of about ½ inch.

Roll the cake up as you did before and frost it with the buttercream. Refrigerate for 15 minutes to allow the buttercream to set.

ROASTED STRAWBERRY-RHUBARB ROSE COMPOTE

3 cups strawberries, hulled and quartered

3 cups rhubarb, cut into ½-inch pieces

½ cup rose syrup, Lyle's Golden Syrup or maple syrup

½ teaspoon freshly ground cardamom seeds from green cardamom pods, if using the rose syrup

Set a rack in the middle of the oven and preheat to 350°F. Line a gratin dish with parchment.

Toss the strawberries and rhubarb with the rose syrup and cardamom. Spread in the prepared gratin dish and bake for 30–40 minutes, or until very tender and the juices have thickened.

Transfer to a container and refrigerate, covered, until cool. Or keep refrigerated for up to 3 days.

VERY LEMONY BUTTERCREAM

1 cup unsalted butter, at room temperature

4¾ cups / 540 grams confectioners' sugar, plus more if needed

3 tablespoons freshly squeezed lemon juice

2 tablespoons limoncello, plus more if needed

2 tablespoons heavy cream, plus more if needed

The grated zest of 2 organic lemons

With a handheld or stand mixer fitted with a paddle or whisk attachment, beat the butter on medium speed until creamy—about 2 minutes. Add the confectioners' sugar, lemon juice, limoncello, heavy cream and zest with the mixer running on low. Increase to high speed and beat for 3 full minutes. Add up to ½ cup more confectioners' sugar if the frosting is too thin or another tablespoon of limoncello or of heavy cream if the frosting is too thick.

VARIATIONS

ELDERFLOWER: Use St-Germain instead of limoncello for a lemon elderflower buttercream. (If doing this, eliminate the cardamom from the compote.)

LEMON ROSE: Use rose water in place of the limoncello.

Grand Gâteau aux Pêches, Rhum et Mascarpone

———— Boozy Peaches and Mascarpone Layer Cake ————

This is a towering, four-layer summer cake. The French, like the Brits, have a great tradition of gathering for big Sunday lunches *en famille*. Unlike our brunch, this is usually in the early afternoon to give everyone time to cook and, in more religious times, to go to Mass. This cake is tall enough to serve a dozen, if the slices are thin. Increasing the amount of peaches, and serving a few slices on the side, will let you extend this dessert if—and this will surely happen—unexpected guests show up, having heard rumors of a certain *grand gâteau aux pêches*.

As there's so much happening in this cake, all-purpose flour can be used instead of cake flour and granulated sugar can be used instead of superfine sugar. No one will notice, so don't rush out to the store unnecessarily. It's not meant to be a refined cake, but rather a big, happy, carefree cake.

GÉNOISE

7 tablespoons unsalted butter

8 large eggs, separated, at room temperature

1¼ cups / 250 grams superfine or granulated sugar

1 tablespoon vanilla extract

2 cups / 240 grams cake or all-purpose flour

½ teaspoon fine sea salt

PEACHES AND CREAM

4 medium peaches, peeled and thinly sliced

⅓ cup / 66 grams granulated sugar

5 tablespoons dark rum

1⅓ cups /333 grams mascarpone

1 cup / 114 grams confectioners' sugar

1½ cups heavy cream

1½ teaspoons vanilla extract

3 perfectly ripe, unbruised peaches, for decoration

GÉNOISE

Preheat the oven to 350°F. Butter two 9-inch cake pans and line each with a round of parchment.

Melt the butter in a small saucepan and set aside.

In a stand mixer or using handheld electric beaters, beat the egg whites until soft peaks form, about 4–5 minutes. Transfer to a clean, cold bowl and set aside.

Combine the yolks and superfine sugar in the mixer and beat at medium-high speed until they are pale and leave a trail of ribbons, about 5–6 minutes. Whisk in the melted butter and vanilla.

Place a sieve over the mixing bowl and sift in the flour and salt. With a light but decisive touch, fold the flour into the yolks. Fold in roughly a third of the beaten egg whites, to lighten the mixture, then fold in the remaining whites, taking care not to deflate the batter. There should be no visible streaks.

Pour the batter into the prepared pans and use an offset spatula to spread it evenly out to the edges. Bake for 25–30 minutes, or until golden and springy to the touch. Transfer to a cooling rack. After 10 minutes, invert onto the rack and let the cakes come to room temperature.

Continued

PEACHES AND CREAM

Place your peeled and sliced peaches in a nonreactive bowl and set aside.

Bring the sugar and rum to a simmer, stirring to dissolve the sugar. Pour this over the peaches and let them mingle for at least 30 minutes at room temperature or up to 2 hours in the fridge.

In a stand mixer or using handheld electric beaters, whisk the mascarpone and confectioners' sugar at low speed to combine. With the mixer still running on low, slowly pour in the cream. Increase the speed to medium-high and whip until the cream becomes thick and forms soft peaks. Mix in the vanilla. Cover and refrigerate until ready to use.

ASSEMBLY

Use a serrated knife to cut each cake horizontally into two layers.

Strain the peaches, reserving the liquid to use as a soaking syrup for the cakes.

Place one cake layer on a platter or cake stand. Brush with the peach syrup. Once absorbed, spread about a quarter of the mascarpone cream onto the cake, then top with a third of the peaches. Place another cake layer on top and repeat the process to make a four-layer cake. The top of the cake should be covered only in cream. Just before serving, peel and slice the remaining peaches and arrange the slices in a pretty pattern on top of the cake.

Serve immediately or refrigerate for 2–3 hours, until ready to serve.

Génoise au Chocolat

— *Chocolate Génoise* —

A chocolate génoise might just be my favorite building block. There's no other base that can so quickly and easily be turned into something fabulously grand. All it needs is a dousing of rum, coffee or Cointreau and a blanket of ganache. Split it in half and fill it with marmalade, raspberry jam, whipped cream, macerated strawberries, ginger curd, chocolate mousse, coffee buttercream, brandied cherries, amaretto apricots, toasted sliced almonds, whipped ganache, or a cardamon caramel buttercream. Top it with ganache, crème Chantilly, berries or all three. In winter, look to candied orange slices, minced crystallized ginger and even crushed peppermint sticks.

This recipe is a bit of a departure from tradition. A classic génoise does not contain butter and the eggs are not separated. But the addition of butter, here, means this génoise skews moist, making it ideal even as a single layer cake. And beating the egg whites gives it levity. This recipe is what the French called *inratable*—foolproof.

This génoise can be made in the morning or, even, the night before, and stored, covered, at room temperature, until dinner. Make a whipped ganache at the last minute and use it to fill and frost the cake, after brushing it with syrup. Final assembly won't take more than ten minutes, and the whole enterprise, start to finish, can be accomplished in well under an hour. I'm including basic guidelines and ideas here. For the classics, turn to page 169.

6 tablespoons unsalted butter

6 large eggs, separated, at room temperature

1¼ cups / 150 grams light brown sugar

¼ teaspoon fine sea salt

¼ teaspoon chocolate extract, optional

¼ cup / 30 grams cornstarch

¼ cup / 30 grams cake flour

⅓ cup / 30 grams unsweetened cocoa powder

Preheat the oven to 350°F. Generously butter a 9-inch springform pan and line the bottom with parchment.

Melt the butter and pour it into a heatproof bowl, leaving the milky solids behind. Set aside somewhere warm.

Continued

In a stand mixer or using handheld electric beaters, whisk the egg whites at medium speed until foamy. Add the sugar and the salt and continue to whisk until they form firm, but not dry, peaks.

In a small bowl, lightly whisk the egg yolks until homogenous. Add the chocolate extract, if using. Pour this mixture over the egg whites and, using a rubber spatula, fold to incorporate. Set a sieve over the mixing bowl and sift the cornstarch, cake flour and cocoa powder onto the eggs. Fold these in until no streaks remain. Fold about half a cup of batter into the melted butter, then fold this butter mixture back into the batter.

Pour the batter into the prepared pan and bake for 25 minutes, or until the surface springs back when touched and a knife inserted in the center comes out clean. Set on a cooling rack for 10 minutes before unmolding.

SIMPLE ASSEMBLY

Slice the génoise in half horizontally once it's cooled to room temperature. Brush each layer with soaking syrup, continuing to add syrup until you feel the cake is moist. You will use more than you expect. If keeping it as a one-layer cake, brush the bottom with syrup, then flip and brush the top with syrup.

For a simple but elegant dessert, brush the cake with rum soaking syrup, then smooth the top of the cake with a thin coating of strained warmed apricot jam. After about 10 minutes, pour ganache onto the center of the cake, so that it casually runs down the sides.

IDEAS

The chocolate génoise. It screams "Kiss me!" With coffee, with rum, with Cointreau, with billowy pillows of Chantilly, with a pouring of ganache or a slathering of buttercream or both! Or perhaps a chaste peck on the cheek with raspberry jam, or perhaps apricot or strawberry and why not add fresh berries? Roll it into a log and you have the makings of a bûche de Noël, layer it and you have a birthday cake, deconstruct it and you have a trifle. A filling of mousse, and you will find yourself in a chocolate dream. Here are some other ideas to get you dreaming.

Soaking Syrups

A génoise is called a sponge cake not, thankfully, because it has that texture, but because that is its calling. A génoise is never meant to be eaten plain, but instead to absorb surprisingly large amounts of flavorful syrup and still maintain its structure. It will not go soggy on you. That is its promise.

Jams

Often a thin layer of jam will be added after the syrup. Raspberry, currant or apricot are most common. If the jam is chunky, or if using marmalade, it's best to warm it, then strain it, as chewy doesn't work here.

Buttercreams

Coffee, chocolate, boozy, spiced, zested—so many good pairings with chocolate.

Whipped Ganache

Fold cooled ganache into Chantilly and use as a filling and frosting for a shortcut to chocolate bliss.

Bits and Pieces

If you'd like a layer of texture, think chopped candied ginger or orange peel or crumbled amaretti cookies or chopped hazelnut praliné.

Mousse

Often a slathering of chocolate mousse will top a layer of génoise.

Fruit

Try berries inside, on top or on the side.

Ganache

This is almost always the frosting of choice for a chocolate génoise and for good reason. Add it only after the cake has absorbed all the liquid and is truly at room temperature.

Nuts

Toasted sliced almonds pressed into the ganache on the sides of your cake add texture, nuttiness and visual appeal.

Decoration

As I've said—no doubt too many times—no Parisian in their right mind would spend an entire day producing elaborate confections that are easily purchased at one of the city's staggeringly high number of pâtisseries. Instead, they streamline. If there's decoration, it most likely will be toasted sliced almonds or a few candied orange peels, purchased at Le Bon Marché.

Dollop

Crème fraîche, crème Chantilly or a combination of the two, flavored and sweetened, or not, adds a welcome tang. In a hurry, you can fill and ice a génoise merely with sweetened whipped cream, so long as you've first given it at least a little brushing of syrup.

A FEW FAVORITE SYRUPS FOR BRUSHING ON A CHOCOLATE GÉNOISE

Heavy Soaking Syrup Base

    2 cups / 400 grams granulated sugar
    1 cup water

Combine the sugar and water in a saucepan and bring to a boil. Stir until the sugar has dissolved. Remove from heat and set aside to come to room temperature before combining with other ingredients.

Stored in the fridge in a sealed jar, it will keep for months. If some of the sugar crystallizes, simply place the jar in a bowl of hot water for half an hour, then shake. It can also be kept at room temperature in a sealed jar for several weeks.

This 2:1 ratio can be increased or decreased, according to need.

Coffee Soaking Syrup

⅓ cup heavy simple syrup

⅓ cup strong espresso

Cardamom Espresso Soaking Syrup

Add 2–3 crushed green cardamom pods to the heavy
soaking syrup when cooking it. Strain just before use.

⅓ cup cardamom-flavored heavy simple syrup

⅓ cup strong espresso

Rum and Coffee Soaking Syrup

⅓ cup heavy simple syrup

¼ cup strong espresso

2 tablespoons dark rum

Really Boozy Soaking Syrup

⅓ cup heavy simple syrup

⅓ cup liqueur

Raspberry Soaking Syrup

⅓ cup heavy simple syrup

⅓ cup crème de framboise or Chambord

Boozy Orange Soaking Syrup

Add the grated zest of 1 organic orange to the heavy
soaking syrup when cooking it. Strain just before use.

⅓ cup orange-infused heavy simple syrup

3 tablespoons freshly squeezed and strained orange juice

3 tablespoons Grand Marnier or Cointreau

Virgin Orange Soaking Syrup

⅓ cup orange-infused heavy simple syrup

⅓ cup freshly squeezed and strained orange juice

Génoise Fourrée au Chocolate

Chocolate Génoise Layer Cake

My go-to. It will be yours, too.

GÉNOISE

6 tablespoons unsalted butter

6 large eggs, separated, at room
   temperature

1¼ cups / 150 grams light brown sugar

¼ teaspoon fine sea salt

¼ teaspoon chocolate extract, optional

¼ cup / 30 grams cornstarch

¼ cup / 30 grams cake flour

⅓ cup / 30 grams unsweetened cocoa
   powder

Preheat the oven to 350°F. Generously butter a 9-inch springform pan and line the bottom with a round of parchment.

Melt the butter and pour it into a heatproof bowl, leaving the milky solids behind. Set aside somewhere warm.

In a stand mixer or using handheld electric beaters, whisk the egg whites at medium speed until foamy. Add the sugar and salt and continue to whisk until they form firm, but not dry, peaks.

In a small bowl, lightly whisk the egg yolks with a fork until homogenous. Add the chocolate extract, if using. Pour this mixture over the egg whites and, using a rubber spatula, fold to incorporate. Set a sieve over the mixing bowl and sift the cornstarch, cake flour and cocoa powder onto the eggs. Fold these in until no streaks remain. Add a soup spoonful of batter to the melted butter and stir to combine. Fold this butter mixture into the batter.

Pour the batter into the prepared pan and bake for 25 minutes, or until the surface springs back when touched and a knife inserted in the center comes out clean. Set on a cooling rack for 10 minutes before unmolding. The cake should come to room temperature before brushing it with soaking syrup.

SOAKING SYRUP

½ cup plus 1 tablespoon / 113 grams granulated sugar

5 tablespoons espresso

4 teaspoons rum, Cognac or coffee liqueur

Melt the sugar in the espresso over low heat. Let it come to a simmer and cook for 1 minute to thicken it slightly. Remove from heat and stir in the liqueur of your choice.

WHIPPED CHOCOLATE GANACHE

2¼ cups heavy cream

280 grams dark chocolate, such as Valrhona Caraïbe 66% cacao

Bring ¾ cup of the cream to a boil and immediately pour over the chocolate. Allow the chocolate to melt for a minute, then whisk to create a smooth ganache. Set aside to come to room temperature. This shouldn't take more than about 10 minutes. If it gets too cold, it will start to solidify, which you don't want. If that happens, warm it up a tiny bit—just enough that it stirs easily.

In a stand mixer or using handheld electric beaters, whip the remaining cream until you see soft, but structured, peaks. Stir a third of this whipped cream into the ganache to lighten it, then fold the remaining ganache into the whipped cream with a rubber spatula. Use immediately.

ASSEMBLY

When the génoise is at room temperature, slice it horizontally into two layers. Brush the inner side of each layer with plenty of the soaking syrup. Set aside until serving time.

When ready to serve, make the whipped chocolate ganache. Blanket the bottom layer with about half the whipped chocolate ganache. Cover with the second layer. Brush any remaining syrup on the surface and ice the cake with the remaining whipped chocolate ganache. Serve right away.

Gâteau Chocolat-Menthe

—— *Mint Chocolate Cake* ——

Christophe Michalak is the charismatic star of the Paris gâteau scene. His master-class book, called *Michalak Masterbook*, is illustrated with rocket ships and the stuff of superhero cartoons—in other words, he plays the boy genius who never grew up. A second look, however, and you'll discover a true and original talent who owns several of the best pâtisseries in Paris. Much awarded, much lauded, published by no less than Alain Ducasse Édition, Michalak is playful, energetic and ready at every turn to flip an idea. He took Paris by culinary storm with his Gâteau Opéra Menthe. The traditional opéra is composed of several thin layers of almond *joconde*, steeped in coffee, slathered with coffee buttercream and dark chocolate ganache and glazed with even more chocolate. Michalak replaced the coffee with mint, producing a cake that tastes like the very best version of an After Eight. This is the cake for those of you who keep their freezers stocked with mint-chip ice cream.

I've stripped away the hours of arduous and intricate labor and simply run with the idea, but the taste is brilliant. Mint appears in three places. The soaking syrup is infused with fresh mint leaves, the Chantilly is infused with either a little crème de menthe liqueur or a little more of the mint soaking syrup and the cake is decorated with candied mint leaves. The quality and freshness of the mint is key. If you don't have access to really fragrant and fresh mint or want a shortcut, Woodford Reserve and Sonoma Syrup Co. both make mint syrups that are easily found online. Either can be used both to steep the génoise and perfume the cream.

1 Chocolate Génoise (page 185), sliced horizontally into two layers

MINT SOAKING SYRUP

½ cup water

¼ cup / 50 grams granulated sugar

20 very fresh mint leaves

Bring the water and sugar to a simmer over low heat and stir to dissolve the sugar. Remove from heat and add the mint leaves. Allow to steep for around 20 minutes before removing the mint.

CANDIED MINT LEAVES

2 large egg whites, whisked until loose

½ cup / 58 grams confectioners' sugar

20 very fresh mint leaves

Place the egg whites in one bowl and the confectioners' sugar in another. Dip each mint leaf into the egg whites, then hold the leaf above the bowl for a few seconds to let any excess egg drip off. Next, dip the leaf into the sugar. Give it a little shake to let any excess fall away. Place the leaf on a parchment-lined baking sheet and set aside to dry. If your kitchen is hot or humid, place in an oven on the lowest setting and turn off the oven. Let the leaves dry out as the oven cools.

Continued

MINT CHANTILLY

2 cups heavy cream

2–3 tablespoons confectioners' sugar

2 teaspoons crème de menthe,
¼ teaspoon mint extract or
2 tablespoons mint simple syrup

In a stand mixer or using handheld electric beaters, whip the cream until it is billowy. Sprinkle with the confectioners' sugar and whisk to incorporate. Drizzle with whatever source of mint you are using and whisk to incorporate.

OR

2 cups heavy cream

20 fresh mint leaves

3 tablespoons confectioners' sugar

Bring the cream to a bare simmer. Add the mint leaves and allow to infuse for 20 minutes. Remove the mint. Refrigerate the infused cream until cold. Close to serving time, whip the cream in a stand mixer or using handheld electric beaters until it is billowy. Sprinkle with the confectioners' sugar and whisk to incorporate.

ASSEMBLY

   Whipped chocolate ganache
      (see page 191)

Brush both halves of the génoise with the mint syrup. Allow to absorb. Repeat. And repeat a third time. Set aside for 10 minutes.

Slather the bottom layer with the whipped chocolate ganache. Cover with the top layer. Ice this with ganache. Decorate by creating a border of candied mint leaves.

Serve with a generous dollop of the mint Chantilly.

Note: *This recipe also makes a fantastic Bûche de Noël Chocolat-Menthe. Use a sheet pan génoise and follow the assembly instructions on page 264. The candied mint leaves will look like fallen tree leaves. Or sprinkle with a crushed peppermint candy cane.*

The
CHIC,
DELICIOUS
and
PLAYFUL

Les Gâteaux Chics,

Gourmands et Fantaisistes

LES DACQUOISES

A dacquoise is a marvelous thing, what with its layers of meringue, buttercream and Chantilly standing tall on a buttery biscuit base. It has serious wow factor, thanks to its towering height and the fragility of its appearance. It's not, however, terribly fragile, nor is it hard to make.

A pâtissier will almost always use multiple flavors of buttercream and bake a thin layer of cake for the base to provide added structure. But a home-baked dacquoise is usually three layers of nut meringue sandwiching either buttercream, mousse or crème Chantilly. A generous blanket of Chantilly on top is de rigueur! The rest is all in the matchmaking, leaving you to pair nut and flavor according to whim, season or what happens to be in your pantry. But there are a few tried-and-true classics.

A dacquoise made with almond and hazelnut meringue and filled with mocha buttercream is light and airy, but with the depth of flavor needed to satisfy winter cravings. On a hot summer's eve, try a lemon-scented almond meringue, filled with lemon buttercream and a neat row of raspberries. I'm partial to certain marriages, such as pistachio and strawberry, chocolate and orange, rose and cardamom, almond and apricot, coffee and rum, chocolate and chestnut, tangerine and yuzu, coconut, lime and mango. Mix and match to the tune of your palate. Sliced fruit is best sandwiched between the layers of meringue. But berries, standing upright, look as sensational holding up the top layer of meringue as they do nestled into a whipped blanket of cream in neat rows or concentric circles. For a lighter and faster dacquoise, use only crème Chantilly, scented and sweetened or not. For a richer dessert, opt for buttercream.

If you think you are going to make a dacquoise and suddenly find yourself with no time to spare, simply pivot and make a Pavlova—one large meringue with a well of whipped cream and fruit. The very ambitious might try a marjolaine, a rectangular chocolate buttercream dacquoise, sporting a glistening chocolate coat. Speaking of meringues, they've been gracing French desserts since the 1600s. We don't know when the first dacquoise was made, but we do know it originated in the town of Dax in southwestern France. A Dacquois is a person from Dax.

What you need to know:

NUTS: I'm including recipes for two types of meringue layers. The first is made with almonds, hazelnuts, pistachios, or a combination of these. Because the chopped nuts are suspended in the meringue, the difference in their oil content will not affect the outcome, as it might in a nut-flour-based cake. Try it with pecans, walnuts or macadamia nuts. The second recipe is for a chocolate meringue.

MERINGUE: To make a neat disk of meringue, a pastry bag is helpful. I use one when making circular meringues, as I like a spiraling shape. But for a rectangular or square meringue, I simply use an offset spatula to create a roughly even layer. The trick is to smooth the meringue without pressing down and deflating the egg whites. While nobody will complain about a two-layer dacquoise, three layers is simply grander and worth the extra effort. Don't hesitate to add a touch of spice, zest, espresso powder or the seeds of a vanilla bean to your meringue batter. Do not add liquid, at least not more than a teaspoon or so.

BUTTERCREAM: Chocolate, coffee, vanilla, chestnut, citrus, boozy are the norm, but don't stop there. Consider cinnamon, cardamom, nutmeg, even chai. And don't forget about the florals: orange blossom, rose, lavender, chamomile, hibiscus. Or the herbs: mint, basil, tarragon, lemongrass. Given the potency of herbs, they're best paired with the mildness of an almond meringue rather than a stronger nut, such as hazelnut or pistachio. A few spoonfuls of cassis or crème de framboise will offer a pink hue and surprising depth. A word of advice: don't hit the palate with too many strong notes. It's all about balance and subtlety. See pages 322–329 for buttercream recipes.

CRÈME CHANTILLY: Flavor as you like—with booze, vanilla, spices, zest, floral waters, extracts, chocolate. Sweeten with confectioners' sugar. Chantilly may replace the buttercream. It may be combined with buttercream or ganache. It is always the top layer.

FRUIT: Fruit can be sandwiched between layers of meringue. Neat concentric circles or rows of raspberries nestled into the top layer of Chantilly make for a beautiful summer's dacquoise.

TIMING: The meringues can be made in advance, as can the buttercream. Crème Chantilly is best made within an hour of serving it and kept refrigerated. Ideally, a dacquoise is assembled at the last minute, but it can be made a few hours in advance and kept refrigerated. Simply remove it from the refrigerator about thirty minutes before serving.

ASSEMBLY: Place one disk (or rectangle) of baked meringue on your cake plate. Slather this with buttercream or Chantilly. Cover with a second disc of baked meringue. Slather this with buttercream or Chantilly. Cover with a third disc of baked meringue. Slather this with buttercream, if using, then Chantilly. If using berries, nestle them lightly into the cream. A dusting of confectioners' sugar is pretty on top. If making a chocolate or mocha dacquoise, consider shaving some chocolate over the surface for decoration, or dusting it lightly with cocoa powder.

SERVING: Use a sharp knife to slice neatly through the layers. But it still won't be neat. And that's part of its charm.

Nut Meringue for a Dacquoise

1 cup / 140 grams almonds, hazelnuts,
    pistachios or a combination of
    almonds and hazelnuts

1 cup plus 2 tablespoons / 130 grams
    confectioners' sugar

7 large egg whites, at room temperature

⅓ cup / 65 grams granulated sugar

Position a rack in the center of the oven and preheat to 225°F. Line an 18 x 13-inch baking sheet with parchment paper. Draw three 10 x 3-inch rectangles at least 3 inches apart on one side of the parchment, then flip it ink side down and liberally coat the top side with butter.

In a food processor, pulse the almonds until ground to a fine powder. Stop grinding as soon as you have a powder. Transfer the nut flour to a medium mixing bowl. Place a sieve over the bowl and sift the confectioners' sugar directly onto the nut flour. Whisk to integrate.

In a stand mixer or using handheld electric beaters, beat the egg whites at medium speed, until they hold soft peaks. To test for the soft-peak stage, stop the mixer and lift the whisk out of the whites; the whites should peak, then droop.

With the mixer running at medium speed, add the granulated sugar in three additions, mixing for 30 seconds after each addition. When all of the granulated sugar has been incorporated, increase the speed to high and beat for about 15 seconds longer. The meringue should be slightly glossy and white and somewhat stiff, but not dry. Scrape the meringue into a large bowl.

Sprinkle the nut-sugar mixture onto the meringue. Working quickly and gently, fold the mixture into the meringue with a rubber spatula, scraping the sides of the bowl to catch any loose nuts. The final consistency will be a little soupy.

Fit a pastry bag with a ½-inch round plain tip (or simply cut a ½-inch opening in a ziplock bag) and fill the bag with the meringue. Following the guidelines you drew on the underside of the parchment, pipe the meringue to "fill in" the rectangles you've drawn. These will be your three meringue layers. Alternatively, spread the meringue with an offset spatula and a light touch to fill the rectangles. Try to create as even a surface as possible without pressing down and deflating the egg whites.

Continued

Bake for 3–3½ hours, or until the meringues are firm to the touch. Turn off the oven, but don't remove the meringues. Leave them in the closed oven for at least 6 hours and up to 12.

Note: *To avoid making nut butter rather than nut flour, try refrigerating the nuts for an hour or so and placing the blade of your food processor in the freezer for 5 minutes before starting the recipe.*

Chocolate Meringue Disks for a Dacquoise

6 large egg whites / 213 grams, at room temperature

¼ teaspoon cream of tartar

Pinch of salt

1 cup / 200 grams granulated sugar

½ cup / 50 grams almond flour

¼ cup / 25 grams unsweetened Dutch-processed cocoa

Put two oven racks equidistant from the top and bottom of the oven and preheat the oven to 225°F. Line two 18 x 13-inch baking sheets with parchment paper. Trace three 8-inch circles on the parchment at least 3 inches apart. Two circles will be on one sheet and the third on the other. Flip the parchment ink side down, then liberally butter the top side.

In a stand mixer or using handheld electric beaters, combine the egg whites, cream of tartar, and salt and beat on medium speed until fine bubbles form. Increase the speed to medium-high and whip until soft peaks form. With the mixer running, gradually add the sugar and whip until the meringue is stiff and shiny, but not dry, another 2–3 minutes.

In a small bowl, whisk together the almond flour and cocoa powder. Sprinkle half of the mixture over the egg whites and, using a rubber spatula, fold to integrate. Repeat with the rest of the cocoa mixture, folding just until combined. Scrape the bottom of the bowl to catch and integrate any stray streaks of almond flour.

Using a piping bag or a small offset spatula, fill the circles with batter.

Bake for 3–3½ hours, or until the meringues are firm to the touch. Turn off the oven, but don't remove the meringues. Leave them in the closed oven for at least 6 hours and up to 12.

Gâteau Concorde

—————— *Concorde Chocolate Meringue and Mousse Cake* ——————

The extraordinary pâtissier Gaston Lenôtre was asked by Air France in the late 1970s to create a cake for the then brand-new Concorde jet that cut flying time between Paris and New York down from seven hours to three. In the late '80s, my mother discovered a way to buy last-minute bucket tickets on the Concorde for the price of a normal fare. I remember how utterly enthralled she was with the aerodynamics and speed of this plane, and how she'd try to hide an irrepressible smile whenever it was time to fly one of these supersonic beauties.

The gâteau Concorde is made with three disks of meringue, filled with an intense egg-less chocolate mousse and decorated with chocolate curls. Not quite as supersonic as its name, the cake needs six hours of refrigeration and can be kept refrigerated for up to forty-eight hours. Please use a chocolate that is around 64%–66% cacao for the mousse. Anything much lower or higher will alter the texture.

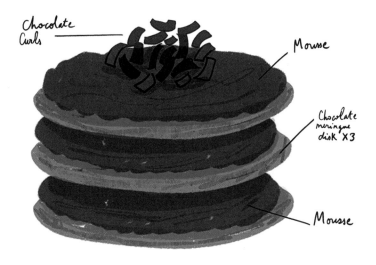

WHIPPED CHOCOLATE (MOUSSE-LIKE) GANACHE

2¼ cups heavy cream

280 grams dark chocolate, such as Valrhona Caraïbe 66% cacao

Bring ¾ cup of the cream to a boil and immediately pour over the chocolate. Allow the chocolate to melt for a minute, then whisk to create a smooth ganache. Set aside to come to room temperature. This shouldn't take more than about 10 minutes. If it gets too cold, it will start to solidify, which you don't want. If that happens, warm it up a tiny bit—just enough that it stirs easily.

In a stand mixer or using handheld electric beaters, whip the remaining 1½ cups of the cream until you see soft, but structured, peaks. Stir a third of this whipped cream into the ganache to lighten it, then fold the remaining ganache into the whipped cream with a rubber spatula. Use immediately.

CHOCOLATE CURLS

Making chocolate curls is too time-consuming to do at home. Instead, I like to use a mandoline to cut fine slices of chocolate off a bar. These shards are more, shall we say, industrial-chic than delicate, but let's not get precious about it. Use at least 200 grams of dark chocolate if you want to cover the entire cake and still allow everyone to sneak a few shards before dinner.

ASSEMBLY

3 Chocolate Meringue Disks for a Dacquoise (page 203)

Lay the chocolate meringue disks on a sheet of parchment. Cover each with a third of the ganache. Then stack them, one on top of the other, on your cake plate. The surface will be ganache. Scatter this with an abundance of chocolate curls or shards. Create a tented dome with aluminum foil over—but not touching—the cake and refrigerate it for at least 6 hours and up to two days. Let it sit at room temperature for about 20–30 minutes to allow the ganache to soften a bit before bringing it to the table.

Tiramisu Français

—— French Tiramisu ——

So easy. So good. A chocolate or nut génoise replaces the ladyfingers. A Chantilly of crème fraîche and heavy cream, accented with rum and coffee, stands in for the mascarpone. The hazelnut génoise I include here is dry enough to absorb four shots of espresso, two shots of rum and another of simple syrup and still maintain a little bite. Such is the beauty of a génoise. It's not overly sweet either, allowing you to go to town on great billowy clouds of sweetened and spiked whipped cream. A dusting of cocoa completes the picture. To keep this recipe even simpler and, in fact, quite pretty, I assemble the tiramisu in the springform pan I used to bake the cake. The only downside is that a cream-based tiramisu won't be good the next day, as the cream holds more water than mascarpone. For anyone with nut allergies, simply use a plain or chocolate génoise. For anyone gluten-intolerant, substitute a gluten-free flour for the cake flour. For anyone avoiding alcohol, replace the rum with additional espresso and add a half teaspoon of freshly ground cardamom to both the batter and the cream. I suppose this would make it a Turkish tiramisu.

HAZELNUT GÉNOISE

8 large eggs, separated, at room temperature

½ cup / 100 grams granulated sugar

The grated zest and juice of 1 orange

400 grams hazelnut flour

2 tablespoons cake flour

½ teaspoon fine sea salt

1 teaspoon vanilla extract

Preheat the oven to 350°F. Butter the sides of a 10-inch springform pan and line the bottom with a round of parchment.

In the bowl of a stand mixer or using handheld electric beaters, beat the egg yolks and granulated sugar together until very pale and voluminous. Add orange zest and juice, hazelnut flour, cake flour, salt and vanilla and beat until homogenous.

In a clean mixing bowl and with a clean whisk or beaters, whip the egg whites. As soon as they form stiff peaks, stop the mixer. Stir one-third of the whites into the batter to lighten it, then, using a rubber spatula, fold in the rest.

Pour the batter into the prepared pan and bake for 15 minutes. Reduce the heat to 325°F and bake for a further 15 minutes, or until a knife inserted in the center comes out clean. Slide onto a cooling rack to come to room temperature. Slice the cake horizontally into two layers.

SOAKING SYRUP

4 short shots / ½ cup strong, hot espresso	2 tablespoons dark rum
	2 tablespoons superfine sugar

Combine the ingredients in a shallow bowl and stir to dissolve the sugar.

CREAM

1½ cups heavy cream	1 tablespoon dark rum
1½ cups crème fraîche	2 tablespoons confectioners' sugar
¼ teaspoon powdered espresso or coffee extract	

Beat the heavy cream and crème fraîche together until they form billowy clouds. Add the remaining ingredients and whisk to integrate.

ASSEMBLY

1 tablespoon unsweetened cocoa powder

Place the bottom layer of génoise back in the springform pan, and brush all of the soaking syrup onto the interior sides of both layers. Slather generously with about half the spiked whipped cream. Place the top layer of génoise back in the pan, syrup side up, and slather the surface with the remaining whipped cream. Secure the sides of the springform, if they're not already locked, tent with aluminum foil, and refrigerate for about 30 minutes and up to 3 hours. Just before serving, dust the surface with the cocoa powder, sifting it over the top through a sieve. Remove the sides of the pan and serve immediately.

Tiramisu mi-Français, mi-Italien

— *Slightly More Italian Tiramisu* —

It's somewhat crazy to even write a recipe for this, as it is meant to be a playful, deconstructed thing of deliciousness. Let me therefore try to describe it. The basic idea is to mix a few strong shots of espresso with a few shots of rum, Cognac or Armagnac and chill it. Dip ladyfingers into this chilled concoction, if you've not succumbed to temptation and drunk it. Whip some cream and crème fraîche together until billowy. Add sugar and more booze, maybe a little vanilla, espresso powder, orange zest or cinnamon. Alternate layers of ladyfingers and cream in a shallow dish. Refrigerate for a few hours and serve dusted with cocoa.

Once you've tried this tiramisu with crème fraîche, you may never go back to mascarpone, let alone the more laborious process of making the required sabayon base. Crème fraîche is, to me, something of a miracle. It's rich and tangy and custard-like in taste and behavior. I say "behavior" because it maintains its smooth, thick texture at nearly any temperature, for as long as you need it to. Well-mannered it is, and always elegant. It lasts in the fridge for weeks, turns a plate of fruit into a sublime dessert and, for that matter, transforms the cooking jus of a roast chicken into a silken gravy in under twenty seconds. I am often teased for keeping a few pints in my fridge at all times, and I just smile knowing it is a secret weapon and a shortcut to Heaven.

SOAKING SYRUP

3 short shots / ⅓ cup strong, hot espresso	3 tablespoons dark rum
	3 tablespoons superfine sugar

Combine the ingredients in a shallow bowl and stir to dissolve the sugar.

CREAM

1½ cups heavy cream	1 tablespoon dark rum
2 cups crème fraîche	2 tablespoons confectioners' sugar
½ teaspoon powdered espresso or coffee extract	

Beat the heavy cream and crème fraîche together until they form billowy clouds. Add the remaining ingredients and whisk to integrate.

ASSEMBLY

45 ladyfingers, store-bought is fine	1 tablespoon unsweetened cocoa powder

One at a time, roll about half the ladyfingers in the syrup and line them in tight rows in the bottom of a 9 x 13-inch Pyrex or baking dish. If you need to, trim any edges.

Spread these ladyfingers with half the cream.

Roll enough ladyfingers in the soaking syrup to tightly line them in a single layer over the whipped cream. Add a final layer of the cream and refrigerate for at least 30 minutes and up to 3 hours. Just before serving, dust the surface with the cocoa powder, sifting it over the top through a sieve.

Alternatively, use a pretty serving bowl and make this in three layers, not two.

Tiramisu aux Framboises et au Limoncello

Limoncello Raspberry Tiramisu

Limoncello is made from Sorrento lemons in southern Italy, where it is often drunk cold, neat and in a small glass, after dinner as a *digestivo*. As there's so much commercial, over-sweetened limoncello on the market, this too often means ending a meal with the liquid equivalent of a lemon jellybean. But the really good limoncellos are natural, barely sweetened and bursting with the taste of Mediterranean lemons at their sun-kissed peak. I don't much like to drink limoncello, but I do love it in cocktails and in desserts. Try it the Corsican way, paired with the French spirit Lillet Blanc and wild elderflower syrup. Or consider a scoop of tart lemon sorbet, a dash of limoncello, a sprig of rosemary in a flute, topped with sparkling wine. Use it to spike lemonade, and you'll find it also intensifies the flavor. Or use it in place of lemon extract, simply increasing the volume by three. Tossed with red berries, it seems to accentuate their flavor, brightening their very berry-ness. There's a wonderful Italian wine store on my childhood street, rue du Cherche-Midi, that sells a Sardinian limoncello called Limonsardo that packs a fabulously zesty punch. It begs to be paired with the creaminess of mascarpone in this summery, chilled riff on a tiramisu. To simplify, replace the mascarpone with a Chantilly made with half crème fraîche and half heavy cream and chill it for only thirty minutes. To build it into a cake, use a lemon-scented génoise in place of the ladyfingers, perhaps adding a layer of lemon curd before the mascarpone. If strawberries are in season, by all means use them. They look fabulous standing, gently nestled in the cream, in neat rows.

5 large eggs, separated, at room temperature

1 cup / 200 grams granulated sugar

1½ cups limoncello

The juice of 6 lemons, and the grated zest of 3 of those lemons

1 cup water

2 cups mascarpone, at room temperature

40–45 ladyfingers, store-bought is fine

4–5 cups raspberries

Confectioners' sugar and thin whisps of lemon zest, for decoration, optional

To make the zabaglione, place the eggs yolks, ¼ cup of the granulated sugar and ½ cup of the limoncello in a double boiler set over low heat. The water should be at a steady simmer. Using handheld electric beaters, immediately start whisking and don't stop until the egg mixture is thick enough to form a ribbon, about 5 minutes. Remove from heat and set aside to cool.

Combine the remaining limoncello, the lemon juice, water and ½ cup of the granulated sugar in a saucepan. Bring to a boil and cook, stirring, until the sugar dissolves and the mixture thickens, about 5 minutes. Transfer to a shallow bowl and set aside to cool.

In a large bowl, whisk the mascarpone to lighten it, then add the lemon zest and whisk until light and creamy.

Using clean handheld electric beaters, whip the egg whites with the remaining ¼ cup of the granulated sugar until they hold nearly firm peaks, 3–4 minutes.

When the zabaglione is cool, use a rubber spatula to fold a third of it into the mascarpone. Fold in the remaining zabaglione in three additions, then, also in three additions, gently fold in the beaten egg whites until no streaks remain.

One at a time, roll about half the ladyfingers in the syrup and line them in tight rows on the bottom of a 9 x 13-inch Pyrex or baking dish.

Spread half the mascarpone mixture over the ladyfingers. Repeat to form second layers of ladyfingers and mascarpone. Cover the tiramisu with plastic wrap and refrigerate for at least 6 hours and up to 24.

Before serving, cover the surface of the tiramisu with rows of raspberries. If you'd like, shower lightly with confectioners' sugar or a little grated lemon zest, or leave as is.

Pavlova

———•———

Created for and named after the Russian ballerina Anna Pavlova, this gorgeous dessert is, indeed, a ballet of meringue, cream and berries. It is ridiculously easy to make, particularly in light of its sumptuous, extravagant appearance. Fruit rests on a pillow of whipped cream that graces a round of meringue. When prepared right, the meringue is marshmallowy on the inside and crisp on the outside, the cream is billowy and the berries are bursting with juice.

When strawberries are at their peak, I like to keep things simple: meringue, whipped cream and sliced strawberries, with a little sugar tossed in. Sometimes I'll sneak in a touch of rose water or limoncello. For a dinner party, I might mix the berries in a raspberry coulis, scented with crème de cassis. When blackberries are at their sweetest, I might, instead, add a touch of lavender extract to the cream. In the dark days of winter, I surprise with sliced tropical fruit and a squeeze of lime juice, and I fold some passion fruit purée into the whipped cream, along with a shot of white rum. Sometimes I spread a thin layer of lemon curd on the meringue before adding the whipped cream. Christian Constant, chef-proprietor of Les Cocottes on the rue Saint Dominique, never fails to have a Pavlova on the menu. In one of my favorites, he laces a lemony whipped cream with ginger syrup. In another, he makes a passion fruit curd and adds a hint of lime zest to the cream. Sometimes a little crème de violette from Toulouse makes its way into the cream, and a few candied violets might be found scattered amongst the berries.

MERINGUE

9 large egg whites, at room temperature	2 teaspoons vanilla extract
¼ teaspoon fine sea salt	1½ teaspoons white vinegar
1½ cups / 300 grams superfine sugar	1 tablespoon cornstarch, sifted

Preheat the oven to 275°F. Line a sheet pan with parchment paper. This generous recipe yields a 12-inch round meringue. If you want a neat circle, draw an outline on the paper, then flip the paper so that the ink is on the underside.

Using a stand mixer or handheld electric beaters, beat the egg whites with the salt at medium-high speed until you see soft peaks form. With the mixer still running, add the superfine sugar in a slow, steady stream and beat at high speed until you see shiny, firm peaks form. Add the vanilla, vinegar and cornstarch and beat to incorporate.

Pour the meringue into the middle of the drawn circle. And, with a light touch so as not to deflate the egg whites, smooth it out to fill the outline of the circle. Using a rubber spatula, create a slight well in the center of the meringue, bringing the rim up a tad higher. Your end goal is a rim that's about ½ inch higher than the well of the meringue, but Pavlovas are not about precision. Some people keep the meringue level, which is easier and very pretty.

Bake for 90 minutes. Turn off the oven but leave the meringue inside for another 2 hours, or until it is no longer sticky to the touch. The exterior should be dry and crackly and the interior moist. It can stay in the oven all day if you want to make the meringue in the morning to have at dinner.

CREAM AND BERRIES

2¼ cups cold heavy cream

⅓ cup / 38 grams confectioners' sugar

1 teaspoon vanilla extract

3 cups berries or other fresh fruit

1 tablespoon granulated or superfine sugar

Just before serving, whip the cream in a stand mixer or using handheld electric beaters at medium speed. When it starts to thicken, add the confectioners' sugar and vanilla and whip until it holds its shape, but is still soft, voluminous and billowy. Toss the berries in the sugar.

Fill the meringue with the whipped cream. Top the cream with the sweetened berries. Serve immediately. A sharp knife will help keep it neat, but neatness isn't the point.

Note: This serves 8 or 9 good eaters. The recipe is easily halved to serve 4 or 5. Simply turn off the oven after 75 minutes, not 90.

Gâteau Revani

—— *Revani Cake* ——

Paris has almost no Greek restaurants, and yet the Greek isles are a favored vacation spot of the French. This *gâteau souvenir* is so good, it conjures the happy memories of a holiday spent barefoot on the beach, toes in the water, the ruins of an ancient temple somewhere close, even if you've never set foot in Greece. Revani is a semolina-almond cake that is drenched just out of the oven in an aromatic syrup. It can be found in nearly every Greek bakery, and it is one of the few Greek recipes (the other being taramasalata) to be adopted by the French. A good amount of beaten egg whites keeps this rich cake surprisingly light, and hints of cinnamon and Cognac (yes, this is via Paris) give it a lingering depth. Semolina's high protein level can somewhat justify the equally high sugar content, and a dollop of Greek yogurt laced with honey might fool you into thinking this a healthy dessert.

Years back, I wrote a piece on revani for the *New York Times Magazine*. For far too many delicious weeks, I tested recipe after recipe of siropiasta—syrup-soaked cakes—searching for the best. Once I discovered cookbook writer Diane Kochilas's Revani Verrias, I could no longer justify further recipe testing, as I had hit on my idea of perfection. But that didn't stop me from playing with the syrup, moving from straightforward lemon-sugar, to warming cinnamon-clove, to the floral whisper of orange blossom. But, for sheer elegance and complexity, I always seemed to return to *liqueur d'orange*. My preference is one called La Lieutenance, an infused Cognac made by Maison Prunier. Complex and nuanced, its notes of orange are far less bright and lively than those of Grand Marnier. I reach for it when I want the warmth of the orange's zest rather than the citrusy burst of its fruit. It works beautifully in this cake, but you can't go wrong with a straight Cognac. Consider it a Greek cake with a very French finish.

SYRUP

3 cups water

1½ cups / 300 grams granulated sugar

1 cinnamon stick

2 tablespoons Cognac

CAKE

2 cups coarse semolina (see Note)

1 tablespoon baking powder

1 cup butter, at room temperature

1½ cups / 300 grams granulated sugar

6 large eggs, separated, at room temperature

1 tablespoon Cognac

1 tablespoon orange juice

½ cup / 50 grams almond flour or finely ground blanched almonds

SYRUP

Bring the water and sugar to a boil in a medium saucepan and stir to dissolve the sugar. Add the cinnamon stick and Cognac and simmer over medium heat until reduced by half, about 15 minutes. Set aside to further infuse and cool.

CAKE

Preheat the oven to 350°F and butter a 10-inch springform pan.

To make the cake, in a bowl, sift together the semolina and baking powder.

In a stand mixer or using handheld electric beaters at medium speed, beat the butter until creamy. Gradually add the sugar, then the egg yolks, one at a time, beating well after each addition. Beat in the Cognac and orange juice. With the mixer on low, sprinkle in the semolina mixture and then the almond flour, and continue beating until homogenous. Transfer to a large bowl.

In a clean bowl, beat the egg whites to soft peaks, then fold these into the semolina batter.

Pour the batter into the prepared pan. Bake until golden and a thin, spongy layer has formed on top, about 45 minutes. Set on a cooling rack. Gently score the cake: draw a sharp knife vertically down the length of the pan and then diagonally to form diamonds. Pour the syrup over the cake while still in its pan. After 10 minutes, unmold and serve it warm or at room temperature with a dollop of crème fraîche, or honey-sweetened whole milk Greek yogurt.

Note: *Coarse semolina is available at www.kalustyans.com and www.sahadis.com.*

Gâteau à la Rose et à la Cardamome

—— Rose and Cardamom Cake ——

The Parisian love for rose water and buttery gâteaux is, in this lovely cake, influenced by the highly fragranced cardamom cakes and puddings found in the Middle East. It is a gem, particularly with a scattering of sugar-dusted rose petals. The scent of it baking will fill the house with a seductive, faintly exotic perfume. In the United States, such a recipe might be reserved for wedding showers and Mother's Day, but not so in Paris. Parisian men never seem remotely embarrassed when ordering rose macarons or petit fours. Come to think of it, there's almost no gender distinction at all in what Parisians eat. It's simply not a culture in which the men at the table will order eight-ounce steaks while the women order salad greens with the vinaigrette on the side. Instead, it's a culture of smaller portions, believing that a little of a good thing focuses the senses and that pleasure is found not in quantity, but in quality and delicacy. And the sight of a handsome Frenchman privately taking in the scent of a rose confection is almost as sexy as this cake.

This recipe calls for a heady dose of rose and cardamom, but more or less of either can be added. I add the full amount of each, but I'm crazy for rose and for cardamom. If you're not a fan of rose, add the juice and zest of a lemon, an orange or two limes instead.

CAKE

10½ tablespoons unsalted butter

4 large eggs, at room temperature

1⅓ cups / 265 grams granulated sugar

1½–2 teaspoons freshly ground cardamom seeds from green cardamom pods

2 teaspoons rose water

1⅓ cups / 160 grams cake flour

¼ teaspoon fine sea salt

ICING

½ cup unsalted butter, at room temperature

2 cups / 227 grams confectioners' sugar, sifted

1–3 teaspoons rose water, to taste

Candied, fresh or dried edible rose petals, for garnish

CAKE

Preheat the oven to 350°F. Butter the bottom and sides of a 9-inch springform pan and line with a round of parchment.

Melt the butter in a small saucepan over low heat. Remove from heat before it starts to brown.

Add the eggs and the sugar to the bowl of a stand mixer or to a metal mixing bowl. Using the mixer or a handheld electric beater, cream the eggs and granulated sugar for a good 5–7 minutes, or until they are pale and have tripled in volume.

Add the cardamom and beat to combine. Sprinkle on the rose water and give the mixture a final beating. Gently, but decisively, fold in the flour and salt with a rubber spatula, until just incorporated. Fold in the melted butter.

Pour the batter into the prepared pan and bake for 35–40 minutes, or until a knife inserted in the center comes out dry. Allow the cake to cool for just 5 minutes, then invert it onto a plate and remove the bottom and sides of the pan. Set aside to come to room temperature before icing.

ICING

Cream the butter using electric beaters or in a stand mixer. Keeping the mixer on low, pour in all but 1 teaspoon of the confectioners' sugar. Raise the speed and beat until the mixture is light and fluffy. Sprinkle with the rose water and beat for another minute to incorporate. Taste and add more rose water, if so desired.

Let the cake cool completely before icing the top of the cake. Decoratively scatter the rose petals over the cake and dust with the remaining teaspoon of confectioners' sugar.

Baba au Rhum

————— Rum Baba —————

A few months ago, we moved into the former apartment of an adored elderly couple. Mr. Rosoff had died in his nineties and his wife, Joanna, had decided to move into a smaller apartment. Everyone in the building had doted on them. Joanna's letter to the board on our behalf is one I've tucked away for safekeeping. She had been a student at Radcliffe when her husband entered Harvard Law. They met, fell in love and went on to spend their lives together and raise three children in the apartment. Mrs. Rosoff had been a book editor and knew that John and I were both writers and the children of writers, and she had read somewhere that we, too, had fallen in love when we were at Harvard. I like to think she could imagine us—vague in appearance but not in emotion—at Café Pamplona, where generations of book-loving students met over espresso. And I could imagine a young Mr. Rosoff carrying Joanna's library books as they walked along the Charles River. When we moved into their former home, I started finding things. Little hooks that, on closer inspection, were carved lions' heads. Silk top hats that, I learned from the doorman, they wore in parades. And then one day I opened a bottom cabinet in the kitchen and discovered a whole collection of baking pans and molds, including a savarin mold and a kugelhopf mold. Clearly fate was at play. This recipe is in honor of Joanna Rosoff, who I think must have made an excellent baba au rhum.

It also happens to be the very dessert of many a great chef, including Alain Ducasse, who holds a record number of twenty-one Michelin stars, and of my friend Daniel Rose, who serves perhaps the best baba in Paris at his restaurant La Bourse et la Vie. So good that I will forgo his chocolate mousse in favor of this boozy, yeasty classic.

A baba au rhum and a savarin are nearly identical and made with the same dough. A savarin, however, is imbued with kirsch and studded with candied fruit. A forkful of rum-soaked baba and Chantilly is one of life's great pleasures. The history of this classic dates back to the early 1700s, when exiled Polish king Stanislas Leszczynski complained to his pastry chef, Nicolas Stohrer, that the kugelhopfs—the prized cake of Nancy, where he was living—were too dry. Stohrer responded by brushing his next kugelhopf with a rum soaking syrup, and a classic was born. Stanislas named it baba after his favorite fictional character, Ali Baba, and the name stuck. When Leszczynski's daughter married King Louis XV, she moved to Paris and brought Stohrer with her—smart woman. He went on to open what remains today one of the great pâtisseries of Paris.

Many pastry chefs I know bake their baba a day in advance to let it really dry out. They then make the syrup in a Dutch oven, such as a round Le Creuset or Staub, and simply immerse the baba in the pot of syrup, ten minutes on one side, ten minutes on the other, a little swirl to wet the sides, and repeat until thoroughly moist but still intact.

The bakers at Stohrer use fresh yeast. I've switched to dry yeast, which I then warm in hot milk. I've also switched from a savarin or kugelhopf mold to the more available Bundt. But I do love the simplicity of a savarin mold, its curved, slender sides and its wide well ready to be filled with Chantilly. This recipe is meant for a ten-cup Bundt. Most savarin and kugelhopf molds are half that size—simply halve the recipe if using one. You'll find babas made with Armagnac and Grand Marnier instead of rum, and those avoiding alcohol will create spiced and citrus-based syrups, often scented with vanilla or orange blossom water. In summer, I like to make a zesty version with limoncello. If it's very hot out, I might fold a little cold passion fruit purée and lime zest into a coconut Chantilly and use a white rum. (See pages 222–225 for more syrup suggestions.) Often, you will find mascarpone whipped into the Chantilly, thickening it slightly so that it can be piped through a pastry bag with a decorative tip.

If you don't make an apricot glaze, you may want to reserve a quarter cup of syrup to give the cake a last-minute drink.

Continued

BABA

4½ teaspoons / 14 grams dry yeast

1 cup whole milk

¼ cup / 50 grams granulated sugar

4 large eggs, at room temperature

2 teaspoons vanilla extract or vanilla paste

3⅓ cups / 400 grams all-purpose flour

½ teaspoon fine sea salt

½ cup unsalted butter, at room temperature

RUM SYRUP

2 cups / 400 grams granulated sugar

2½ cups water

1½ cups good dark rum

The zest of 1 organic orange, in strips

GLAZE

1 cup apricot jam

2 tablespoons rum

CHANTILLY

3 cups cold heavy cream

3 tablespoons confectioners' sugar

The seeds of 2 vanilla beans

BABA

Empty the packets of yeast into a stand mixer fitted with the dough attachment or into a mixing bowl.

In a small saucepan, heat the milk to 115°F, then pour it over the yeast and stir. Add the granulated sugar, stir and leave to rest for 10 minutes. Turn the mixer on low and add the eggs, one by one, then the vanilla, flour, salt and butter. Beat at medium-high speed for 6 minutes. The dough should be very elastic. Remove the bowl from the stand (if using) and form the dough into a soft ball. Cover the bowl with a damp towel and leave it to rise for about 90 minutes, or until it has doubled in size.

Generously butter a 10- or 12-cup Bundt pan. Transfer the dough to the Bundt and set aside for 1 hour, or until the dough has risen to the top of the pan.

Preheat the oven to 375°F. Bake the cake for 30 minutes, or until a knife inserted in the center comes out clean. (If you halve the recipe and use a savarin mold, which is quite shallow, it will be done in 20–25 minutes.)

RUM SYRUP

While the baba is baking, prepare the syrup. In a medium saucepan, bring the granulated sugar and water to a simmer and stir until the sugar has dissolved. Off heat, stir in the rum and the zest. Set aside to infuse somewhere warm. Before using, remove the strips of zest and discard.

Transfer the baked baba to a cooling rack. Let it rest for 10 minutes, then slowly pour about a quarter of the rum syrup onto the cake. Let the cake absorb this for 5 minutes, then invert the cake onto the cooling rack. Slide a piece of parchment or foil under the rack to catch excess liquid. Pour all of the remaining rum syrup very slowly and in stages onto the warm cake, allowing it to soak in thoroughly as you go. Trust me—the cake will and should absorb all the liquid, so use every last drop.

GLAZE

To make the glaze, heat the apricot jam with the rum in a microwave or over low heat to liquefy the jam. Press this through a sieve and discard the solids. Brush the cake, once it's at room temperature, with the apricot glaze.

CHANTILLY

Right before serving the baba, whip the cream with the confectioners' sugar and vanilla seeds until it is abundant and billowy. Serve each portion of baba with an excessive dollop of Chantilly.

BABA'S SYRUPS: Needless to say, baba au rhum calls for rum. Lots of it, in fact. And the best rum you can afford to liberally douse on a cake. The Ritz Hotel in Paris makes an absurdly indulgent baba with Zacapa, a rum that's been aged twenty-three years. Ludicrous! A rum that good should be drunk neat, at room temperature, not mixed with sugar and poured on cake. But the quality of the rum you use does matter, as it is the predominant taste in a classic rendition of the great baba.

But let the variations begin . . . In the winter, I add a little Grand Marnier and orange zest or perhaps simmer the syrup with cinnamon sticks, cloves and a star anise for a deeper, warming flavor. In the spring, I might use lemon zest for a bright, sunny taste. Or I might make a tropical syrup. In late summer, I'm likely to move from berries to stone fruit and add the seeds of a vanilla bean. The autumn calls for a Calvados syrup and sauteed apples. One of my favorite renditions calls for no rum but instead uses limoncello. Call this a baba Italienne.

But don't forget about the absolutely essential crème Chantilly. This, too, can be accented with flavor and even booze. The trick is to consider yourself a mixologist and choose complementary flavors that might pair well in a cocktail. The soaking syrup, the crème Chantilly and the accompanying fruit, if serving, should marry to great effect.

ARMAGNAC SYRUP

    2 cups / 400 grams granulated sugar

    2½ cups water

    1½ cups good Armagnac

Serve in winter with prunes soaked in Armagnac and crème fraîche Chantilly.

CALVADOS SYRUP

    2 cups / 240 grams light brown sugar

    2½ cups water

    1½ cups good Calvados or other apple brandy

    1 cinnamon stick

Serve in the autumn with apples sautéed in a little brown butter and light brown sugar.

CARDAMOM RUM SYRUP

This is nuanced with spice and softened with honey. I add a little quince paste to further round out the flavors. It's a beauty of a syrup and can easily be used in a much smaller quantity over any number of autumn or winter cakes. When I think cardamom, rose leaps to mind and so I've added candied petals for decoration. A sprinkling of pistachios, ground to a fine powder, would be striking.

  2 cups water

  1½ cups / 120 grams light brown or raw sugar

  1 cup honey

  2 teaspoons quince paste, optional

  3 cinnamon sticks

  2 cloves

  20 green cardamom pods

  The zest of 1 organic orange, in strips

  The zest of 1 organic lemon, in strips

  1¼ cups good dark rum

  Candied rose petals, for decoration

  ¼ cup whole pistachios, ground to a powder

In a medium nonreactive saucepan, bring the water, sugar, honey, quince paste, spices and zest to a simmer and stir until the sugar has dissolved. Off heat, set aside to infuse for a few hours. Or refrigerate for a day or two in a covered jar. Remove the spices and strips of zest before using. Gently reheat the syrup, remove from heat and stir in the rum. Decorate the baba with the rose petals and pistachio powder.

CITRUS RUM SYRUP

  2 cups / 400 grams granulated sugar

  2½ cups water

  1½ cups good dark rum

  2 tablespoons Grand Marnier

  The zest of 1 organic orange, in strips

  The zest of ½ lemon, in strips

GRAND MARNIER AND RUM SYRUP

2 cups / 400 grams granulated sugar

2½ cups water

1¼ cups good dark rum

¼ cup Grand Marnier

The zest of 1 organic orange, in strips

LIMONCELLO SYRUP

1½ cups / 300 grams granulated sugar

2½ cups water

2 cups limoncello

The zest of 1 organic lemon, in strips

SPICED RUM SYRUP

½ vanilla bean

3 cinnamon sticks

2 cloves

½ star anise

2 cups / 400 grams granulated sugar

2½ cups water

1½ cups good dark rum

Add the vanilla and spices when dissolving the sugar in the simmering water. Set aside to infuse for a few hours. Remove the spices, reheat the syrup, remove from heat and stir in the rum.

TROPICAL SYRUP

2 cups / 400 grams granulated sugar

2½ cups water

1½ cups rum

2 tablespoons Cointreau

The zest (in strips) and juice of 2 organic limes

VANILLA RUM SYRUP

2 cups / 400 grams granulated sugar

2½ cups water

1½ cups good dark rum

2 teaspoons vanilla extract

APOLLONIA'S BRIOCHE AU RHUM

Apollonia Poilâne may run the world's best-known bread bakery, but she is nothing if not frugal. This is not to say she's austere, as she's anything but, nor that she's parsimonious, as she couldn't be more generous—what she has is that very French frugality that's a mixture of practicality and a deep-rooted belief in the value of things. Stale bread becomes breadcrumbs or appears in cake or granola. Stale brioche becomes this riff on a baba au rhum.

What you need to know: Use whole (not sliced!) brioche (or challah) that is stale—at least a few days old. (It must be made by hand or by a bakery. The supermarket variety is too filled with preservatives and therefore too soft and prone to disintegrate.) Pour the rum syrup of choice over the brioche and let it rest, covered, in the fridge for at least 6 hours and up to 24. Every few hours, turn the brioche over so that each side absorbs the soaking syrup. Just before serving, place about a quarter cup of rum in a skillet and use a long-handled match to carefully ignite it. (Apollonia suggests a *rhum agricole*, which is made with cane sugar and not molasses, making it a little less sweet and a little more aromatic.) When the flames have died down, pour the rum over the brioche, and serve with Chantilly.

Charlotte à la Crème de Marron
et à la Mousse au Chocolat

————— Charlotte with Chocolate Mousse and Chestnut Cream —————

A disclaimer. This is not your classic charlotte. It's simply what I like to eat and imagine you might as well. There's nothing more to it than ladyfingers rolled in Armagnac, a sensational chocolate mousse—thank you, Julia Child—and a dreamy, billowy blanket of chestnut Chantilly. A layer of Comice pear slices sautéed in beurre noisette and sandwiched between the chocolate and chestnut would be well worth the fuss, and a decorative round of candied chestnuts would, indeed, be sweet. But I relish the almost Eton Mess–like quality of this normally rather formal dessert and so have done away with the génoise, the buttercreams and fragile leaves of gelatin and ladyfingers that stand up straight with such impeccable posture that they need no securing.

I confess I use store-bought, packaged ladyfingers, and I always buy extra. If they absorb too much liquid, they can disintegrate. And one or two in a pack will inevitably be broken. This recipe is for a small charlotte, but it can easily be doubled or tripled. Have a nice wide ribbon handy. My one nod to formality, here, is a pretty bow, as it will hold your charlotte together. You will also need a charlotte mold or a soufflé bowl with high, straight sides or use the sides of a small springform pan placed on a cake plate. If you have none of these, lay the ladyfingers on their sides and called it a tiramisu. I buy tins of Clément Faugier chestnut purée, or *crème de marrons*. It's sweetened and contains a touch of vanilla. Candied chestnuts add another layer of indulgence and texture. Shavings or shards of dark chocolate look dramatic and taste delicious. Or let the chestnut Chantilly effortlessly entice.

Mousse au Chocolat (page 334)

½ cup Armagnac

24 ladyfingers

1¾ cups heavy cream

½ cup chestnut purée, preferably from Clément Faugier

Candied chestnuts and shards of chocolate, if decorating

Prepare the chocolate mousse and refrigerate it until well-chilled.

If using a charlotte mold or straight-sided bowl, line it with plastic wrap, leaving several inches of overhang. This will allow you to remove the charlotte with ease. If using the sides of a springform pan, simply place it on a serving plate.

Pour the Armagnac into a shallow bowl. Roll a ladyfinger in the Armagnac—do this swiftly, as you don't want to saturate the cookie, just moisten and perfume it—then stand it upright against the side of the mold. Repeat with enough ladyfingers to create a full circle, with each ladyfinger standing right up against her neighbor.

Fill the circle of ladyfingers with chocolate mousse. The mousse should come anywhere between halfway up and all the way up the sides of the cookies. Place a layer of plastic wrap directly onto the mousse while also covering the ladyfingers and refrigerate for at least 2 hours and up to 6.

Close to serving time, whip the cream until stiff peaks have formed (add a spoonful of Armagnac if you have some left over). Stir about a fifth of the whipped cream into the chestnut purée, then fold this mixture back into the remaining whipped cream. Streaks are just fine here, so there's no need to overfold. This can sit in the fridge, well covered in plastic wrap, for 2 hours, while you eat dinner.

To serve, remove the charlotte from the mold and onto a pretty plate. Immediately tie a wide ribbon securely around its circumference. Top the charlotte with clouds of whipped chestnut cream and pass a bowl of whatever remains.

If using candied chestnuts, use only enough whipped cream to come halfway up the sides of the ladyfingers. When adding the cream, level it off evenly, so that it forms a flat surface, bordered by the tops of the ladyfingers. Decorate with a circle of candied chestnuts.

As to slicing this frivolous delight, hats off to whoever does it neatly. My advice is simply to cut between ladyfingers, and always cut when it's cold.

MADELEINES
FINANCIERS
VISITANDINES

La Madeleine Classique

—— *The Classic Madeleine* ——

This is the classic. Quick to prepare, quick to bake—and, yet, exquisite. But the beauty of a madeleine is fleeting. From the minute they are removed from the oven, the clock begins to tick. Eat them within five minutes, and you will fall silent in awe. After fifteen minutes, you might close your eyes in bliss. After thirty minutes, you will find these delicious, but not transcendent. After an hour, they will please, but not delight, unless you dip them in a cup of tea, as Proust was wont to do.

The timing shouldn't dissuade you from making these. Quite the opposite. The batter needs to be refrigerated for at least six hours and preferably overnight. You can do this in a sealed container. Or, better yet, you can spoon the batter into prepared madeleine molds, cover them tightly with plastic wrap and refrigerate until you are ready to pop them into the oven. This is what most of my French friends do, as it makes serving them effortless.

6 tablespoons unsalted butter,
   preferably European

⅔ cup / 80 grams cake flour

¾ teaspoon baking powder

⅛ teaspoon fine sea salt

The grated zest of 1 organic lemon

½ cup / 100 grams granulated sugar

2 large eggs, at room temperature

1 teaspoon vanilla extract or 2 teaspoons
   orange blossom water

Butter 12 metal madeleine molds, dust with flour and turn upside down and tap to get rid of excess flour. If using silicone molds, simply place them on a baking sheet.

Melt the butter in a small saucepan and set aside to come to room temperature.

Whisk together the flour, baking powder and salt in a small bowl.

In the bowl of a stand mixer or in a large mixing bowl, combine the zest and sugar. Using your fingertips, rub them together a bit to release the citrus oil. Add the eggs and beat at medium-low speed until the mixture is pale and homogenous and the sugar has dissolved, about 2 minutes. Add the vanilla and beat for another 30 seconds.

Fold the dry ingredients into the batter with a rubber spatula in quick and decisive, but gentle strokes. Fold in the melted butter.

Fill the prepared madeleine molds with batter, cover with plastic wrap and refrigerate for 6–24 hours.

Preheat the oven to 385°F. Discard the plastic wrap and bake the madeleines for 11–13 minutes, or until they are golden.

Serve immediately!

Note: *This recipe yields a dozen standard-sized madeleines. If you have a mini madeleine mold rather than a standard or large-sized one, simply reduce the baking time to about 8–10 minutes. This recipe will yield 36 mini madeleines.*

Madeleines au Miel

—— Honey Madeleines ——

Orange, honey and rum. It could be a hot drink on a cold winter's night. This recipe is close to what is sold in most pâtisseries, as the honey extends the madeleine's fleeting moment of perfection by perhaps an hour or two. But I still recommend baking these to order, as part of the magic of a madeleine is its tender, fragile warmth. The tiny bit of rum hovers in the background, a faint haunting. The orange teases. It's a beautiful balance.

Tricks of the trade: Thermal shock makes the famous bump, like a camel's hump, on the back of the madeleine. Cold batter and a hot oven are a must. If using metal molds, chill them first. Make sure the plastic wrap touches the batter rather than loosely covering the dish. And there's no need to overbeat the eggs and sugar. Aerating is not the goal, creating a homogenous mixture is.

- 6 tablespoons unsalted butter
- ¾ cup / 90 grams cake or all-purpose flour
- ½ teaspoon baking powder
- ¼ teaspoon fine sea salt
- The grated zest of 1 orange

- ⅓ cup / 66 grams superfine or granulated sugar
- 2 large eggs, at room temperature
- 2 tablespoons honey, such as orange blossom or wildflower
- 2 teaspoons rum, orange blossom water or orange juice

Melt the butter in a small saucepan and set aside to come to room temperature.

Whisk together the flour, baking powder and salt in a small bowl.

In the bowl of a stand mixer or in a large mixing bowl, combine the minced zest and the superfine sugar. Using your fingertips, rub them together a bit to release the citrus oil. Add the two eggs and beat until the mixture is quite pale and frothy. Add the honey and rum and beat for another minute.

Fold the dry ingredients into the batter with a rubber spatula in quick and decisive but gentle strokes. Pour in the melted butter and stir to combine.

You now have two options. You can refrigerate the batter in a sealed container for at least 6 hours and ideally overnight. Or you can first spoon the batter into prepared madeleine molds, cover them tightly with plastic wrap and refrigerate until ready to pop them into the oven. To prepare, thoroughly butter 12 metal madeleine molds, dust with flour and turn upside down and tap to get rid of excess flour. If using a silicone mold, simply set it on a baking tray.

Preheat the oven to 400°F. Reduce the heat to 375°F just after placing the madeleines in the oven. Bake the madeleines for 11–13 minutes, or until they are golden. Remove from their molds and serve immediately.

Madeleine Variations

———•———

There are times not to tamper with the classics, and then there are times you want that extra kick of zest or a smooth whiff of Armagnac. Maybe it's Key lime season or wild blueberries are at the farmers' market. Madeleines take to all sorts of spices, fruits, liqueurs, diced fruit and finely chopped nuts. When trying any of the following variations, use the classic recipe on page 230 and simply replace the lemon zest and vanilla—or not. Your choice. Just note that you don't want to add more than a tablespoon or two of liquid or weigh down the batter with too many solid additions. I tend to go bold on flavor, which isn't always the most subtle approach. Think about the occasion. For a morning madeleine, I do like a true burst of citrus, whereas a faint hint of lavender makes for a dreamy bedtime treat.

SPICE

Chai: Add 2 teaspoons ground chai spice. These are lovely dipped in chocolate.

Maple: Replace the granulated sugar with maple sugar. Add 1 tablespoon grade B maple syrup and ¼ teaspoon ground ginger.

Pain d'Épices: Add 2 teaspoons pain d'épices spice mix (see page 261).

Ras el Hanout: Add 2 teaspoons ras el hanout, ½ teaspoon cinnamon and 1 teaspoon rose or orange blossom water.

Vanilla: Fold in the scraped seeds of 2 vanilla beans along with 2 teaspoons vanilla paste or vanilla extract. This version is particularly good if you brown the butter—use an extra 2 teaspoons butter, as some of its water evaporates during browning.

CITRUS

Agrumes: Agrumes means citrus and, in desserts, usually implies a mix of several. Fold in the zest of 1 orange, 1 lemon and 1 lime. Squeeze in 2 tablespoons juice from the orange. This has serious pucker to wake you up! I consider it my breakfast madeleine.

Lime: Add the zest and juice of 3 Key limes or 2 regular limes.

Lemon Basil: Fold in the zest of 1 lemon, 2 tablespoons limoncello and ½ cup finely slivered fresh basil leaves.

Lemon Lavender: Fold in the zest of 1 organic lemon and 1 teaspoon finely ground lavender flowers or 2–3 drops lavender extract.

Lemon Rose: Add 1 tablespoon lemon juice and 2 teaspoons rose water to the batter. Once baked, spritz on a third teaspoon of rose water or sprinkle it on. This last step is optional but adds a beautiful aroma.

Lemon Rosemary: Fold in the zest of 2 lemons and 2 tablespoons lemon juice. Add 2 teaspoons minced fresh rosemary leaves. You may also want to add 3 tablespoons pine nuts. Try this with orange or Meyer lemons.

Lemon Thyme: Fold in the zest of 1 lemon, 2 tablespoons limoncello and 1 tablespoon lemon thyme leaves, each little leaf plucked from its neighbors.

Meyer Lemon: Fold in the zest of 3 Meyer lemons and 2 tablespoons of their juice.

Orange Blossom: Fold in 1–1½ tablespoons orange blossom water and the zest of 1 clementine as a last step. To give it extra perfume, sprinkle or spritz a bit more orange blossom water on once baked and right before serving.

Orange, Candied: Fold in the zest of 1 orange and ⅓ cup finely chopped candied orange tossed in 1 teaspoon flour.

Orange Cardamom: Fold in the zest of 1 orange and ½ teaspoon freshly ground cardamom seeds from green cardamom pods.

Orange Clove: Add ¼ teaspoon ground cloves to the melted butter and fold in the zest of 1 orange.

Orange Fennel: Fold in the zest of 1 orange and add 1 teaspoon ground fennel seeds. You might even want to add a light sprinkle of coarse semolina to the top before baking.

Orange Ginger Jasmine: Fold in the zest of ½ orange, 2–3 drops culinary jasmine essential oil, and 3 tablespoons minced crystallized ginger tossed in 1 teaspoon of flour.

Orange Grand Marnier: Fold in the zest of 1 organic orange and 2 tablespoons Grand Marnier as a last step.

Orange Jasmine: Fold in the zest of ½ orange and 2–3 drops culinary jasmine essential oil.

Triple Orange: Fold in the zest of ½ orange, 1 tangerine or mandarin and 1 clementine. These are particularly delicious in the morning.

Yuzu: Add 2 tablespoons concentrated pure yuzu juice and the zest of 1 mandarin.

FRUIT

Apricot Almond: Fold in ¼ cup toasted sliced almonds, 8 fresh apricots that have been diced, and either ¼ teaspoon almond extract or 1 tablespoon amaretto or 1 tablespoon Abricot du Roussillon (apricot liqueur) or 1 tablespoon orange blossom water.

If using dried apricots: Finely dice 8 dried apricots. Warm 3 tablespoons Abricot du Roussillon or black tea to nearly a simmer and pour it over the apricots. Let them plump up for 10 minutes. Add the apricots, the liqueur, if using, and ¼ teaspoon almond extract to the batter as a last step. A sweet wine may be used in place of the Abricot du Roussillon, as can amaretto or orange blossom water.

Armagnac Prune: Warm 3 tablespoons Armagnac to nearly a simmer and pour it over ½ cup diced pitted prunes. Let them plump up for 10 minutes. Fold in the prunes and Armagnac as a last step. If you can find prunes from Agen, even better.

Coconut: Add ½ teaspoon coconut extract, and fold in ⅓ cup shredded sweetened coconut as a last step.

Dried Cherry and Kirsch: Warm 3 tablespoons kirsch to nearly a simmer and pour it over ½ cup dried cherries. Let them plump up for 10 minutes. Fold in the cherries and kirsch as a last step.

Lingonberry: Fold in ½ cup lingonberry preserves and ¼ teaspoon almond extract.

Raspberry: Fold in 20 halved raspberries and 2 tablespoons crème de framboise or Chambord.

Strawberry—Intense: Fold in ¾ cup diced strawberries that have been tossed with 1 tablespoon crème de fraise des bois.

Strawberry Lemon: Fold in ¾ cup diced strawberries that have been tossed with 1 tablespoon limoncello.

Strawberry Rose: Fold in ¾ cup diced strawberries. Sprinkle or spritz the baked madeleines with rose water just before serving them. Alternatively, add ¼ teaspoon rose extract to the batter.

Strawberry-Rose Geranium: Fold in ¾ cup diced strawberries and add a few drops culinary essential oil of rose geranium.

Rhubarb: Fold in ½ cup finely chopped rhubarb that has been baked or stewed and either 1 tablespoon rose syrup or a simple syrup made with hibiscus. Try adding ½ teaspoon freshly ground green cardamom seeds from green cardamom pods if using the rose syrup.

Rum Raisin: Warm 3 tablespoons dark rum to nearly a simmer and pour it over ½ cup raisins. Let them plump up for 10 minutes. Fold in the raisins and their rum as a last step.

Verbena: Fold in the zest and juice of 1 lemon and ¼ cup very finely slivered fresh, tender verbena leaves.

Wild Blueberry: Wild blueberries tend to be smaller and more concentrated in flavor. Fold in the zest of 2 lemons, 1 tablespoon limoncello and ¾ cup wild blueberries. Blueberries are also good in the maple variation; simply omit the lemon and limoncello.

NUT

For walnut, hazelnut, pecan, pine nut or pistachio madeleines, simply add ½ cup finely chopped toasted nuts to the batter. If you have a hazelnut or walnut liqueur, go ahead and add a tablespoon. Nut madeleines are particularly good with chocolate. Try dipping these into melted chocolate, the way you might strawberries.

For almond or hazelnut madeleines, fold in ½ cup chopped toasted nuts or chopped praliné and 1 tablespoon amaretto (for almond) or Frangelico (for hazelnut).

CHOCOLATE

For chocolate madeleines, see page 243. But, if simply adding chocolate, use ½ cup mini chocolate chips or chopped chocolate lightly tossed in 1 teaspoon flour.

Madeleines au Miel Épicé

—— *Chile-Infused Honey Madeleines* ——

Hot chile pepper–infused honey gives these innocuous-looking beauties a fiery kick. This is my own crazy, but truly delicious concoction and, in the spirit of full disclosure, I need to tell you that the only thing that makes these even remotely French is that I've baked them for a Parisian friend, and she loved them. Serve these madeleines before dinner with a good Manchego and a glass of aged reposado tequila, straight up, with a twist of orange. They are also terrific with a glass of Champagne, sparkling Saumur, or Cava. Or drop a sugar cube and a few sprinkles of orange bitters into a chilled flute glass before topping it off with a dry sparkling wine.

When possible, I buy Mike's Hot Honey to make this recipe, to drizzle onto fresh ricotta or yogurt, to whip with butter and serve with cornbread, and for making a hot honey simple syrup for mixing cocktails. But hot honey is easy to make and allows you to adjust the heat, so I've provided a recipe.

Now a quick story. When I dreamed up these madeleines and put them in the oven, I stepped out to the garden and . . . suddenly received a fierce bite on my ankle, and immediately an intense poison shot up my body, from my ankle to—oddly, I'll admit—the back of my ears. I'd never felt such a direct hit of toxicity. I could trace its every movement inside me, like a mapping of my veins. I'd been bitten by one of those killer hornets that has started appearing on our shores. I'd no idea that I was allergic. It was terrifying. I grew very hot and very red. I looked at my timer: two minutes since the madeleines had gone in the oven. I texted John, who was upstairs on a zoom meeting: "I need you to take me to the hospital in nine minutes." Something about the nine minutes must have mitigated any sense of urgency, and so he stayed on Zoom . . . for exactly nine more minutes. When he came downstairs, I was pulling the madeleines out of the oven. I turned around and caught his expression. I'm not sure if it was the deep red hue of my skin or the fact that I was still baking that disturbed him so profoundly. I grabbed the madeleines. He grabbed the car keys. We sped to the ER. An IV of five different antihistamines and two tranquilizers later, I was released. "But they were really good, weren't they?" I murmured, as we drove home after midnight, a prescription for an EpiPen clutched in my hand.

And, yes, the answer was yes. They were really good.

6 tablespoons unsalted butter

¾ cup / 90 grams cake or all-purpose flour

½ teaspoon baking powder

¼ teaspoon fine sea salt

The grated zest of 1 orange

⅓ cup / 66 grams superfine or granulated sugar

2 large eggs, at room temperature

2 tablespoons Chile-Infused Honey (page 242)

2 teaspoons tequila or orange juice

Melt the butter in a small saucepan and set aside to come to room temperature.

Whisk together the flour, baking powder and salt in a small bowl.

In the bowl of a stand mixer or in a large mixing bowl, combine the minced zest and the superfine sugar. Using your fingertips, rub them together a bit to release the citrus oil. Add the eggs and beat until the mixture is quite pale and frothy. With the mixer still running, add the honey and tequila and beat for another minute.

Fold the dry ingredients into the batter with a rubber spatula in quick and decisive but gentle strokes. Pour in the melted butter and stir to combine.

You now have two options. You can refrigerate the batter in a sealed container for at least 6 hours and ideally overnight. Or you can first spoon the batter into prepared madeleine molds, cover them with plastic wrap and refrigerate ready to pop into the oven. To prepare, thoroughly butter 12 metal madeleine molds, dust with flour, turn upside down and tap to get rid of excess flour. If using a silicone mold, simply place it on a baking tray.

Preheat the oven to 400°F. Reduce the heat to 375°F right after placing the madeleines in the oven. Bake for 11–13 minutes, or until they are golden. Remove from their molds and serve immediately or, ideally, within 30 minutes.

Continued

Chile-Infused Honey

6 dried chiles de arbol

1½ cups honey, such as wildflower, orange blossom or clover

¼ teaspoon fine sea salt

Finely chop 5 of the chiles. Combine these with the honey and salt in a saucepan. Cook over low heat for 15 minutes without allowing it to reach a simmer. Remove from heat and set aside to cool for an hour or two.

Place the remaining chile in a pint-sized glass jar. Strain the honey through a fine sieve into the jar. Discard the solids. Stored with its lid on tightly, at room temperature and away from direct sunlight, the honey will last for at least 1 year.

Madeleines au Chocolat

—— *Chocolate Madeleines* ——

These have a way of vanishing like a magic trick. They are irresistible. And they are light, as light as a feather, despite the butter. When you prepare the batter, you'll have a moment of wondering why it is so loose. Trust me and bake them. I have a thing for chocolate and orange, as you may have noticed. But if you prefer a vanilla accent, scrape the seeds of a vanilla bean into the batter or use a half teaspoon of vanilla paste. A quarter teaspoon of chocolate extract, if you have it, gives additional depth. Unlike other madeleine batters, this one does not need to be refrigerated, but it can be kept tightly covered in plastic wrap and chilled for up 24 hours.

12 tablespoons unsalted butter, preferably European

3 large eggs, at room temperature

½ cup / 100 grams granulated sugar

The grated zest of 1 orange, ½ teaspoon vanilla paste or the seeds of 1 vanilla bean

6 tablespoons / 45 grams all-purpose flour

6 tablespoons / 36 grams unsweetened cocoa powder, preferably Valrhona

½ teaspoon baking powder

¼ teaspoon fine sea salt

Confectioners' sugar, for dusting and decorating, optional

Preheat the oven to 375°F. Butter and dust 24 madeleine molds with cocoa powder or set a silicone mold on a baking sheet.

Brown the butter by heating it in a skillet over medium heat until it turns a dark golden. Set aside to cool slightly—it should still be pourable but not hot to the touch.

Combine the eggs, granulated sugar and orange zest in a mixing bowl. Beat with electric handheld beaters or in a stand mixer for 5 minutes, or until the mixture has tripled in volume.

Place a sieve over the mixing bowl and sift in the dry ingredients. With the mixer on its lowest speed, whisk just to integrate. With the mixer still running on low, pour in the melted butter and whisk to integrate. Stop as soon as it is homogenous.

Continued

Fill the molds with the batter and place in the oven. Immediately reduce the heat to 350°F and bake for 12 minutes. A knife inserted in a madeleine should come out slightly moist but not streaked with batter.

After 2 minutes, pop them out of their molds. Serve immediately, as is, or dusted with confectioners' sugar. Eat within the hour! Or later, dunked in coffee.

VARIATIONS

CHERRY: Plump ½ cup dried cherries in 3 tablespoons warm kirsch for 10 minutes. Fold into the batter as a final step. Alternatively, use Luxardo cherries.

CHOCOLATE ALMOND: Add 60 grams melted bittersweet chocolate and ⅓ cup toasted sliced almonds to the batter as a last step. For a more pronounced almond flavor, add ¼ teaspoon almond extract as well. You may also add 1 tablespoon booze to the mix— Cognac, rum and amaretto are all good options.

CHOCOLATE CHIP: Fold in ½ cup mini chocolate chips that have been tossed in 1 teaspoon flour.

CHOCOLATE ORANGE: Fold in the zest of 1 orange and add either 1 tablespoon Grand Marnier or 3 tablespoons minced candied orange zest.

DRIED CHERRY AND CHOCOLATE: Plump ½ cup dried cherries in warm water for 10 minutes. Drain and discard the water. Add the cherries and 100 grams melted bittersweet chocolate to the batter as a last step. You may replace the cherries with dried cranberries.

FIG: Warm 3 tablespoons port to nearly a simmer and pour it over ½ cup diced dried figs. Let plump for 10 minutes. Fold the figs and port into the batter as a final step.

GINGER: Fold in ½ cup minced candied ginger that has been tossed in 1 teaspoon flour. If you have ginger syrup or ginger liqueur, add a tablespoon as well.

HAZELNUT: Fold in ½ cup chopped toasted peeled hazelnuts or chopped hazelnut praliné.

MOCHA: Fold in 1 teaspoon espresso powder or ½ teaspoon coffee extract.

PECAN OR PISTACHIO: Fold in ½ cup chopped pecans or pistachios.

PORT: Fold in 3 tablespoons ruby port.

RASPBERRY: Fold in ½ cup raspberries and 3 tablespoons crème de framboise.

Madeleines au Chocolat Fourrées de Ganache au Chocolat Noir de Jean-Paul Hévin

—————— *Jean-Paul Hévin's Ganache-Filled Chocolate Madeleines* ——————

A cake might be festive, romantic, empathetic and celebratory and, certainly, a cake is never less than an expression of care and thoughtfulness. But a madeleine is more akin to a private kiss, a moment stolen in a hallway or staircase that, romantic or familial, is so full of love that you'll carry it about the rest of your day. At a dinner party, madeleines will create a momentary hush connecting everyone in a moment of intense, shared pleasure.

These are not the faintly fragranced cakes of Proust's Combray. No, these are filled with rich, dark chocolate ganache. Created by Parisian master *chocolatier* Jean-Paul Hévin, the recipe is a brilliant one. A perfect, delicate madeleine, sporting a nice, tall hump, offers a mouthful of molten chocolate at its center. The trick is to freeze little nuggets of ganache and bake the cakes in a very hot oven for a very short time—just enough to melt the chocolate.

An additional piece of equipment is needed here—a silicone mini ice cube tray. These are inexpensive and easily ordered online. The good news is that you can use these to add most anything to small sweet or savory cakes—jam, coulis, chestnut paste, chèvre, feta, pesto. For years, I avoided pastry bags, thinking they added unnecessary fuss and mess and that their special tips were best left to cake decorators. Then I watched my friend Delphine and her daughter Lila pipe batter into two trays of madeleine molds in about fifteen seconds flat, and I realized I had it all backward. A ziplock bag with a corner cut off will work nearly as well as a professional pastry bag.

As with all madeleines, these should be eaten immediately. Make the batter in advance and bake them to order.

BATTER

- 50 grams dark chocolate, preferably Valrhona Caraïbe 66% cacao
- 14 tablespoons unsalted butter
- 5 large eggs, at room temperature
- 1 cup minus 1 tablespoon / 195 grams superfine sugar

- 1⅓ cups / 170 grams cake flour
- 1¾ teaspoon baking powder
- ½ cup / 50 grams unsweetened cocoa powder, preferably Valrhona

FROZEN GANACHE INTERIOR

- ¾ cup plus 1 tablespoon heavy cream

- 150 grams dark chocolate, preferably Valrhona Caraïbe 66% cacao

For the batter, in a double boiler, melt the chocolate and butter together and stir until smooth. Remove from heat and set aside.

In a stand mixer or using handheld electric beaters, whisk the eggs and sugar until homogenous and smooth and pale. Stir about ⅓ cup of this mixture into the chocolate-butter mixture.

Set a sieve over the mixing bowl and sift in the flour, baking powder and cocoa powder. Fold these in with a rubber spatula until no streaks of flour remain. Fold in the chocolate mixture.

Pour the batter into an airtight container and refrigerate for at least 2 hours and up to 48.

FROZEN GANACHE INTERIOR

Bring the cream to a boil and immediately pour over the chocolate. Stir until melted and smooth. Pour this ganache into mini ice cube trays and place in the freezer for at least 1 hour and up to 48. (If freezing them longer than 2 hours, cover the tray with two layers of plastic wrap to prevent freezer burn.)

When ready to bake the madeleines, preheat the oven to 475°F. Butter and dust 30 metal madeleine molds with cocoa. (Or save some of the batter for another time.) If using a silicone mold, simply set it on a baking sheet.

Using a pastry bag, fill each mold about one-quarter full with batter. Place a frozen cube of ganache on top and then cover with batter. The molds can be nearly but not completely full. Bake for 8 minutes. Transfer to a cooling rack. Wait 5 minutes, unmold and serve immediately.

Financiers

These treats were created in the late 1800s by a pâtissier named Lasne as a rich snack for the bankers on their way to and from the Bourse, Paris's former stock exchange. Their shape—a small rectangle—was a nod to the bars of gold that presumably fueled ambition. Today, you'll often see them baked in boat-shaped molds, but why argue with a brick of gold? In a pinch, use a mini muffin pan.

Financiers might taste a little eggy when just out of the oven, but after sitting for an hour, they have the loveliest nutty taste. They're best eaten the day they are baked, but the batter can be chilled for a few days. Sometimes, you'll find a raspberry or two buried inside. Simply press the fresh fruit lightly into the surface before baking. If serving for dessert, I bake them in small silicone *tartelette* molds, covered with almond slices. A dusting of confectioners' sugar and a small spoonful of crème fraîche turn them from snack into dessert. The use of almond extract is not traditional, but it does the trick if you're using store-bought almond flour rather than grinding your own. A small amount is all that's needed, because these are all about the beurre noisette.

12 tablespoons unsalted butter, preferably European

1 cup / 200 grams granulated sugar

1 cup / 100 grams almond flour

6 large egg whites

¾ cup / 90 grams cake flour

¼ teaspoon fine sea salt

¼ teaspoon almond extract

½ teaspoon vanilla extract

Cut the butter into about a dozen pieces and melt it in a skillet over low heat. Once the butter has melted, raise the heat to medium and bring it to a boil. The butter will foam, then start to darken in color. Once it is a deep golden-brown, immediately remove from heat. Set this beurre noisette aside somewhere warm.

Combine the sugar, almond flour and egg whites in a medium heavy-bottomed pot and whisk to thoroughly combine. Place the pot over low heat and cook, stirring, for approximately 2 minutes, or until hot to the touch and the consistency of runny honey.

Off heat, using a rubber spatula, fold in the cake flour and salt. Fold in the browned butter and the almond and vanilla extracts. Fold just until no streaks of flour remain.

Butter and dust 12 metal financier molds with flour or set a silicone mold on a baking sheet. Pour the batter into the prepared molds, cover the entire pan with plastic wrap and refrigerate for 2 hours. Alternatively, once the batter is at room temperature, place in an airtight container and refrigerate for up to 3 days.

Preheat the oven to 400°F. Bake for 12–14 minutes, or until the tops are golden and spring back when touched. A knife inserted in the center should come out clean. Set on a cooling rack for 5 minutes, unmold and serve once they've come to room temperature.

PISTACHIO FINANCIERS: To make pistachio financiers, the French turn to pistachio paste. As that's not widely available in the U.S. and, as each brand has a different consistency, I recommend simply grinding pistachios into a sandy flour and using this in place of the almond flour. Pistachio financiers are particularly good with a bit of raspberry jam hidden in their centers. Omit the almond and vanilla extracts and use the freshest, greenest pistachios you can find.

Financiers aux Noisettes

———— Hazelnut Financiers ————

Hazelnut flour augments the taste of the beurre noisette that distinguishes a financier. Ideally, toast and grind peeled hazelnuts to order, as the taste of nut flours dissipates after sitting on a shelf too long. There, I've told you. Now let me also tell you that I almost never do this. If I want extra hazelnut taste, I add a teaspoon of Frangelico to the batter. (Unnecessary and entirely optional, but delicious.) European butter, well browned, gives these the true richness that belies the ten minutes they take to make. The batter should chill in the fridge for at least an hour and up to three days. Going from cold to hot shocks the batter into rising—you'll see that no leavener is used, although you're welcome to add half a teaspoon with the flour if you appreciate a safety net. The trick of starting with a very hot oven and reducing the temperature midway through baking is one I learned from Patricia Wells, whose book *Bistro Cooking* was seminal to me when I was in my twenties. I must have cooked my way through that classic, start to finish, in what was my first kitchen away from home.

Financier molds run about 2 x 4 inches. Oval barquette or tartlet molds are also options. And, yes, so are small muffin pans.

¾ cup unsalted butter, preferably European

2 teaspoons Frangelico, optional

1¾ cups / 200 grams confectioners' sugar

1 cup / 90 grams hazelnut flour

⅔ cup minus 1 tablespoon / 70 grams cake flour

¼ teaspoon fine sea salt

6 large egg whites

Cut the butter into about a dozen pieces and melt it in a skillet over low heat. Once the butter has melted, raise the heat to medium and bring it to a boil. The butter will foam, then start to darken in color. Once it is a deep golden-brown, immediately remove from heat. Measure out ¾ cup of this beurre noisette to use in this recipe. Any remainder can be stored in the fridge. Stir in the Frangelico, if using.

Combine the sugar and hazelnut flour in a mixing bowl and whisk to combine. Set a sieve over the bowl and sift in the cake flour and salt. Add the egg whites and stir well to combine. Thoroughly stir a spoonful of the batter into the melted butter, then fold the beurre noisette into the batter.

If using a metal mold, butter and dust 20 wells with flour. If using a silicone mold, simply place it on a baking sheet. Pour the batter into the prepared molds, cover with plastic wrap and refrigerate for 2 hours.

Preheat the oven to 450°F. Bake the financiers for 7 minutes. Reduce the heat to 400°F and bake for another 7 minutes. Turn the oven off and let the financiers sit in the cooling oven for a final 7 minutes.

Place the financier molds on a cooling rack. After about 15 minutes, flip to let them pop out. If not eating within a few hours, let them come truly to room temperature, then place them in an airtight container and store. These are best within 36 hours, but good for 48.

Financier au Chocolat

Chocolate Financiers

These financiers are so good and so quick and simple to make they just might be your undoing. So think like a Parisian and make them only moments before friends are arriving for an afternoon coffee or pop them into the oven when you sit down to lunch or dinner *en famille* or with good friends. They will disappear. Having already taken an urban revisionist hand to the venerable brown-butter classic, consider spicing or spiking these.

1¼ cups / 125 grams almond flour

¼ cup /30 grams unsweetened cocoa powder

1¼ cups / 145 grams confectioners' sugar

5 tablespoons / 40 grams cake flour

¼ teaspoon baking powder

4 large egg whites

9 tablespoons unsalted butter, melted and cooled to room temperature

Preheat the oven to 375°F. If using a metal mold, butter and dust 12 wells with cocoa powder. If using silicone, simply place it on a baking sheet.

In a large mixing bowl, whisk together the dry ingredients.

In a small bowl, whisk the egg whites with a fork until loosened, combined and only just starting to froth.

In two steps, whisk the egg whites into the dry ingredients. Then whisk in the melted butter. Continue to whisk until the batter is completely smooth.

If possible, refrigerate the batter for 1 hour and up to 2 days. In a rush? Simply let the batter rest for 15 minutes at room temperature before baking the financiers.

Pour the batter into the prepared molds and bake for 10–12 minutes. If the batter has been refrigerated, the financiers may need a minute or two more. When a knife inserted in the center comes out clean, they are ready. Unmold and serve the day they are baked or store in an airtight container overnight.

VARIATIONS

CHOCOLATE ALMOND: Add ¼ teaspoon almond extract with the melted butter and fold in ¼ cup toasted almond slices as a last step. Or lightly press untoasted almond slices into the surface of the financiers before baking them.

CHOCOLATE CARDAMON: Add ½ teaspoon ground cardamom seeds from green cardamom pods.

CHOCOLATE CHERRY: Add 1 teaspoon kirsch to the melted butter and nestle a Luxardo maraschino cherry or two into the top of each financier before baking.

CHOCOLATE GINGER: Add 2 tablespoons minced crystallized ginger to the batter after the melted butter.

CHOCOLATE ORANGE: Add the zest of 1 orange to the warm melted butter. This is delicious.

CHOCOLATE PEAR: Add 2 teaspoons Poire Williams to the melted butter. The flavor with chocolate is exceptional.

CHOCOLATE PISTACHIO: Replace the almond flour with finely ground pistachios. This is excellent with either cherries or cardamom or both. Press a few chopped pistachios into the top of each financier before baking.

CHOCOLATE RASPBERRY: Add 1 teaspoon crème de framboise to the melted butter and nestle a raspberry or two into the top of each financier before baking.

GIANDUJA: Replace the almond flour with hazelnut flour and decrease the butter by 1 teaspoon, as hazelnuts have a higher oil content.

MEXICAN CHOCOLATE: Add 1 teaspoon cinnamon and ¼ teaspoon dried chipotle pepper to the dry ingredients.

MOCHA: Add 1 teaspoon instant espresso or ¼ teaspoon coffee extract to the dry ingredients.

VANILLA AND CHOCOLATE: Scrape the seeds of a vanilla bean into the warm melted butter.

Gâteau Financier aux Framboises

—— *Raspberry Financier Cake* ——

This cake is absurdly easy and fabulously tasty. It's nothing more than a financier made in a cake pan, but the switch turns a delicious snack *à goûter* into dessert. This is the cake for supper *en famille* or for a small dinner party. The raspberries can be replaced with most any fruit. Blackberries, sliced pear, sliced apricots—any fruit that isn't too watery will work beautifully, as will no fruit at all. Notice the unusual baking temperature. It's hot enough to make the batter stand tall and low enough to keep the cake moist. I keep a photo of this recipe on my phone for last-minute plans and for those days when suddenly there's only ten minutes to make dessert before the doorbell rings. If your almond flour has been sitting in the cupboard and has lost its almondyness, add a quarter teaspoon of almond extract when adding the vanilla.

½ cup unsalted butter	¼ teaspoon fine sea salt
½ cup / 60 grams all-purpose flour	4 large egg whites
⅞ cup / 90 grams almond flour	½ teaspoon vanilla extract
1½ cups / 170 grams confectioners' sugar	1 cup / 125 grams fresh raspberries

Preheat the oven to 365°F. Butter and flour an 8-inch cake pan.

Cut the butter into about a dozen pieces and melt it in a skillet and over low heat. Once the butter has melted, raise the heat to medium and bring the butter to a boil. It will foam, then start to darken in color. Once it is a deep golden brown, immediately remove from heat and set aside somewhere warm.

In a mixing bowl, whisk the all-purpose flour, almond flour, sugar and salt to combine.

In another mixing bowl, whisk the egg whites and vanilla until frothy.

Using a rubber spatula, fold the egg whites into the dry ingredients. Then fold in the melted butter. Pour the batter into the prepared cake pan. Scatter with the raspberries. Bake for 40 minutes, or until a knife inserted in the center comes out clean.

Visitandines

Little Almond Cakes

This recipe, more or less, dates back to the seventeenth century, when the Catholic Order of the Visitandines in the Haute-Savoie region of western France started making these moist little cakes with nothing more than almonds, sugar, butter, flour and eggs. Today, they tend to be made with an added note of flavor—a bit of zest, a drop of almond or vanilla extract, a spoonful of rum or kirsch—but they really are kind of perfect without any additions. I make these in mini muffin pans. No doubt the nuns used less frivolous bakeware. But I can't say I was surprised to read that the Order of the Visitation of Holy Mary welcomed those not keen on practicing the austerity required in other orders, such as the dreaded and required fast. The Order also sensibly moved the daily chanting of the canonical office from the cold, dark hours of the night to a more reasonable eight-thirty in the evening. I like to think this ritual was followed by a nighttime cake, perhaps with a bit of sweet, if not necessarily holy, wine. And, on that note, may I recommend sprinkling the hot cakes with a little more of the kirsch or rum?

½ cup plus 2 tablespoons / 125 grams granulated sugar

1¼ cups / 125 grams almond flour

¼ teaspoon fine sea salt

5 tablespoons / 40 grams all-purpose flour

4 large egg whites

14 tablespoons unsalted butter, melted and slightly cooled

1 tablespoon kirsch or dark rum or 1 teaspoon vanilla extract

¼ teaspoon almond extract

Butter a 24-well metal mini muffin pan and dust with flour. A metal pan will produce the most golden exterior, but silicone is fine. If using a silicone mold, simply set it on a baking sheet.

Stir the sugar, almond flour and salt together in a mixing bowl. Set a sieve over the bowl and sift in the all-purpose flour. Whisk to integrate. Lightly whisk 3 of the egg whites to loosen them, then fold them in. Fold in the melted butter, kirsch and almond extract until fully incorporated.

Beat the fourth egg white until it forms soft peaks. Gently fold into the batter.

Fill the molds three-fourths full, cover with plastic wrap and refrigerate for at least 1 hour and preferably overnight.

Preheat the oven to 425°F.

Bake the visitandines for 12–15 minutes, or until golden and a knife inserted in the center comes out clean. While still warm, overturn the pan and let the cakes fall out. These are irresistible straight from the oven, but try to let them rest 15 minutes to allow the flavors to bloom. These cakes keep well and will stay moist in an airtight container overnight.

Note: *If room is tight in your fridge, as it is in mine, simply chill the batter in the mixing bowl and transfer to the pan just before baking. If your pan isn't chilled, the cooking time may be a minute shorter.*

HOLIDAY
CAKES

Les Gâteaux de Fête

Pain d'Épices Moelleux

—— *Spice Cake* ——

This is not your traditional *pain d'épices*, which is made with rye flour and no butter and is significantly stiffer and drier. That version lasts a week, getting better by the day, and is delicious toasted and smeared with butter, but, in my opinion, not very good untoasted. This version is a tender loaf cake, also made with honey and spices, but moist and baked for more or less immediate consumption. This will perfume your house with spice. It's less of a dessert and more of a tea cake. Ideally, serve it with black tea. The first day, it is delicate of crumb and lovely. The second day, the top has a slightly sticky chewiness that is equally hard to resist. Giving a pain d'épices to friends around the holidays is a time-honored custom. This recipe is easily doubled, but best not to make a larger loaf, as that will alter the cooking time and texture. Instead, make two medium loaves. If you are a fan of chai, you can also make this using ground chai spices.

⅓ cup whole milk

½ cup wildflower or orange blossom
   honey

5 tablespoons unsalted butter,
   preferably European

1 large egg yolk

½ cup / 60 grams light brown sugar

The grated zest of 1 organic orange

1⅓ cups / 160 grams cake flour

1½ tablespoons Mes Épices (recipe
   follows)

1 teaspoon baking soda

⅛ teaspoon fine sea salt

Preheat the oven to 315°F. Generously butter an 8½ x 4½-inch loaf pan or line it with parchment paper.

In a medium saucepan, heat the milk and honey over low heat, stirring, until warm to the touch and well combined. Set aside.

In a small saucepan or microwave, melt the butter and set aside.

In a stand mixer or using handheld electric beaters, beat the egg yolk with the brown sugar until smooth. Add the orange zest. With the mixer running, pour in the warm milk and honey and beat until well combined.

Place a sieve over the bowl and sift in the flour, spice mix, baking soda and salt. Fold in these dry ingredients with a rubber spatula. Add the melted butter and fold that in.

Pour the batter into the prepared pan and bake for 50–60 minutes, or until a knife inserted in the center comes out clean. Allow to come to room temperature on a cooling rack, as any cake containing baking soda needs an hour to settle and rid itself of the any lingering baking soda taste.

Mes Épices

This is the mix of spices I use when making pain d'épices. I happen to like a little less star anise than is customary and so break one in half, and I like a little more cinnamon and ginger. I also add a touch of mace. It's a gentler mix than the British use in gingerbread and a less sweet mix than American pie mix. It's easily procured in France, particularly around the holidays, but a word of warning: it's not the same as the five-spice Asian mix available in U.S. supermarkets. This recipe yields enough for 2 loaves.

4 teaspoons ground cinnamon	3 cloves
1½ teaspoons ground ginger	Half a star anise
¼ teaspoon ground coriander	Half a small nutmeg, grated
⅛ teaspoon ground mace	3 green cardamom pods

Combine all of the ingredients in a spice grinder, clean coffee grinder or high-powered blender, such as a Vitamix, and grind to a fine powder.

Mocha Bûche de Noël

— *Mocha Yule Log* —

When I was a little girl, this yule log was always my favorite. Now the coffee, no longer illicit, isn't quite so exotic, but this bûche remains my preferred way to end Christmas dinner. A dedicated espresso drinker, I brush a little extra onto the génoise before blanketing it with buttercream. A dusting of confectioners' sugar and cocoa tends to be my only decoration, with perhaps some chocolate-covered espresso beans scattered about. The 364 days a year that are not Christmas, you could make it as a simple rouleau and add a bit of cinnamon or cardamom or rum, maybe a thin drizzle of ganache. As well you should! I make it only on Christmas, as I relish the intensity of experience that comes with ritual and with tasting something I love merely once a year.

The recipe may look elaborate but, broken down, it's quite simple. All you are really doing is making a génoise in a sheet pan, rolling it up so it stays malleable, brushing it with coffee, slathering it with buttercream, rolling it back up, running the tines of a fork over the buttercream, dusting it with sugar and cocoa, et voilà! You will need a candy thermometer and two 10 x 15-inch rimmed baking sheets.

ALMOND GÉNOISE

4 large eggs, at room temperature

⅔ cup / 132 grams granulated sugar

1 teaspoon almond extract

¼ teaspoon fine sea salt

1 cup / 120 grams cake flour

Confectioners' sugar, as needed

MOCHA BUTTERCREAM

4 large egg whites, at room temperature

85 grams dark chocolate, preferably around 70% cacao

¾ cup / 150 grams granulated sugar

⅔ cup water

½ teaspoon instant espresso powder

½ teaspoon vanilla extract

¾ cup unsalted butter, at room temperature

TO ROLL AND SOAK

Confectioners' sugar, as needed

2 tablespoons espresso or 1 tablespoon espresso mixed with 1 tablespoon of dark rum

DECORATION

1 tablespoon unsweetened cocoa powder

2 tablespoons confectioners' sugar

Chocolate-covered espresso beans, for fun, optional

ALMOND GÉNOISE

Preheat the oven to 400°F. Butter the sides of a 10 x 15-inch rimmed baking sheet or jelly roll pan and line it with parchment paper.

In a stand mixer or using handheld electric beaters, whisk the eggs until thick and foamy, about 5 minutes at medium speed. Add the granulated sugar, almond extract and salt and, increasing the speed to high, beat for 2 minutes.

Place a sieve over the mixing bowl and sift in the cake flour, about a third at a time, folding it in with a rubber spatula until no streaks of flour remain. Pour the batter into the prepared pan and, with a light touch, spread it into an even layer. Bake for 12–14 minutes, or until the center springs back when gently pressed and the edges have just started to pull away from the pan.

Let the cake cool for about 5 minutes. Dust the entire surface with a little confectioners' sugar. This will help to prevent sticking. Cover the cake with a clean tea towel and the back of a second jelly roll pan and invert the cake onto the back of the second pan. Peel off the parchment and dust this side with confectioners' sugar as well. Turn the cake so that you are facing its length, not its width. Use the tea towel to roll the cake. The towel both helps the rolling and mimics the eventual filling. Set the cake aside to cool to room temperature, while rolled and wrapped in the towel, seam side down.

MOCHA BUTTERCREAM

In a stand mixer or using handheld electric beaters, beat the egg whites until they form soft peaks. Set aside. Melt the chocolate in a microwave or in a double boiler and set aside.

In a small saucepan, bring the sugar and water to a boil and cook to 240°F on a candy thermometer, or the soft-ball stage.

Restart the mixer, beating the egg whites on high speed. With the mixer running, pour the hot sugar syrup down the side of the bowl and into the eggs in a slow but steady stream.

Pour the melted chocolate, espresso powder and vanilla into the egg whites and continue beating until the meringue has fully cooled to room temperature, about 5 minutes.

Keeping the mixer on high, add the butter to the meringue, a tablespoon or two at a time, and continue to beat until integrated. *Note: If the buttercream becomes runny during this process, refrigerate it until it is cool to the touch. Then continue the process of beating the butter into the meringue.*

ASSEMBLY

Unroll the cake and brush it with the espresso. Allow the liquid to be absorbed, then spread the cake with about half of the buttercream, smoothing it into an even layer and leaving an inch at the bottom seam unfrosted.

Gently roll the cake back into a log. If you'd like, cut a thin piece off each end on the bias. This makes it a bit neater. Ice the log with the remaining buttercream. Drag a dinner fork down the length of the log so that the tines create the impression of a tree bark. Repeat until the entire log is etched this way.

Chill the cake before serving to allow the buttercream to set. It can be made up to 1 day in advance and kept covered with a tent of aluminum foil. Right before serving, combine the cocoa powder and confectioners' sugar and lightly dust this over the cake to give the impression of snow that's fallen on a tree trunk. Scatter about some chocolate-covered espresso beans, if you have them.

Bûche de Noël au Chocolat

———— *Chocolate Yule Log* ————

Chocolate on chocolate never fails. Add a little rum and espresso, and you're off to the races. A dusting of confectioners' sugar will turn it into a snowy winterscape, while a line of chocolate-covered espresso beans down the center will give it grown-up elegance.

CHOCOLATE GÉNOISE

5 tablespoons unsalted butter

6 large eggs, at room temperature

¾ cup / 150 grams granulated sugar

1 teaspoon vanilla extract or 2 teaspoons rum

⅔ cup / 80 grams cake flour

⅓ cup / 30 grams unsweetened cocoa powder

⅛ teaspoon baking soda

Cocoa powder or confectioners' sugar, for dusting

Heat the oven to 350°F. Butter a 10½ x 15½-inch jellyroll pan or a 10 x 15-inch rimmed baking sheet. Line with parchment. Butter the sides.

In a small saucepan over low heat, melt the butter. Set aside in a warm place.

Bring the water for a bain-marie to a simmer. Reduce the heat and maintain the water just below a simmer.

Combine the eggs and sugar in the bowl of your stand mixer. Place this over the bain-marie and vigorously whisk for 3 minutes to warm the mixture and dissolve the sugar. Remove from heat and immediately lock the bowl into place in the stand mixer and set the speed to high. It will take about 8 minutes for the eggs to triple in size and become quite pale. Reduce the speed to medium, add the vanilla and beat for 2–3 minutes more, or until fabulously voluminous.

Set a sieve over the mixing bowl and sift the flour, cocoa and baking soda directly onto the batter. Stop three times and, using a rubber spatula, fold the dry ingredients in with a light but determined touch. No streaks of flour should remain.

Continued

Stir about ⅓ cup of the batter into the melted butter. Fold this mixture back into the batter.

Spread the batter evenly in the prepared pan and bake until the cake springs back when touched in the center, 15–20 minutes. Don't overbake or the cake will crack. Transfer to a cooling rack and let sit until cool enough to handle, 2–3 minutes, before inverting it onto a second rack. Peel off the parchment.

Dust the surface with cocoa powder and run a knife around the edges of the pan. Invert onto a clean tea towel and dust with more cocoa. Starting with one of the short sides facing you, roll up the cake along with the towel inside. Set aside to cool to room temperature, rolled up in the towel, until ready to assemble.

SOAKING SYRUP

½ cup plus 1 tablespoon / 113 grams granulated sugar

5 tablespoons espresso

4 teaspoons rum, Cognac or coffee liqueur

Melt the sugar in the espresso over low heat. Let it come to a simmer and cook for a minute to thicken it slightly. Remove from heat and stir in the rum.

DARK CHOCOLATE BUTTERCREAM

115 grams dark chocolate, preferably Valrhona Guanaja 70% cacao

1 cup / 200 grams superfine sugar

3 large egg whites, at room temperature

¼ teaspoon fine sea salt

¼ teaspoon coffee extract

18 tablespoons unsalted butter, at room temperature

Melt the chocolate in a microwave or double boiler and set aside somewhere warm.

Heat the sugar and egg whites in a double boiler, whisking occasionally, until the sugar has dissolved. Transfer to a stand mixer or mixing bowl and beat at medium-high speed until it is glossy and holds its shape. With the mixer running, add the salt, extract and then the butter, tablespoon by tablespoon, waiting until each piece is fully incorporated before adding the next one. If it starts to separate, set in the fridge for a few minutes to chill before continuing.

With the mixer still running, add the melted chocolate and whisk until no streaks remain. If not using right away, cover and refrigerate. It may then need a few minutes at room temperature to make it spreadable.

ASSEMBLY

Unroll the cake and brush with the soaking syrup. Allow to absorb for a few minutes, then spread with about half of the buttercream, smoothing it into an even layer and leaving bare about an inch at the bottom seam.

Gently roll the cake back into a log. If you'd like, cut a thin piece off each end on the bias. This makes it a bit neater. Ice the log with the remaining buttercream. Drag a dinner fork down the length of the log so that the tines create the impression of a tree bark. Repeat until the entire log is etched this way.

Chill the cake before serving to allow the buttercream to set. It can be made up to 1 day in advance and kept covered with a tent of aluminum foil. Give it a last-minute dusting of confectioners' sugar to create the effect of just-fallen snow.

Note: This buttercream recipe may also be used in layer cakes and to fill and frost dacquoises. This quantity will frost a 9-inch layer cake. If you are making a dacquoise or gâteau Concorde, double the quantities, as you will be icing three layers. Please note that using a chocolate that is significantly lower or higher in its cacao will affect the texture. Stick to a chocolate that is between 65% and 72% cacao.

Bûche de Noël au Bourbon

— *Bourbon Yule Log* —

I've had the good luck to have had a fabulous intern who has become a dear friend. This book coincided with the birth of Chrissy's second baby and the pandemic, and so, naturally, I didn't expect to hear more than a peep from her. And then one morning, I opened my inbox to find this amazing recipe. It's a happy threesome of American bourbon, French génoise and Italian mascarpone, all rolled into one. To serve it as bûche de Noël for Christmas, ice it with ganache, then run the tines of a fork along the ganache to make it look like the bark of a tree. To serve it year-round as a rouleau au bourbon, skip the ganache and simply dust it with confectioners' sugar.

PECAN GÉNOISE

¼ cup unsalted butter

½ cup / 60 grams pecans, toasted and
  cooled

1 tablespoon potato starch

⅔ cup / 75 grams cake flour

1 teaspoon baking soda

5 large eggs, at room temperature

⅔ cup / 125 grams granulated sugar

Confectioners' sugar, for dusting

BOURBON SOAKING SYRUP

3 tablespoons / 38 grams granulated
  sugar

⅓ cup water

2 tablespoons bourbon

MASCARPONE CREAM FILLING

1 cup heavy cream

2 teaspoons vanilla extract

1 tablespoon confectioners' sugar

3 tablespoons mascarpone

PECAN GÉNOISE

Preheat the oven to 325°F. Line a 13 x 17-inch sheet pan with parchment paper and butter the sides.

Make a beurre noisette by melting the butter in a small skillet over medium heat. When melted, raise the heat and continue to cook, watching carefully, as the solids will go from brown to burned quickly. As soon as it smells nutty and the solids have turned a dark golden brown, pour it into a heatproof measuring cup.

In a food processor, grind the pecans and potato starch until you have a uniform flour. Add the cake flour and baking soda and pulse several times to integrate.

Make a bain-marie. Combine the eggs and granulated sugar in a mixing bowl or the bowl of your stand mixer and set it over the simmering water. Whisk for 2–3 minutes, until the mixture is hot to the touch. Lock the bowl into the stand mixer or use handheld electric beaters and set to high. Whisk for 8 minutes, or until the mixture is thick, pale and leaves a ribbon in its wake.

Using a rubber spatula, gently but decisively fold the dry ingredients into the egg mixture until no streaks of flour remain. Fold in ½ cup of the beurre noisette until thoroughly integrated.

Pour the batter into the prepared pan and bake for 18–20 minutes, or until the center feels set when lightly pressed, and the edges start to shrink away from the sides of the pan.

Dust the surface with confectioners' sugar, then flip the cake onto another piece of parchment. Dust this side with confectioners' sugar. Use the parchment underneath the cake to help you roll the cake into a snug coil and rest seam side down. Set aside to come to room temperature. The cake can also sit like this for a few hours if you wrap it in plastic once it has cooled to room temperature.

BOURBON SOAKING SYRUP

Combine the sugar and water in a small saucepan and bring it to a simmer. Cook, stirring, until the sugar has dissolved. Remove from heat and add the bourbon. Set aside.

MASCARPONE CREAM FILLING

Beat the cream, vanilla and confectioners' sugar in a large mixing bowl or the bowl of a stand mixer until the cream holds stiff peaks. Whisk in the mascarpone until it disappears.

Continued

ASSEMBLY

When the cake has come to room temperature, unroll it and brush its surface with the syrup. Use all the syrup, pausing as you go, to let it soak in.

Spread the mascarpone cream evenly over the cake and carefully roll it back up.

If not serving this within the hour, wrap it in aluminum foil and refrigerate it for up to 3 hours. Let it come back to a cool room temperature before serving it. Dust it with confectioners' sugar last minute, if not icing it with ganache.

Note: *Due to the mascarpone cream, this cake is best eaten within a few hours of being assembled.*

Bûche de Noël à la Noix de Coco
et à la Crème de Yuzu

———— *Coconut Yule Log with Yuzu Buttercream* ————

For a brief spell, serving fresh-squeezed grapefruit juice at the end of dinner parties was all the rage in Paris. Not at the table, but toward the end of the night, long after dessert and espresso and even Cognac. The ritual reminded me of those restaurants that signal the staff is leaving by turning the lights up—not the subtlest approach. But, in truth, the juice was refreshing and seemed to inject a bit of purpose or ambition into whatever decadent languor might have set in. This ambition might merely have been along the lines of walking home rather than calling a taxi or taking the Metro, and, on a clear night, there's no more beautiful city for a midnight stroll. The grapefruit juice trend faded as suddenly as it appeared, because long, decadent, languorous nights should move gently and without interruption into dreams. But ending a rich dinner with a bit of citrus gives a little wake-up shake to the palate. Yuzu is one of the most fragrant members of the citrus family. Like bergamot, it leads with its perfume, rounding its pucker with a floral note. It's vibrant. I love it. And, here, I pair it with a coconut génoise for a rouleau, or a bûche de Noël, that conjures sunshine and the memory of holidays. If serving it at Christmas, a shower of shredded coconut isn't a half-bad stand-in for snow.

The options here are many. Replacing the yuzu curd with lime curd, preferably made with Key limes, is maybe more Florida than Paris, but who's fussing? Chocolate and coconut are, of course, a happy, candied match. Ginger, mango, even roasted banana would be delicious whipped into the buttercream or into a Chantilly. As would be a double dose of coconut—filling, that is, the coconut génoise with whipped coconut cream instead of mascarpone. A rum buttercream would be the adult match.

A small note: *It's nearly impossible to buy fresh yuzu, but if you happen upon it, do add the zest. I've never been able to find one, and I sometimes dream of starting an orchard with bergamots, yuzu and pomelos.*

Continued

YUZU CURD

½ cup / 100 grams granulated sugar

The grated zest of 1 yuzu, optional

⅔ cup pure yuzu juice

7 large egg yolks, at room temperature, lightly broken up with a fork

6 tablespoons unsalted butter

In a small saucepan set over medium heat, whisk the sugar, yuzu zest, if using, yuzu juice and egg yolks. Cook, stirring constantly with a rubber spatula, until the mixture thickens enough to coat the spatula, 4–5 minutes.

Remove from heat and stir in the butter, a pat at a time, until all the butter has melted into the curd and the mixture is homogenous.

Pour the curd through a sieve into a bowl and immediately place a piece of plastic wrap directly on its surface and put it in the fridge to cool completely—an hour should be enough, but it can be refrigerated up to a few days.

BUTTERCREAM

½ cup / 100 grams granulated sugar

½ cup water

3 large egg whites

Pinch of cream of tartar

12 tablespoons unsalted butter, at room temperature

1 teaspoon vanilla extract

In a small saucepan over medium heat, bring the sugar and water to a boil. Keep it boiling until it forms a syrup and reaches 238°F on a candy thermometer. This is called the soft-ball stage.

Meanwhile, place the egg whites in the bowl of a stand mixer or in a mixing bowl using handheld electric beaters and whisk at low speed until foamy. Add the cream of tartar and increase the speed to medium-high. Beat until stiff, but not dry. It is important not to overbeat. Stop when the peaks hold their shape.

With the mixer running, add the sugar syrup to the whites in a slow but steady stream, beating on high speed for 3 minutes. Add the butter, 1 tablespoon at a time, and beat until the mixture is spreadable, 3–5 minutes. Beat in the vanilla. If the buttercream starts to curdle, simply continue to beat it until it is smooth or place it in the freezer for 2 minutes, then proceed to beat it until smooth.

COCONUT GÉNOISE

4 large eggs, at room temperature

⅔ cup / 140 grams granulated sugar

1 teaspoon coconut extract

¼ teaspoon fine sea salt

1 cup plus 2 tablespoons / 140 grams cake flour

Confectioners' sugar, for dusting

Preheat the oven to 400°F. Line a 10 x 15-inch rimmed baking sheet or jelly roll pan with parchment paper and butter its sides.

In a stand mixer or using handheld electric beaters, whisk the eggs until thick and foamy, about 5 minutes. Add the sugar, coconut extract and salt and continue to beat for another 2 minutes. Place a sieve over the bowl and sift the cake flour onto the egg mixture, stopping a few times to fold it in with a rubber spatula. Fold gently but decisively, until no streaks of flour remain.

Pour the batter into the parchment-lined pan and, with a light touch, spread it evenly over the surface without deflating it. Bake for 12–14 minutes, or until the center springs back when gently pressed and the edges have just started to pull away from the pan.

Allow the cake to cool for 5 minutes. Dust the entire surface with a little confectioners' sugar to prevent it from sticking, then cover it with a clean tea towel and invert it. Peel off the parchment and dust this side with confectioners' sugar.

With a short end facing you, roll the cake, leaving the tea towel inside. Let the cake cool completely while rolled and wrapped, seam side down.

ASSEMBLY

Unsweetened dried coconut flakes, toasted (or untoasted, if for a wintery bûche de Noël)

Unroll the cake and remove the tea towel.

Mix ½ cup of the buttercream into the yuzu curd and spread this mixture over the surface of the cake, leaving an inch bare at the short ends. Starting at a short end, roll the cake up and set seam side down on a serving dish. Ice the cake with the remaining buttercream.

Serve at room temperature within several hours, showering it at the last minute with the coconut. If serving the following day, refrigerate it, tented in aluminum foil. Allow it to come to a cool room temperature before serving it.

Bûche de Noël Pistache, Cerises Morello, Ganache

Pistachio Roulade with Morello Cherries and Chocolate Frosting

This is a riff on *La Forêt Noire*—a much-loved cake made with layers of chocolate *joconde* or génoise and filled with cherries and cream—that is not unsimilar to our Black Forest cake. La bûche de Noël Forêt Noire is a popular one, for good reason. I make mine with a pistachio génoise, as I love the combination of pistachios and cherries. To guarantee a decadent amount of chocolate, I use a whipped ganache. And I serve the crème Chantilly on the side, instead of as a filling, so that the cake can be made in advance. The sequence is roughly as follows. Bake a pistachio génoise, brush it with kirsch soaking syrup, slather it with ganache, dot it with kirsch-soaked Morello cherries, roll it, ice it and serve.

I take a delicious shortcut and use Griottines, easily purchased online. These are jarred wild Morello cherries macerating in kirsch and brandy syrup from Distilleries Peureux. A fourteen-ounce jar is just right for this recipe. But I've also included a quick way to make cherries in syrup. The question of whether or not to toast the pistachios is a personal one. I like them raw and bright green, but most people toast them in a 350°F oven for about five minutes.

For a simple version, consider a pistachio génoise, brushed with kirsch, filled with whipped cream to which Morello cherries have been folded in, rolled and dusted with confectioners' sugar. For the chocolate lover, use the Chocolate Génoise (page 185) and shave strips of dark chocolate over the top.

PISTACHIO GÉNOISE

½ cup / 70 grams shelled pistachios

4 large eggs, separated, at room temperature

⅔ cup / 133 grams granulated sugar

2 tablespoons hot water

½ cup / 60 grams cake flour

1 teaspoon baking powder

¼ teaspoon fine sea salt

Confectioners' sugar, for dusting

Preheat the oven to 400°F. Butter a 9 x 13-inch quarter sheet pan and line it with parchment. Place the blade of your food processor in the freezer for 5 minutes.

Place the pistachios in the bowl of a food processor and grind until fine. Stop well before they turn to paste.

In a stand mixer or using handheld electric beaters, whisk the egg yolks and granulated sugar at medium speed for about 5 minutes until thick and creamy. Slowly pour in the hot water, mixing until just combined. Sprinkle the ground pistachios evenly over the top. Using a rubber spatula, gently fold them in.

Place a sieve over the bowl and sift the flour, baking powder and salt directly onto the egg yolk and pistachio mixture. Using the rubber spatula, gently fold in the dry ingredients, until no streaks of flour remain.

In a clean and dry bowl in the stand mixer or using clean handheld electric beaters, beat the egg whites at medium-high speed to a soft peak. Using a rubber spatula, gently fold these into the pistachio mixture, in three batches.

Scrape the batter onto the prepared sheet pan and bake for about 15 minutes, or until the cake springs back when lightly touched in the center. Remove the cake from the oven and let cool for 5 minutes.

Run a knife around the edges to separate the cake from the pan. Sift a tablespoon or so of confectioners' sugar evenly over the surface of the cake, then cover with a clean tea towel and then a cooling rack. Flip the cake out of the pan so the towel is in between the cake and the rack. Peel off the parchment and sift a little more confectioners' sugar evenly over the cake.

With a short end of the génoise facing you, roll up the still-warm cake with the tea towel inside and set it aside to come to room temperature.

Continued

KIRSCH SOAKING SYRUP

¼ cup / 50 grams granulated sugar

½ cup water

3 tablespoons kirsch

Bring the sugar and water to a simmer in a small nonreactive saucepan and stir to dissolve the sugar. Off heat, stir in the kirsch. Set aside to come to room temperature.

CHERRIES IN KIRSCH

1 cup / 200 grams granulated sugar

½ cup water

2 pounds pitted cherries, such as Bing or
    Rainier

1 cup kirsch

2-3 tablespoons lemon juice

In a nonreactive pot, combine the sugar and water and bring to a simmer over low heat. Stir to dissolve the sugar. Cook for 2 minutes to thicken slightly. Add the cherries and cook, tossing them in the liquid, for 5 minutes to soften the fruit. Off heat, pour in the kirsch and lemon juice and toss the cherries. Allow to sit at room temperature for a few hours, occasionally giving the cherries a stir. If using immediately, pluck the cherries you need and set them on a few layers of paper towels. For this recipe, you want the cherries to be plump and boozy but not dripping wet.

Store the rest of the cherries in their syrup in a covered glass jar for up to 5 days. If longer, you will want to sterilize and seal the jar. Go ahead and use thawed frozen cherries if fresh ones are out of season. They won't be as perky and pretty, but they won't be visible either, and they may even taste better. They need only 2–3 minutes over heat and an hour to macerate.

WHIPPED GANACHE

1¾ cups heavy cream

400 grams dark chocolate, preferably
    Valrhona, such as Caraïbe 66% cacao

Bring the cream to a simmer and pour it over the chocolate. Stir until the chocolate has melted and the mixture is smooth. Set aside for 10 minutes, stirring occasionally, then refrigerate for 15 minutes. The ganache should be cold, not rock solid. If it is too cold, simply leave it at room temperature to soften a bit. Transfer the ganache to the bowl of a stand mixer or use handheld electric beaters. With the speed set at low, start to whip the cold ganache. Continue beating, raising the speed incrementally. What you want is a voluminous ganache, akin to whipped cream.

DECORATION

¼ cup unsalted shelled pistachios,
    ground to a fine powder

ASSEMBLY

Brush the surface of the génoise with the soaking syrup. Let it absorb. Repeat. And repeat a third time. Allow it to sit for ten minutes.

Using a small offset spatula, spread a roughly ⅓-inch-thick layer of the whipped ganache evenly over the surface of the cake, leaving an unfrosted border of about ½ inch.

Dot the ganache in a crisscross pattern with the cherries, spacing them about 1½ inches apart, then roll the cake up as you did before, this time without the tea towel inside.

Ice the cake with more of the whipped ganache and run the tines of a fork lengthwise from one end to the other to create the appearance of a tree bark. Do this over the entirety of the log. Traditionally, the log is then cut on the bias at each end, so that the rolls are exposed. (Eat these two small wedges or give to someone you love.) If not eating within a few hours, create a tented dome with aluminum foil over the bûche de Noël and refrigerate it for up to a day.

About half an hour before serving the cake, remove it from the fridge and transfer it to a serving platter. Dust the top of the log with the pistachio powder—it will look like forest moss.

Serve with a big dollops of crème Chantilly.

Bûche de Noël Pistache, Chocolat Blanc et Framboise

Pistachio Roulade with White Chocolate Cream —— *and Raspberries*

This pretty log appears to have been covered in a blanket of snow. A row of raspberries and a dusting of ground pistachios hint at its interior. The snow is a white chocolate ganache made with cream, mascarpone and a touch of lemon extract to cut the sweetness. If you're lucky enough to have a source of fresh red currants, try them in place of the raspberries. If you'd like to accentuate the flavor of the berries, try replacing the kirsch in the soaking syrup with Chambord liqueur. If love is on your mind, try a white chocolate rose ganache. All thoughts of austerity should be banished over the holidays.

PISTACHIO GÉNOISE

½ cup / 70 grams shelled pistachios

4 large eggs, separated, at room temperature

⅔ cup / 130 grams granulated sugar

2 tablespoons hot water

⅔ cup / 70 grams cake flour

1 teaspoon baking powder

¼ teaspoon fine sea salt

Confectioners' sugar, for dusting

Preheat the oven to 400°F. Butter a 9 x 13-inch quarter sheet pan and line with parchment. Place the blade of your food processor in the freezer for 5 minutes.

Place the pistachios in the bowl of a food processor and grind until fine. Stop well before they turn to paste.

In a stand mixer or using handheld electric beaters, whisk the egg yolks and granulated sugar at medium speed for about 5 minutes until thick and creamy. Slowly pour in the hot water, mixing until just combined. Sprinkle the ground pistachios evenly over top. Using a rubber spatula, gently fold them in.

Place a sieve over the bowl and sift the flour, baking powder and salt directly onto the egg yolk and pistachio mixture. Using the rubber spatula, gently fold in the dry ingredients, until no streaks of flour remain.

In a clean and dry bowl in the stand mixer or using clean handheld electric beaters, beat the egg whites at medium speed to a soft peak. Using a rubber spatula, gently fold these into the pistachio mixture, in three batches.

Scrape the batter onto the prepared sheet pan and bake for about 15 minutes, or until the cake springs back when lightly touched in the center. Remove the cake from the oven and set aside for 5 minutes.

Run a knife around the edges to separate the cake from the pan. Sift a tablespoon or so of confectioners' sugar evenly over the surface of the cake, then cover with a clean tea towel and then a cooling rack. Flip the cake out of the pan so the towel is in between the cake and the rack. Peel off the parchment and sift a little more confectioners' sugar evenly over the cake.

With a short end of the génoise facing toward you, roll up the still-warm cake with the tea towel inside and set it aside to come to room temperature.

Continued

KIRSCH SOAKING SYRUP

¼ cup / 50 grams granulated sugar

½ cup water

3 tablespoons kirsch or Chambord

Bring the sugar and water to a simmer in a small, nonreactive saucepan and stir to dissolve the sugar. Off heat, stir in the kirsch. Set aside to come to room temperature.

WHITE CHOCOLATE CREAM

200 grams white chocolate, preferably Valrhona Ivoire or Dulcey

6 tablespoons unsalted butter, at room temperature

1 cup mascarpone

1¼ cups heavy cream

¼ teaspoon lemon extract, the grated zest of 1 lemon or 1 tablespoon limoncello

Place the chocolate in the top of a double boiler set over a pan of simmering water and stir until melted. Remove from heat and set aside to cool slightly.

In a stand mixer or using handheld electric beaters, whisk the butter at a medium-high speed for 30 seconds, until smooth, then add the mascarpone. Beat well to combine, then add the melted chocolate. Continue to beat until smooth, then add the cream and lemon extract. Continue to beat until the mixture starts to billow. If it separates, don't panic. Simply place the bowl back over the double boiler to warm it back up while whisking vigorously for a minute or two. Once it's warm to the touch, remove it from heat and continue to beat it until it is billowy and abundant.

ASSEMBLY AND DECORATION

2 cups raspberries

2 tablespoons unsalted shelled pistachios, ground to a fine powder, for dusting

When ready to assemble, unroll and remove the towel. Brush the surface of the génoise with the soaking syrup. Let it absorb. Repeat. And repeat a third time. Allow it to sit for 10 minutes.

Using a small offset spatula, spread a layer, roughly ⅓-inch thick, of the whipped white chocolate ganache evenly over the surface of the cake, leaving an unfrosted border of about ½ inch.

Dot the ganache in a crisscross pattern with all but 12 of the raspberries, then roll the cake up as you did before, this time without the tea towel inside.

Use a small spatula or piping bag with a decorative attachment to frost the cake with the remaining white chocolate cream. Arrange the dozen remaining raspberries in a row down the center of the cake.

If not serving within a few hours, cover the bûche with a tented dome of aluminum foil and refrigerate for up to 8 hours. About half an hour before serving the cake, remove it from the fridge and transfer it to a serving platter. Dust with the pistachio powder.

VARIATIONS

STRAWBERRY ROSE: In late spring, you could easily turn this into a strawberry rouleau with a white chocolate and rose ganache and candied rose petals on top. Simply cut the strawberries into thin, flat slices and place them as you would the raspberries.

LAVENDER BLACKBERRY: In summer, consider replacing the lemon extract with ½ teaspoon lavender extract and the raspberries with blackberries that have been tossed in a bit of granulated sugar and lemon zest.

Galette des Rois

—— *Kings of the Epiphany Galette* ——

This is not a cake and therefore does not technically belong in this book. But if you make it and—especially—eat it, I believe you will understand why I've included it here. A galette des rois is composed of two layers of puff pastry that sandwich a rich filling of tender frangipane. It is served at the Feast of the Epiphany on January sixth. Did I mention that Parisians adhere, be they religious or not, with religious fervor to rituals? Well, they do. This galette is named after the three kings—*les rois*—who came to visit the newborn Jesus. And that's pretty much where religion stops and custard sets in. Traditionally, a *fève* is added to the batter. This might be a trinket or it might be a dried bean. If your slice contains the fève, you are crowned king or queen for the day and given a gold crown to wear.

I still remember the first and only time my slice held the magic fève. I must have been quite little, but I didn't think of myself, at the time, as being even remotely little. It's that funny, persistent discrepancy between reality and experience that can make it so hard to accurately place a memory. But the intensity of my desire for the fève speaks to my tender age, as does my belief in the magic of it all. Now I understand that our lovely hostess picked me because I was the youngest and a guest. She must have made a hidden mark on the galette for just such a purpose. A mother now, I fervently believe in these little cheats. What is cake's greatest purpose, after all, if not creating moments of intense pleasure that then sweeten our memories?

Trinket aside, this very traditional cake, which is not really a cake but a galette, is sublime. It is French baking at its rich, buttery, layered best. Which is no doubt why pâtisseries in Paris extend the galette de rois season beyond the Day of the Epiphany, otherwise known as Twelfth Night. It can be found in shops the entire month of January. If, however, you crave—and you will—this beauty of a dessert the remaining eleven months of the year, you'd better learn to make your own. This is when Parisians turn to store-bought puff pastry, a shortcut I lazily endorse if you can find a good one, such as that made by Dufour.

The frangipane interior of the galette is what makes it worthy of its noble name. It is sometimes flavored. Chocolate being, of course, the most popular variation. I like to add bits of candied orange or chopped pistachios or even chocolate chips. But before you stray, try this pure, classic version. Few tastes and textures are quite as satisfying.

Continued

2 large or extra-large eggs, at room
   temperature

1 teaspoon milk

6 tablespoons unsalted butter,
   preferably European, at room
   temperature

¾ cup / 85 grams confectioners' sugar

¾ cup plus 1 tablespoon /85 grams
   almond flour

¼ teaspoon fine sea salt

4 teaspoons dark rum

½ teaspoon vanilla extract

¼ teaspoon almond extract

Two 9-inch circles of puff pastry dough,
   preferably homemade or from a
   14-ounce box of Dufour

Separate one of the eggs. Place the yolk in a small bowl, add the milk and break the yolk apart with a fork. Cover and refrigerate. Mix the whole egg and remaining egg white and set aside.

In a stand mixer or using handheld electric beaters set at medium-high speed, beat the butter and sugar together until pale. Add the almond flour and salt and continue to beat until thoroughly incorporated. Add the reserved whole egg and egg white and beat to combine. Add the rum and the vanilla and almond extracts and beat to incorporate. Cover the filling and refrigerate for at least 1 hour and up to 24.

If you've refrigerated the filling for more than a couple of hours, remove it and let it soften for 15 minutes, then beat with electric handheld beaters for 1 full minute before proceeding. If you refrigerated it for an hour, proceed directly.

Line a baking sheet with parchment paper. Set one of the puff pastry circles on the parchment. Spread with the filling, leaving a 1-inch border bare. Even out the filling so it is of a uniform thickness. If using a fève, place it in the filling, not too close to the center. (I usually make a small mark on the parchment so that I know where the trinket is.) Dip your fingers in cold water and lightly moisten the border of the dough. Place the second round of dough over the first and lightly press the border to seal. You do want to make sure the border is well sealed. Refrigerate for 30 minutes.

Preheat the oven to 425°F. Lightly brush the surface of the galette with the yolk-milk wash, avoiding the border. With the tip of a sharp knife, pierce the surface to create small steam vents. Six should be plenty, if well spaced.

Place the galette in the oven and immediately reduce the temperature to 400°F. Bake for approximately 30–35 minutes. If it starts to brown, tent it with foil. The galette is done when it is a deep golden color and nicely puffed up in the center. Slide it onto a cooling rack. If the location of the fève is important to you, keep a note of where it is. Say, by keeping it at 2 o'clock or giving it a tiny mark. Allow the galette to come to room temperature before serving. It is best served the day it is made. It will deflate, but its character will not be diminished.

Galette des Rois au Chocolat

———— Chocolate Frangipane Epiphany Galette ————

This is a chocolate frangipane version of the classic. I often add a little chopped-up candied orange or a handful of sliced almonds, but neither is needed. Simply use good chocolate and fresh almond flour. I've also made this with ground pistachios in place of the almond flour, but do beware of tampering with this beloved classic if serving to anyone French. The rules of a galette are rightly taken seriously and held dear.

150 grams chocolate, preferably Valrhona Caraïbe 66% cacao

⅓ cup unsalted butter, at room temperature

¾ cup / 150 grams granulated sugar

2 large or extra-large eggs

1½ cups / 150 grams almond flour

¼ teaspoon fine sea salt

1 tablespoon dark rum or amaretto

¼ cup chopped candied orange, optional

Two 9-inch circles of puff pastry dough, preferably homemade or from a 14-ounce box of Dufour

1 teaspoon whole milk, for the egg wash

1 additional egg yolk, for the egg wash

Melt the chocolate in a double boiler, remove from heat and set aside.

Using a stand mixer or handheld electric beaters at medium-high speed, beat the butter and sugar together until pale. One at a time, add the eggs and beat until incorporated. With the mixer still running, add the melted chocolate. Add the almond flour and salt and continue to beat until thoroughly incorporated. Add the rum and beat until the mixture is smooth. If adding candied orange, fold it in at this time. Cover the batter and refrigerate for at least 1 hour and up to 24.

If you've refrigerated the filling for more than a couple of hours, remove it and let it soften for fifteen minutes, then beat with electric handheld beaters for 1 full minute before proceeding. If you refrigerated it for 1 hour, proceed directly.

Line a baking sheet with parchment paper. Place one of the puff pastry circles on the parchment. Spread with the filling, leaving a 1-inch border bare. Even out the filling so it is of a uniform thickness. If using a fève, place it in the filling, not too close to the center. (I usually make a small mark on the parchment so that I know where the trinket is.) Dip your fingers in cold water and lightly moisten the border of the dough. Place the second round of dough over the first and lightly press the border to seal. You do want to make sure the border is well sealed. Refrigerate for 30 minutes.

Preheat the oven to 425°F. Mix the milk and egg yolk. Lightly brush the surface of the galette with the yolk-milk wash, avoiding the border. With the tip of a sharp knife, pierce the surface to create small steam vents. Six should be plenty, if well spaced.

Place the galette in the oven and immediately reduce the temperature to 400°F. Bake for approximately 30–35 minutes. If it starts to brown, tent it with foil. The galette is done when it is a deep golden color and nicely puffed up in the center. Slide it onto a cooling rack. If the location of the fève is important to you, keep a note of where it is. Say, by keeping it at 2 o'clock or giving it a tiny mark. Allow the galette to come to room temperature before serving. It is best served the day it is made.

SAVORY
CAKES

———◦❦◦———

Les Cakes Salés

Cake Croque Monsieur

—— *Ham and Cheese Savory Loaf* ——

I call this a Cake Croque Monsieur, as it has all the melted cheesy, hammy goodness of the iconic sandwich baked into one loaf that happens to have the delicate texture of a giant gougère. But there's even more to love. This beauty can be dressed down for lunch with a salad, dressed up with an aperitif before dinner, or undressed for a midnight snack. It feels particularly indulgent eaten warm, but the flavors are more notable at room temperature. It can be wrapped and tossed in a weekend tote bag and, if made on a Friday, will still be delicious, toasted, late Sunday night. I know of no better picnic food, as it requires nothing more than a napkin and glass of wine.

There's a secret ingredient in this recipe: raw leeks. Leeks and shallots are essential to Parisian cooking, almost more so, even, than yellow onions. Shallots are minced and added to vinaigrettes, braised until meltingly tender and sweet, and add structure to many a classic sauce. Leeks are served every which way—drizzled with vinaigrette, adding intrigue to potatoes in a vichyssoise, sliced paper thin in a salad. A few years ago, I began adding a bit of finely minced leek to my grilled cheese sandwiches. The leek seems to cut through the richness of the melted cheese, while also heightening its flavor. And that is what it does here. But if you prefer a mellower loaf, simply sauté the leeks until translucent before adding them to the batter. Should you want a more assertive allium, use shallots. The chives make a vivid addition. It's customary to chop the ham somewhat coarsely, but I prefer using sliced ham. I'm less interested, I suppose, in biting into a cube of ham than I am in having thin bits of it lace this cake. The use of buttermilk is an idea I owe to my friend and colleague Melissa Clark, and her wonderful book *Dinner in French*. It has a similar tanginess to crème fraîche and is often easier to find at the market. Look for a whole artisan buttermilk that is rich and creamy. If all you can find is the watery, skimmed version, avoid it. Use crème fraîche instead.

- 4 tablespoons unsalted butter
- 2 large eggs, at room temperature
- 1 cup whole buttermilk
- 1 tablespoon extra-virgin olive oil
- 2½ cups / 300 grams all-purpose flour
- 1½ teaspoons baking powder
- ½ teaspoon baking soda
- 1 teaspoon fine sea salt
- Several grindings of black pepper

- 2 cups / ½ pound / 227 grams grated Comté, Gruyère or cheddar
- 1 cup / ½ pound / 227 grams chopped or torn-up ham
- 3 tablespoons minced leeks (white and pale green parts only) or 1 tablespoon minced shallots
- 1 tablespoon chopped chives

Preheat the oven to 350°F. Butter a metal 9 x 5-inch loaf pan and dust it with flour.

Melt the butter and set aside for 5 minutes to cool slightly.

In a small mixing bowl, whisk the eggs, buttermilk and oil. Continue to whisk as you pour in the melted butter.

In a larger mixing bowl, whisk the flour, baking powder, baking soda, salt and pepper. Stir in the cheese, ham, leeks and chives. Add the wet ingredients to the dry and fold together with a rubber spatula until no streaks of flour remain.

Pour into the prepared pan and bake for 45–50 minutes, or until a knife inserted in the center comes out nearly clean.

Let the savory cake cool for 5 or 10 minutes before unmolding it. It is delicious warm, straight from the oven, but the flavors deepen and the crumb grows tender if you let it rest for an hour or two. It can sit at room temperature, wrapped in plastic, for much of the day. Overnight, it should be refrigerated, but be sure to bring it to room temperature before serving it. On the third day, it will be best toasted.

Time for a glass of wine or an aperitif? Cut thick slices into batons and stack on a plate.

Cake d'Alsace

Alsatian Bacon, Caramelized Onion and Gruyère Loaf

If bacon, caramelized onion and Gruyère doesn't sell you, there's nothing I can say that will. This can be brunch, lunch, picnic, snack, aperitif, supper. Try it in a lunch box; bring it on a plane or train. In fact, this is what so many Parisians take on the TGV (high-speed train) on weekends. No refrigeration or utensils needed.

5 tablespoons unsalted butter, plus more if needed

½ pound / 227 grams bacon, cut into lardons

1 medium yellow onion, thinly sliced

2 large eggs, at room temperature

1 cup whole buttermilk

1 tablespoon extra-virgin olive oil, plus more if needed

2½ cups / 300 grams all-purpose flour

1½ teaspoons baking powder

½ teaspoon baking soda

½–1 teaspoon fine sea salt, depending on the saltiness of the bacon

Several grindings of black pepper

½ pound / 227 grams grated Comté, Gruyère or cheddar (approximately 2 cups)

3 tablespoon minced flat-leaf parsley

Preheat the oven to 350°F. Butter a metal 9 x 5-inch loaf pan and dust it with flour.

Melt the butter and set aside. It should be warm, but not hot, when you use it.

In a large skillet, over low heat, cook the lardons until they render their fat. Remove with a slotted spoon and set aside. If there's not much fat in the pan, add a little olive oil and butter. Add the onion and sauté over low heat, stirring occasionally, until it starts to turn golden.

In a small mixing bowl, whisk the eggs, buttermilk and oil. Continue to whisk as you slowly pour in the melted butter.

In a larger mixing bowl, whisk the flour, baking powder, baking soda, salt and pepper. Stir in the cheese, bacon and parsley. Add the wet ingredients to the dry and fold together with a rubber spatula until no streaks of flour remain.

Transfer to the prepared pan and bake for 45–50 minutes, or until a knife inserted in the center of the loaf comes out nearly clean.

Let the savory cake cool for 5 or 10 minutes before unmolding it. It is delicious warm, straight from the oven, but the flavors deepen and the crumb grows tender if you let it sit for an hour or two. It can sit at room temperature, wrapped in plastic, for much of the day. Overnight, it should be refrigerated, but be sure to bring it to room temperature before serving it. On the third day, it will be best toasted.

VARIATIONS

SAVOYARD: Add 4 ounces / 113 grams of Reblochon cheese to the Gruyère and reduce the bacon to 170 grams.

SWISS: Add 4 ounces / 113 grams raclette cheese to the Gruyère and reduce the bacon to 170 grams. Serve with cornichons.

Note: I cook bacon lardons my mother's way—over low heat for a long time, letting them render their fat and crisp without burning. Give it a try.

Cake Roquefort et Noix

—— *Roquefort and Walnut Savory Loaf* ——

Roquefort is an assertive cheese, but not terrifically pungent compared to some blues. It is a prized classic for a reason—it's sharp, salty, distinctive and intricately veined. But try some of the artisan American blues, many of which are at a better price point for baking. To choose the cheese, smell it. If you want to breathe in its scent, it is the right one. If you want to back three feet away, it's not for you. And, conversely, if you need to really sniff to get a sense of its character, then it is too weak. Roquefort lovers, go ahead and use a cup and a quarter in this recipe. For the uninitiated, start with a scant cup. The trick to crumbling cheese is to freeze it for twenty to thirty minutes before breaking off bits with the tip of a sharp knife. The pieces should be roughly the size of green peas. Anything smaller, and they will melt—albeit deliciously—into the batter. I make two versions of this savory cake. One with diced pear, the other with browned lardons of bacon. The latter was inspired by one of my favorite salads—frisée lettuce, Roquefort, and lardons with a shallot vinaigrette. And do serve this with salad. It's a rich loaf, and vinaigrette is the ideal counterpoint. If you are making it with pear, choose a pear that is ripe but still offers a bit of resistance. Peel it and dice it and add it with the cheese. It will punctuate the cake with little bursts of sweetness. As to the bacon, save anything that is maple-cured for breakfast. Applewood-smoked is fine.

4 tablespoons unsalted butter

1 cup bacon lardons

2 large eggs, at room temperature

1 cup whole buttermilk

1 tablespoon extra-virgin olive oil

1 tablespoon minced shallots or the whites of a leek

2½ cups / 300 grams all-purpose flour

1½ teaspoons baking powder

½ teaspoon baking soda

1 teaspoon fine sea salt

Several grindings of black pepper

1–1¼ cups blue cheese, preferably Roquefort, crumbled

1¼ cups walnuts, lightly toasted and roughly chopped

1 tablespoon finely chopped flat-leaf parsley, if you'd like a bit of green

Preheat the oven to 350°F. Butter a metal 9 x 5-inch loaf pan and dust it with flour.

Melt the butter and set aside somewhere warm.

Sauté the bacon lardons in a good-sized skillet over low heat until they have rendered their fat and just started to crisp. Discard the fat or save for another use.

In a small mixing bowl, whisk the eggs, buttermilk and oil. Continue to whisk as you pour in the melted butter.

Rinse the minced shallots in cold water for 10 seconds. Drain and pat dry.

In a larger mixing bowl, whisk the flour, baking powder, baking soda, salt and pepper. Stir in the Roquefort, walnuts, shallots, parsley and lardons. Add the wet ingredients and fold with a rubber spatula until no streaks of flour remain.

Transfer to the prepared pan and bake for 45–50 minutes, or until a knife inserted in the center of the loaf comes out nearly clean.

Let the savory cake cool for 5 or 10 minutes before unmolding it. Wait half an hour before serving, if you can resist the smell. The flavors will settle and deepen. The cake can sit at room temperature, wrapped in plastic, for much of the day. Overnight, it should be refrigerated, but be sure to bring it to room temperature before serving it. On the third day, it will be best toasted, perhaps with a pat of butter or drizzle of good olive oil.

Cake Salé aux Tomates, Mozzarella et Basilic

———— Tomato, Mozzarella and Basil Savory Loaf ————

This cake salé has the summer freshness of a caprese salad—ripe tomatoes, tangy mozzarella, bright, spicy and sweet basil. Just don't be tempted by the fabulous milky buffalo mozzarella we all like to eat, but which contains too much water for baking. For this recipe, you want a good artisan mozzarella that isn't sitting in water. Something you can slice through, without it being squidgy. As ripe tomatoes are also filled with water and vary in taste, I roast mine. But there are, in fact, three ways to prepare the tomatoes, and they're all equally good. They can be baked in a 250°F oven for an hour or two. They can be roasted in a hot oven, as I do here, for a mere fifteen minutes. Or, if they are truly flavorful, they can be sliced, sprinkled with salt and set over a sieve for a few hours to shed some of their excess liquid. As mozzarella is a great absorber of flavor but not inherently flavorful, I add garlic to the cake twice, more salt than usual, a spoonful of Parmesan, plenty of basil and some chives for kick. If you want a spicy cake, add some crushed red pepper. Olives and sun-dried tomatoes can join the party, too. But what I love about this recipe is that it reminds me of that last bite of a Caprese salad—you know the one, when you slide an end of bread across the plate, catching the stray bits of mozzarella, a sliver or two of basil and a shimmer of olive oil, flecked with sea salt. The good news is that this cake can be made any time of year, as roasting the tomatoes draws forth their flavor, making something intense out of even those chilled supermarket things that offer no raw pleasure.

1½ cups cherry tomatoes, halved

¼ cup extra-virgin olive oil

2 garlic cloves, minced, plus 1 whole clove

2 teaspoons fine sea salt

4 tablespoons unsalted butter

2 large eggs, at room temperature

1 cup whole buttermilk

2½ cups / 300 grams all-purpose flour

1½ teaspoons baking powder

½ teaspoon baking soda

1 tablespoon grated Parmesan

2 teaspoons fine sea salt

Several grindings of black pepper

1 tablespoon chopped chives

20–25 leaves basil, julienned or torn up

2 cups mozzarella that has been cut in ⅓-inch cubes

Preheat the oven to 400°F.

On a rimmed sheet pan or in a baking dish large enough to accommodate all the cherry tomatoes in one layer, toss the tomatoes, olive oil and minced garlic together, then shake to spread them out. Sprinkle with a bit of the salt. Roast for 15 minutes. Remove from the oven and set aside. When cool enough to handle, tilt the pan and gather 1 tablespoon of the olive oil, which will be deliciously perfumed with the garlic and sweetened with juice from the tomatoes. Set this aside and save the rest to drizzle on toast.

Lower the oven temperature to 350°F. Butter a metal 9 x 5-inch loaf pan and dust it with flour.

Peel the whole garlic clove and slice it horizontally in half. Melt the butter in a small saucepan with the garlic halves, then set aside for five minutes to infuse. Remove and discard the garlic.

In a small mixing bowl, whisk the eggs, buttermilk and the tablespoon of yummy tomato-garlic-olive oil from the pan. Continue to whisk as you pour in the garlic-infused butter.

In a larger mixing bowl, whisk the flour, baking powder, baking soda, Parmesan, salt and pepper. Stir in the chives, basil, cherry tomatoes and mozzarella. Fold in the wet ingredients with a rubber spatula until no streaks of flour remain.

Pour into the prepared loaf pan and bake for 45–50 minutes, or until a knife inserted in the center comes out nearly clean.

Remove the savory cake to a wire rack and let it cool for 5 minutes before unmolding it. It is delicious warm, straight from the oven, but the flavors deepen and the crumb grows tender, if you let it sit for an hour or two. Store at room temperature, wrapped in plastic or in an air-tight container. It should be refrigerated overnight, but be sure to bring it back to room temperature before eating it. On the third day, it will be best toasted and drizzled with olive oil.

Cake Salé à la Feta,
aux Tomates Séchées et aux Olives

—— Feta, Sun-Dried Tomato and Olive Savory Cake ——

The flavors here are strong but softened by the gentle crumb of this savory cake. It is Mediterranean through and through. Serve it with a crisp white wine.

4 tablespoons unsalted butter

2 large eggs, at room temperature

1 cup whole buttermilk

1 tablespoon extra-virgin olive oil

2½ cups / 300 grams all-purpose flour

1½ teaspoons baking powder

½ teaspoon baking soda

1 teaspoon fine sea salt

Several grinds of black pepper

Pinch of Aleppo pepper, optional

1 tablespoon chopped fresh oregano, basil or flat-leaf parsley

2 cups / 8 ounces / 227 grams feta cheese, crumbled

⅔ cup sun-dried tomatoes, slivered or chopped

½ cup pitted olives, such as kalamata, halved

Preheat the oven to 350°F. Butter a metal 9 x 5-inch loaf pan and dust it with flour.

Melt the butter and set aside for 5 minutes to cool.

In a small mixing bowl, whisk the eggs, buttermilk and oil. Continue to whisk as you pour in the melted butter.

In a larger mixing bowl, whisk the flour, baking powder, baking soda, salt and pepper. Stir in the Aleppo pepper, oregano, feta, sun-dried tomatoes and olives. Fold in the wet ingredients with a rubber spatula to combine. Don't overmix, but don't leave streaks of flour either.

Pour into the prepared pan and bake for 45–50 minutes, or until a knife inserted in the center comes out nearly clean.

Transfer the savory cake to a cooling rack and let it rest for 5 minutes before unmolding it. It is delicious warm, straight from the oven, but the flavors deepen and the crumb grows tender, if you let it sit for an hour or two. If you are not eating it within a few hours, wrap it in plastic wrap and store at room temperature. It should be refrigerated overnight, but be sure to bring it back to room temperature before eating it. On the third day, it will be best toasted and drizzled with olive oil.

Note: If you are using a very wet feta, crumble it, set it in a sieve and let some of its liquid drip off before adding it to the batter. French feta is ideal for this recipe, as it is neither too dry, nor too salty, but any good feta will do.

Cake Chorizo, Piquillo, Chèvre
—— *Chorizo, Piquillo and Chèvre Savory Loaf* ——

My friend Stephanie and I cooked up a crazy idea of opening a tequila pop-up shop near her apartment in Paris that would travel to Provence in the summer. We never pursued it, but I dreamed up this aperitif loaf to serve during tastings. Tastings would be de rigueur. Parisians don't "do" shots and so approach tequila with the same aesthetic curiosity they reserve for cognac. They study, they taste, they ponder, they discuss, and they buy only when they've found their ideal match. At home, a small glass of anejo or reposado might be served as an aperitif, perhaps alongside a few slices of dried chorizo or serrano ham. Always straight up, perhaps with an orange twist. But come summer, all bets are off. As Parisians flock to the South, they leave their finicky selves behind and turn to rosé and cocktails. Pair this cake with a good tequila, a paloma or a chilled Provençal rosé, and you're in for a treat.

Fresh chorizo varies in heat, spice and size. The rule of thumb applies: bake with what you like to eat. Piquillo peppers may be replaced with roasted red bell peppers, even those right from a jar. But piquillo peppers have a smoky, tangy sweetness that is worth trying if you haven't. Due to the heat of the chorizo, I chose chèvre as a soft and mild counterpoint. I love biting into the sudden warm cloud of it. For a bolder taste, replace it with two cups of grated manchego. Choose a young manchego, as an aged one will be too potent. If you don't eat meat, eliminate the chorizo and add two cups of corn kernels and triple the amount of smoked paprika.

5 tablespoons unsalted butter

14 ounces / 400 grams fresh chorizo, about 3 sausages

2 large eggs, at room temperature

1 cup whole buttermilk

1 tablespoon extra-virgin olive oil

2½ cups / 300 grams all-purpose flour

1½ teaspoons baking powder

½ teaspoon baking soda

½ teaspoon smoked paprika

½ teaspoon fine sea salt

Several grinds of black pepper

1½ cups / 8 ounces / 227 grams crumbled fresh chèvre

½ cup roasted piquillo peppers, julienned

2 tablespoons chopped chives

Preheat the oven to 350°F. Butter a metal 9 x 5-inch loaf pan and dust it with flour.

Melt the butter and set aside for 5 minutes to cool.

Warm a skillet over medium-high heat. Crumble the chorizo and add to the skillet. Brown them on one side, breaking them into smaller bits with a metal spatula, as they fry. Toss and continue until browned on all sides. Transfer the sausages to a paper towel–lined plate to absorb excess oil. You should have roughly 2 cups of chorizo, but a little more or less won't hurt and there's no reason to measure.

In a small mixing bowl, whisk the eggs, buttermilk and oil. Continue to whisk as you pour in the melted butter.

In a larger mixing bowl, whisk the flour, baking powder, baking soda, smoked paprika, salt and pepper. Toss in the crumbled chèvre, browned chorizo, julienned piquillo peppers and chopped chives. Fold in the wet ingredients with a rubber spatula until no streaks of flour remain.

Pour into the prepared pan and bake for 55 minutes, or until a knife inserted into the center of the loaf comes out nearly clean. If your knife comes out covered in chèvre, try another spot.

Let the savory cake sit for 5 or 10 minutes before unmolding it. It is delicious warm, straight from the oven, but the flavors deepen and the crumb grows tender if you let it rest for an hour or two. It can sit at room temperature, wrapped in plastic, for much of the day. Overnight, it should be refrigerated, but be sure to bring it to room temperature before serving it. On the third day, it will be best toasted.

Madeleines aux Noix, Poire et Roquefort

—— Walnut, Pear and Roquefort Madeleines ——

This recipe appeared in the first article I ever published. It was for the *New York Times Magazine* and, at the time, I certainly didn't imagine it would lead to fifteen years as a food columnist. I simply had a subject I wanted to investigate, and Amanda Hesser, then the editor of the magazine's food pages, decided to take a gamble on me. No doubt this beauty of a recipe, courtesy of the Parisian blogger Clotilde Dusoulier, ensured the article would not be my last. People literally swoon when they bite into these. The yielding pleasure of the moist, tender crumb, the unexpected sweetness of pear, the sharp, distinctive edge of Roquefort and the crunch of walnuts . . . These madeleines are meant to be eaten with an aperitif before dinner, but they become truly extravagant when paired with a vintage port and served in lieu of a cheese or dessert course.

And so we come full circle, and I leave you with this final recipe.

1¼ cups / 150 grams all-purpose flour

1 tablespoon baking powder

3 large eggs, at room temperature

½ teaspoon fine sea salt

½ teaspoon freshly ground pepper

2 tablespoons extra-virgin olive oil

½ cup whole buttermilk

3 ounces Roquefort, crumbled

1 ripe pear, peeled, cored and diced

⅓ cup walnuts, roughly chopped.

Preheat the oven to 350°F and butter 24 madeleine molds.

Combine the flour and baking powder in a small mixing bowl.

In a medium mixing bowl, whisk together the eggs, salt and pepper. Add the oil, buttermilk and cheese, and whisk again until well blended.

Place a sieve over the bowl and sift the flour mixture into the egg mixture, then stir with a wooden spoon until incorporated—the batter will be thick. Don't overmix; it's okay if a few lumps remain. Fold in the pear and walnuts and stir to combine.

Spoon the batter into the molds, filling them by two-thirds. Bake until puffy and golden, 12–16 minutes. Transfer to a cooling rack for 2 minutes, unmold and serve immediately.

To SOAK

To SAUCE

To COAT

To FILL

To ICE

To DRIZZLE

To SPOON

To GLAZE

and PERCHANCE *to* DOLLOP

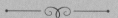

Au Dessus et À Côté

Crème Chantilly

Big clouds of whipped cream! What could be better? I remember a friend of my son's coming over and asking me how whipped cream was made—the jump from liquid to billowy confection is indeed mysterious. The simple answer of air was even more perplexing to his young mind, but that is all it is. The thing I always forget is that Chantilly does actually last a little bit in the fridge if stored in a covered cold metal mixing bowl. It will need a bit of rewhipping, but you can prepare it before dinner to serve at dessert.

There's not much to know when it comes to technique. Start with the mixer at low and increase to medium-high. Stop when the cream is as light as a cloud. Don't make butter. If you are filling a rouleau, you may want to beat it a bit longer, so that it maintains its structure. If topping a Pavlova, it should be pillowy and soft. If you are planning on eating it right away, it can be on the looser side, so it seems to gently fold over, say, a slice of cake. Or it can be full-on voluminous and able to hold its shape. There's no wrong here. Only right.

As to quantities, more is more. Meaning, a tiny amount of Chantilly is downright wrong in spirit. I'm not one to waste food, but I do think a big bowl or big dollops of whipped cream are the point. Chantilly is festive, generous, playful—the very opposite of austere. For four people, I'll use one and a half cups of heavy cream; for six people, two cups and on upward. Generally, I like about two teaspoons of sugar for every cup of cream, but most people prefer a tablespoon.

If you can find a local heavy cream that is not ultra-pasteurized, this is the time to use it. It will have a wholesomeness that's hard to define.

Now for myriad possibilities.

Traditional whipped cream is just that, often with a little confectioners' sugar and perhaps a touch of vanilla. But the French were onto something when they invented crème fraîche. It is rich and sensual but with a little tang. It's this little tang that makes it the perfect foil for a rich cake. That and its coolness. Even at room temperature, crème fraîche has a coolness to it. At home, Parisians are more likely to serve cake with a dollop of crème fraîche than to whip up a Chantilly, but, when they do, they often mix crème fraîche and heavy cream. And the ratio—well, that depends on either what the cake needs or how much of each is in the fridge. I tend to think three parts heavy cream to one part crème fraîche is the gold standard.

And sugar? Confectioners' is best, but superfine works well, too. Here, less is more. Unless your cake isn't terribly sweet, you'll want the Chantilly to be a counterpoint to the cake's sweetness, so keep it barely sweetened. The trick is to add, whip, taste, repeat until you've found, well, your sweet spot.

Crème Chantilly has a great purity to it, but it also takes kindly to extracts, liqueurs, vanilla seeds, spice, cocoa, floral waters, jam, curd, marmalade, zest and ganache. As cream is a fairly blank canvas, a little goes a long way. And, where liquid or heavier additions like jam are concerned, use only a small amount, so as not to deflate the Chantilly or liquefy it. If I'm using a cup of cream, for example, I won't add more than a tablespoon of liquid, and I will use confectioners' sugar rather than granulated, as confectioners' sugar helps the cream hold its shape. Add, whip, taste, repeat is, again, the rule of thumb.

Ganache Chantilly

This is the go-to when a light, chocolate cloud is what's needed. It's also a shortcut filling and frosting for those days when the idea of making a buttercream elicits a yawn or a sigh or an anxious look at the clock. It's the quickest route to dacquoise or génoise bliss. The only catch is the cacao percentage. If you are like me and prefer bittersweet chocolate to semisweet, know that you can inch up to about 66% but that anything higher might yield a slightly grainy texture. Still delicious, but not as smooth and glorious.

113 grams chocolate, 52%–66% cacao   **1 cup heavy cream**

Break the chocolate into smallish pieces and set them in a mixing bowl or in the bowl of a stand mixer. Bring the heavy cream to a simmer in a small saucepan or heat it in a microwave and pour it onto the chocolate. Stir until melted, then set aside to cool to room temperature, about 30 minutes, giving it a stir once or twice along the way. Do not overcool it, as it will not whip to a smooth consistency.

Beat the ganache at low speed until soft, slightly floppy peaks form, about 1–2 minutes. Stop before you would when making an all-cream Chantilly, as the ganache will thicken at room temperature and overbeating may alter the texture. It's at its peak if used soon after making, but it will keep for a day in the fridge, if kept in an airtight container. It can also be left at cool room temperature for a few hours. If storing overnight, do refrigerate it, as you would with most dairy products.

Of course, you can always melt the ganache Chantilly, chill it and whip it all over again, should you need to.

Chocolate Ganache

It's nearly impossible to walk more than five minutes in Paris without passing one of its three hundred or so chocolate shops. To call them shops is a bit ridiculous. They are temples to the city's favorite sweet, with neat rows of impeccable handmade confections that astonish in their craftsmanship, tantalize in their myriad flavors and will easily melt the stoniest amongst us at first bite. But good chocolate is also a pantry staple. Melted in a little warm cream, it becomes ganache, the simplest, most perfect recipe ever to grace this earth. I mean this sincerely. No wonder, then, that Parisians make it more than any other icing, glaze or dessert sauce. It is poured over ice cream, cakes, and towering meringue dacquoises. It is a dunking and dipping favorite, whether coating candied orange zest or Proustian madeleines, set over a flame for fondue or in the freezer to enrobe a *petit four*. It is the filling and icing of choice for most every chocolate dessert made at home. But all ganache is not equal. Chocolate is the star. The better the chocolate, the better the ganache. If you can find a heavy cream from a local dairy that isn't ultra-pasteurized, all the better.

What you need to know is common sense, really. A thicker ganache is best when frosting a cake, a thinner one when pouring or drizzling. Adjust the ratio of chocolate to cream accordingly. To frost, you'll want a ganache that's come to room temperature or been briefly chilled. To pour, you'll want it warm. Flavor options abound, but the true chocolate lover may want it served neat. Or not. I am a true chocolate lover, and I most always tilt tipsy.

Continued

CLASSIC GANACHE

227 grams dark chocolate, 60%-66% cacao

1 cup heavy cream

3 tablespoons spirits or liqueur, such as rum, bourbon, whiskey, crème de framboise, Grand Marnier or Cointreau, or 1 teaspoon vanilla extract (see Choices)

Break the chocolate into smallish pieces.

Bring the cream to a simmer over a double boiler. Add the chocolate and stir until melted. Immediately remove from heat and stir in the liqueur.

If you are pouring the ganache like a glaze, use it while warm, but not hot.

If you are using the ganache like a sauce, use it while hot. (I use it in place of hot fudge on ice cream. And my mother pours it over red wine–poached pears and vanilla ice cream.)

If you are using it as a frosting, wait until it comes to room temperature and thickens. It can be refrigerated for 3 days and brought back to room temperature. Don't stir ganache when it is cold, as it will break.

CHOICES

Use up to 3 tablespoons of liquid. This can include liqueur, coffee or vanilla, orange or almond extract. More than 1 teaspoon of vanilla extract will, in my opinion, dampen the intensity of the chocolate. Use no more than ¼ teaspoon orange or almond extract, as they are surprisingly strong. Rum, bourbon, whiskey, crème de framboise, Grand Marnier and Cointreau all add wonderful notes. What to choose will depend upon the gâteau you are making. One of my favorite combinations is 1 tablespoon dark rum, 5 teaspoons strong coffee and 1 teaspoon vanilla extract. Another favorite is 2 tablespoons Grand Marnier and 1 teaspoon vanilla extract. Ginger liqueur, chai tea, Armagnac, amaretto, Kahlúa, tequila, port, even grappa . . . the list goes on. And, of course, you can skip the liquid altogether and simply enjoy the purity of chocolate and cream.

Sometimes it's nice to add a hint of spice. A quarter teaspoon of ground cardamom or half a teaspoon ground cinnamon are good choices. A pinch of cayenne or chipotle powder will add heat, and a pinch of black pepper will sharpen it. Spice should be added to the cream as you are heating it.

To, paradoxically, lighten the ganache, stir in a tablespoon of butter when you add the chocolate.

If you use a chocolate with a percentage of cacao over 66%, you will want to increase the amount of cream or add a touch of butter or it will not be spreadable. For 66%–68% cacao chocolate, use 1¼ cups cream. For 70% cacao, you will want to use about 1½ cups of cream. Avoid using chocolate over 70% cacao when making a ganache, as it will produce an inferior texture.

Use leftovers to make an amazingly rich hot chocolate or to warm up and pour over ice cream. Dip fruit—strawberries, dried apricots, even bananas—in ganache and allow to set.

For an exquisite dessert, use two spoons to shape a portion into a quenelle and serve dusted with Maldon sea salt, orange zest and a whisper of fabulous olive oil.

GLISTENING GANACHE

If you want a bit of shine, replace the 3 tablespoons liquid with honey or Lyle's Golden Syrup. Alternatively, keep the liquid and add 3 tablespoons honey and 1 ounce unsweetened chocolate. The honey should be stirred in off heat.

THINNER, POURING GANACHE

If you want a ganache to drizzle rather than spread, use 113 grams chocolate, ½ cup heavy cream and 2 tablespoons liqueur. Drizzle while still warm.

MILK CHOCOLATE GANACHE

For a milk chocolate ganache, use 454 grams milk chocolate, around 40% cacao, and 1⅛ cups heavy cream.

Continued

WHITE CHOCOLATE GANACHE

1 cup heavy cream   12 ounces white chocolate

Note the shift in ratio. Same preparation.

WHITE CHOCOLATE ROSE GANACHE

½ cup heavy cream   1–3 tablespoons rose water, to taste
7 ounces white chocolate

Bring the cream to just short of a simmer in a double boiler. Add the chocolate and stir until melted. Remove from heat and let it cool for 3 minutes, then stir in the rose water.

To give this the pale pink hue of tea roses, either add an all-natural food coloring or reduce the heavy cream by 1 tablespoon and add 1 tablespoon of the juice of crushed blackberries when adding the rose water.

Coulis

———— • ————

A great favorite among pastry chefs and home cooks, this simple and fresh light sauce is most often made with raspberries, but any berry, or a mix thereof can be used. Drizzled on a plate or spooned over a cake, it offers a burst of color and bright berry-ness. There's no exact ratio of berry to sugar, as it depends on the sweetness of the berries and how you intend to use the coulis. Just taste until you smile. I usually add a little matching liqueur or rose water. Crème de framboise or crème de cassis give dimension to a raspberry coulis. Rose water and strawberries is a fragrant match. A spoonful of Champagne, if you've opened a bottle, perks up blueberries and blackberries. Alternatively, lemon or limoncello will give it zest.

Fresh or frozen berries

Superfine sugar

Crème de cassis, lemon juice or rose water, to taste (see Note)

Preferably in a Vitamix or other powerful blender, purée the berries and sugar. Add the crème de cassis, if using, and blend until smooth. If the mixture is too thick, add a touch of water. Strain into a pitcher. Coulis is best used right away, but it can be refrigerated overnight in a sealed jar. It will need to be re-blended or well shaken before using.

Note: *If planning to store the coulis, lemon juice is the best addition, as it helps lock in the color.*

Caramel Sauce

———•———

Unlike American caramel sauce, which tends to include butter and brown sugar, French caramel sauce is usually made with heavy cream and the sugar is cooked until it caramelizes to a deep amber color. I mix traditions, cooking it the French way and adding bourbon at the end. This recipe makes about 1 cup and has a pouring consistency.

1 cup / 200 grams granulated sugar	½ teaspoon vanilla extract
½ teaspoon fine sea salt	2 teaspoons rum, Cognac, whiskey, Grand Marnier or bourbon, optional
¼ cup water	
½ cup heavy cream	

In a tall, narrow pot or high-sided saucepan, combine the sugar, salt and water over medium heat. Stir until the sugar dissolves and the syrup is transparent. Bring to a boil and continue to cook, swirling the pan occasionally, until the syrup is a deep amber, about 10 minutes.

Immediately remove from heat. Standing back to avoid being splattered, pour in the cream, vanilla and rum, if using. When the mixture stops bubbling, start stirring to create a smooth sauce. Set aside to come to room temperature and refrigerate, if not using within a few hours.

Notes: Caramel can splatter and burn something awful. Be careful. I use a high-sided pot and wear mitten potholders, and, despite the deliriously good smell, I keep my face averted.

A bit of orange zest or a touch of spice can be stirred in with the cream. If you want a more pronounced salty note, simply omit the salt in the sauce and sprinkle each serving with some flaky Maldon sea salt.

Soaking Syrups

These are also called brushing syrups, as they can be brushed on with a pastry brush. Or they can be spooned over and sort of pushed around the surface of a cake with the back of a spoon. Soaking syrups are at the essence of many French cakes, including all génoise creations, be they layered or rolled, and of baba au rhum and savarin cakes. They're a godsend when you've overcooked a cake or want to remoisten it after a day or two. The trick is to add enough to moisten but not so much as to wet and possibly cause the cake to disintegrate. That said, génoises and babas are meant to absorb a surprisingly large quantity of syrup and have the structure to stand up tall even when drenched. They're made for that very purpose, and syrup is an integral part of their recipe. If you're worried, simply place the cake on the cooling rack with a piece of foil or parchment underneath to catch excess liquid when you add the syrup. This will ensure that your cake isn't sitting in a puddle. The other trick is to wait until the cake has come to room temperature. The same is true for the syrup. Don't add hot syrup to a hot cake. Everyone needs a beat to rest and cool before meeting and mingling.

Brush; wait for the cake to absorb the syrup. Repeat. When the cake stops absorbing the syrup, and the liquid seems to sit on top and not sink in, stop. Leave the cake at room temperature, uncovered, if serving it within the day. If keeping it overnight, cover it with a cake dome or a tented piece of foil. Save any extra soaking syrup, as you might want to add another spoonful just before serving the cake.

You'll find many soaking syrup recipes on pages 188 and 189. But there's no reason to stop there. The basic recipe is this: create a simple syrup (1:1 ratio of sugar to water), as you would when making a cocktail, or a heavy simple syrup (2:1 ratio of sugar to water). Feel free to use granulated, raw, brown or muscovado sugar. Honey and maple syrup work here as well. If not using it right away, store the syrup a covered glass jar in the fridge for up to a month. If using right away, add desired flavors.

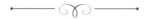

Continued

SIMPLE SYRUP

This is a 1:1 ratio.

Bring 1 cup / 200 grams sugar and 1 cup water to a boil, stir to dissolve the sugar and remove from heat.

Use this simple syrup if flavoring with spices, powders, zests or extracts—such as cinnamon sticks, espresso powder, strips of citrus zest or vanilla extract.

HEAVY SIMPLE SYRUP

This is a 2:1 ratio.

Bring 2 cups / 400 grams sugar and 1 cup water to a boil, stir to dissolve the sugar and remove from heat.

Use this heavier simple syrup if you will be adding additional liquid, such as liqueur, citrus juice, a shot of espresso, floral waters.

QUICK ESPRESSO RUM SYRUP

½ cup plus 1 tablespoon / 113 grams granulated sugar

5 tablespoons espresso

4 teaspoons rum, Cognac or coffee liqueur

This is for true coffee lovers, as there's no water to dilute things.

In a small saucepan, dissolve the sugar in the espresso over low heat. Let it come to a simmer and cook for a minute to thicken it slightly. Remove from heat and stir in the rum.

Glazes and Drizzles

———•———

When the French frost, they do so with buttercream. But Parisians would not look like Parisians if they did that very often. Rather, a not-too-heavy blanket of dark chocolate ganache is used on most anything calling for chocolate or more chocolate. For most every other cake, the simplest of glazes is used. Sometimes the glaze skews thicker and will set with a little time or dry heat—even five minutes in the lowest setting on your oven. Sometimes it's nearly liquid and can be poured or drizzled on with a flick of the wrist. There's not much to these glazes—mix a liquid into confectioners' sugar and stir. But try to keep extra ingredients on hand. That way, if you squeeze in too much lemon juice, you need only add more confectioners' sugar or, if you shake in too much confectioners' sugar, you have an extra half lemon to squeeze.

Citrus glazes are the most common, as the tart burst of a lemon or orange or lime will counter the sugar with sass. These bring liveliness. Also common is the use of a little coffee to accentuate or balance the flavors of a cake. For example, a walnut cake loves a coffee glaze, while a cake made with coffee might like a boost in flavor. Parisians are far more likely to keep floral waters in their pantry than Americans, and they make good use of them in glazes. A little rose water glaze on a pistachio cake or a little orange blossom water on an almond cake gives new dimension. Crushing blackberries can add a little color and provide a vehicle for a few drops of lavender extract. Likewise freeze-dried raspberries, pulverized to a powder, can add color and flavor, but they will need additional liquid from, say, lemon juice.

And then there are boozy glazes. Rare is the Parisian meal without wine on the table and brandy in the food. Rum, Armagnac, Calvados, Cognac, *eau-de-vie*, Chambord, Grand Marnier, Cointreau, kirsch, crème de cassis, crème de framboise, crème de pêche, crème de mûre, Abricot du Roussillon—two or three tablespoons of any of these stirred into a cup of confectioners' sugar and, suddenly, you're in business. Think of it this way: You bake two quick yogurt and apple cakes. One you save for after-school snacks, the other you drizzle with a Calvados glaze and serve at dinner. Parisians are ever practical, even—especially— in their insistence on the pleasures of eating well. The intensity of flavor in liqueur means a spoonful or two can add depth, elegance and nuance in one quick step.

Continued

The following glazes are favorites. Two tablespoons of liquid will give you a glaze, three will give you something to pour or drizzle. There's no need to weigh the sugar and measure precisely—you'll know when you have the consistency you want. For example, I'll mix, say, a big mug of confectioners' sugar with the juice of a tangerine and the juice of half a lemon and perhaps a dash of orange blossom water. I use a tiny whisk, but a fork or spoon works just fine. If, by the way, you taste your glaze and want something mellower, but not sweeter, simply add a spoonful of heavy cream.

LEMON GLAZE

1 cup / 114 grams confectioners' sugar

2-3 tablespoons freshly squeezed lemon juice

The grated zest of 1 lemon

LIMONCELLO GLAZE

1 cup / 114 grams confectioners' sugar

1 tablespoon freshly squeezed lemon juice

1-2 tablespoons limoncello

ORANGE GLAZE

1 cup / 114 grams confectioners' sugar

1-2 tablespoons freshly squeezed orange juice

1 tablespoon Grand Marnier, optional

ORANGE BLOSSOM GLAZE

1 cup / 114 grams confectioners' sugar

1 tablespoon orange blossom water

1-2 tablespoons freshly squeezed orange juice

LIME GLAZE

1 cup / 114 grams confectioners' sugar

1-2 tablespoons freshly squeezed lime juice

1 tablespoon white rum or coconut cream, optional

BLOOD ORANGE GLAZE

1 cup / 114 grams confectioners' sugar

1–2 tablespoons freshly squeezed blood orange juice

1 tablespoon Solerno, optional

CITRUS GLAZE

1 cup /114 grams confectioners' sugar

1½ tablespoons freshly squeezed Meyer lemon juice

1½ tablespoons freshly squeezed mandarin juice

YUZU GLAZE

1 cup / 114 grams confectioners' sugar

2–3 tablespoons undiluted yuzu juice

ROSE GLAZE

Note: *This glaze depends greatly on the strength of your rose water and on personal preference. Create the balance you like, adding more or less lemon juice as you go.*

1 cup / 114 grams confectioners' sugar

1 tablespoon rose water

About 1 tablespoon freshly squeezed lemon juice

LAVENDER GLAZE

1 cup / 114 grams confectioners' sugar

2 tablespoons freshly squeezed lemon juice

¼ teaspoon lavender extract

A few drops natural purple food coloring, optional

ELDERFLOWER GLAZE

1 cup / 114 grams confectioners' sugar

2 tablespoons St-Germain

1 tablespoon freshly squeezed lime juice

INFUSION GLAZE

1 cup / 114 grams confectioners' sugar

2–3 tablespoons strong infusion/tea, such as hibiscus, chamomile, lime blossom or verbena

COFFEE GLAZE

1 cup / 114 grams confectioners' sugar

2–3 tablespoons strong espresso

¼ teaspoon coffee extract, or mix 1 teaspoon instant espresso into the strong espresso, optional

COFFEE RUM GLAZE

1 cup / 114 grams confectioners' sugar

1½ tablespoons strong espresso

1 tablespoon dark rum

⅛ teaspoon coffee extract, optional

BOOZY GLAZE

1 cup / 114 grams confectioners' sugar

2–3 tablespoons spirits or liqueur, such as rum, Cognac, kirsch or Grand Marnier

COCONUT GLAZE

1 cup / 114 grams confectioners' sugar

2–3 tablespoons coconut cream

¼ teaspoon coconut extract or 1 teaspoon coconut liqueur

The grated zest of 1 lime

TROPICAL GLAZE

1 cup / 114 grams confectioners' sugar

2 tablespoons freshly pressed pineapple juice

1 tablespoon dark rum

The grated zest of 1 lime

MINT GLAZE

Note: I recommend just a drizzle of this rather than a full glaze.

1 cup / 114 grams confectioners' sugar

3 tablespoons crème de menthe

A few drops of natural green food coloring, optional

MARGARITA GLAZE

1 cup / 114 grams confectioners' sugar

2 tablespoons freshly squeezed lime juice

1 tablespoon silver tequila

GLAÇAGE DE CHRISTOPHE MICHALAK

2½ cups / 286 grams confectioners' sugar

⅓ cup freshly squeezed lemon juice

3 tablespoons extra-virgin olive oil

This glaze is adapted from one that pâtissier Christophe Michalak makes. Use an excellent buttery, not herbaceous, olive oil. All the ingredients should be mixed until smooth. Michalak then glazes the cake or loaf and places it in a 425°F oven for exactly 2 minutes to set the glaze. The high heat works quickly and will not affect the timing of any but the most delicate of cakes. I particularly love this one on cakes and loaves that have an herb ingredient or are citrus based. It's a natural fit for a quatre-quarts scented with rosemary and lemon or blood oranges or with any polenta or semolina cake, as those grains have a slightly savory and rustic note. At the Ritz Paris, you'll find a tea cake layered with raspberry jam and graced with this glaze. I like to serve it with fresh berries tossed in a spoonful of limoncello. This yields enough glaze to coat a large 10- to 12-inch cake or 24 cupcakes.

Buttercreams

———•———

Few things are as synonymous with French pâtisserie as buttercream. It is that rich, silken layer in cakes and pastries that fills your mouth with a sudden, unabashed rush of sensuality. But it's no quick affair. A sugar syrup needs to reach exactly 242°F before it is carefully and slowly poured into whisked eggs. And then? Well, a shocking amount of butter goes in, bit by bit. If you have a candy thermometer, success is within easy reach. If you attempt to wing it, be prepared for failure. I've included as streamlined a recipe as possible. I've also included far easier buttercreams that need no apology for being quick. These may not be transcendent, but they are damn good. For a dark chocolate meringue buttercream, turn to page 266.

THE CLASSIC FRENCH BUTTERCREAM

Call me a wimp, but pouring boiling sugar syrup into a spinning, whisking bowl is not my idea of happy baking. But for special occasions, I do relent. And if you use pot holders, there's not really any risk. But please don't even think about attempting this without a stand mixer. It requires constant whisking for nearly twenty minutes. This recipe is deliberately low on the sugar spectrum. In that, it differs greatly from American frosting. The idea behind French buttercream is twofold. One to create an indulgent, buttery, billowy layer to put in and on a cake. The other is as a foil for flavor. There's a lot of butter in here, so flavor boldly. You may add cocoa, espresso powder, praliné in any texture from chopped to paste. More common is the addition of extracts and liqueur. Think chocolate, coffee, almond, hazelnut, lemon, orange, raspberry, lavender, rose and mint. Rum, Cognac, crème de cassis, limoncello, bourbon, whiskey, Solerno and amaretto are all strong enough to stand up to this confection with some serious gumption. Blitzed freeze-dried fruit adds flavor and color. And bits of candied ginger or orange give texture. As with any frosting, you can add food coloring. This is an excellent buttercream for piping into decorative swirls and shapes, but a surface smoothed with an offset spatula has its own natural beauty that, to me, speaks volumes. As to quantity, the best approach is to add a teaspoon, taste and repeat, until it meets your fancy and is proportionally subtle or intense. A strongly flavored cake may want a subtle buttercream, whereas a mild génoise with a simple soaking syrup may want something that packs a greater wallop. Trust yourself.

2 cups unsalted butter, preferably
    European, at cool room temperature

10 large egg yolks, at room temperature

⅛ teaspoon fine sea salt

1 cup / 200 grams superfine sugar

⅓ cup water

The seeds from 2 vanilla beans

1 tablespoon dark rum or 2 teaspoons
    extract of your choice

Slice the butter into pieces, about 1 tablespoon each. Set aside. The butter should be at cool room temperature, starting to soften but not even close to losing its shape or resistance when you press it. This is important.

In a stand mixer, whisk the egg yolks until foamy and just starting to thicken. Add the salt and beat another few seconds.

Heat the sugar and water in a small saucepan, preferably one with a spout, over medium heat. Stir to help dissolve the sugar as you bring the mixture to a full boil. Carefully, use a candy thermometer to check the temperature. When it hits 242°F, remove it immediately from heat.

Restart the mixer, this time at low speed. Keep it running as you pour in the hot syrup in a very slow but steady stream. Take care to use a pot holder and avoid splatters. Sugar burns badly.

Increase the mixer speed to medium-high and whisk until the mixture cools, a full 10 minutes. The bowl should no longer be warm to the touch. With the mixer still running, begin adding the pieces of butter, one at a time, waiting until the mixture is homogenous before adding another. Add the vanilla and rum. Mix for another 4 minutes.

EASY BUTTERCREAMS FOR DACQUOISES, GÉNOISES, BÛCHES DE NOËL AND MORE

Unlike classic buttercreams, these contain no eggs and require no heat. But they are rich and buttery. Play with the flavors but stick to the ratios provided. It's all about the balance between solids and liquid, which is where extracts come in handy. For example, I add coffee extract to the espresso buttercream rather than adding more espresso and risking a runny buttercream. If you want a lighter, fluffier buttercream, fold in a little whipped cream. If you want a fruity buttercream, fold in a little jam. Better yet, add a thin layer of jam before the buttercream. Buttercream can easily take a few solid additions, such as a handful of minced candied ginger or minced candied orange peel or mini chocolate chips. Keep chilled if not using right away, particularly in summer, but remove it from the fridge about fifteen minutes before using, so it returns to a spreadable consistency. You can always give it another quick whipping or vigorous stirring to quickly fluff it back up. These recipes make enough buttercream to fill a three-layer dacquoise or a two-layer génoise, sides and surface included.

Chocolate Buttercream

- 1 cup unsalted butter, at room temperature
- 4½ cups / 540 grams confectioners' sugar, plus more if needed
- 2½ tablespoons heavy cream, plus more if needed

- 3-5 teaspoons chocolate extract, or to taste
- ¼ teaspoon coffee extract
- Pinch of fine sea salt

In a stand mixer or using handheld electric beaters at medium speed, beat the butter until creamy, about 2 minutes. At low speed, add the confectioners' sugar, cream, the chocolate and coffee extracts and the salt. Increase the mixer speed to high and beat for 3 minutes. Taste.

Add up to ½ cup more confectioners' sugar if you'd like a thicker buttercream or another tablespoon of cream for a looser one.

Lemon Buttercream

1 cup unsalted butter, at room temperature

4½ cups / 540 grams confectioners' sugar, plus more if needed

2½ tablespoons lemon juice

2 tablespoons heavy cream, plus more if needed

2 teaspoons lemon zest, plus more if needed

A few drops of lemon extract, optional

In a stand mixer or using handheld electric beaters at medium speed, beat the butter until creamy, about 2 minutes. On low speed, add the confectioners' sugar, lemon juice, cream and zest. Increase the speed to high and beat for 3 minutes. Taste.

Add additional zest or a few drops of lemon extract if you want more pucker.

Add up to ½ cup more confectioners' sugar if you'd like a thicker buttercream or another tablespoon of cream for a looser one.

Variations: Use limes, Key limes, mandarins, clementines, grapefruit or Meyer lemons in place of the lemons. Another beauty: 3 tablespoons concentrated yuzu juice and the zest of 2 mandarins.

Boozy Orange Buttercream

1 cup unsalted butter, at room temperature

4½ cups / 540 grams confectioners' sugar, plus more if needed

2½ tablespoons Grand Marnier, Cointreau or freshly squeezed and strained orange juice

2 tablespoons heavy cream, plus more if needed

2–3 teaspoons grated orange zest

In a stand mixer or using handheld electric beaters at medium speed, beat the butter until creamy, about 2 minutes. Reduce the speed to low and add the confectioners' sugar, Grand Marnier, cream and zest. Increase the speed to high and beat for 3 minutes. Taste.

Add up to ½ cup more confectioners' sugar if you'd like a thicker buttercream or another tablespoon of cream for a looser one.

Espresso Buttercream

1 cup unsalted butter, at room
temperature

4½ cups / 540 grams confectioners'
sugar, plus more if needed

2½ tablespoons espresso, at room
temperature

2 tablespoons heavy cream, plus more if
needed

¼ teaspoon coffee extract

Pinch of fine sea salt

In a stand mixer or using handheld electric beaters at medium speed, beat the butter until creamy, about 2 minutes. Reduce the speed to low and add the confectioners' sugar, espresso, cream, extract and salt. Increase the speed to high and beat for 3 minutes. Taste.

Add up to ½ cup more confectioners' sugar if you'd like a thicker buttercream or another tablespoon of cream for a looser one.

Variations: For a spiked version, reduce the espresso to 2 tablespoons and add 1 tablespoon dark rum. For a cinnamon version, add 1 teaspoon cinnamon powder to the sugar. For an American riff, fold in a handful of mini chocolate chips.

Vanilla Buttercream

1 cup unsalted butter, at room
temperature

4½ cups / 540 grams confectioners'
sugar, plus more if needed

3 tablespoons heavy cream, plus more if
needed

1 tablespoon vanilla extract

Pinch of salt

In a stand mixer or using handheld electric beaters at medium speed, beat the butter until creamy, about 2 minutes. Reduce the speed to low and add the confectioners' sugar, cream, vanilla and salt. Increase the speed to high and beat for 3 minutes. Taste.

Add up to ½ cup more confectioners' sugar if you'd like a thicker buttercream or another tablespoon of cream for a looser one.

Note: *Add the seeds of 2 vanilla beans for a stronger perfume and for their appearance.*

Berry Boozy Buttercream

1 cup unsalted butter, at room
temperature

4½ cups / 540 grams confectioners'
sugar, plus more if needed

¼ cup crème de cassis, framboise, mûre
or fraises de bois

1 tablespoon heavy cream, if needed

In a stand mixer or using handheld electric beaters at medium speed, beat the butter until creamy, about 2 minutes. Reduce the speed to low and add the confectioners' sugar and crème de cassis. Increase the speed to high and beat for 3 minutes. Taste.

Add up to ½ cup more confectioners' sugar if you'd like a thicker buttercream or the tablespoon of cream for a looser one.

Note: *If you want a stronger pink hue, add a drop or two of natural food coloring or the juice of a few crushed blackberries.*

Orange Blossom Buttercream

1 cup unsalted butter, at room
temperature

4½ cups / 540 grams confectioners'
sugar, plus more if needed

1-2 tablespoons orange blossom water

2½–3½ tablespoons heavy cream, plus
more if needed

1 teaspoon grated orange zest

In a stand mixer or using handheld electric beaters at medium speed, beat the butter until creamy, about 2 minutes. Reduce the speed to low and add the confectioners' sugar, orange blossom water, heavy cream and zest. Increase the speed to high and beat for 3 minutes. Taste.

Add up to ½ cup more confectioners' sugar if you'd like a thicker buttercream or another tablespoon of cream for a looser one.

Amaretto Buttercream

1 cup unsalted butter, at room
 temperature

4½ cups / 540 grams confectioners'
 sugar, plus more if needed

2½ tablespoons amaretto

2 tablespoons heavy cream, plus more if
 needed

½ teaspoon vanilla extract

¼ teaspoon almond extract

In a stand mixer or using handheld electric beaters at medium speed, beat the butter until creamy, about 2 minutes. Reduce the speed to low and add the confectioners' sugar, amaretto, cream and vanilla and almond extracts. Increase the speed to high and beat for 3 minutes. Taste.

Add up to ½ cup more confectioners' sugar if you'd like a thicker buttercream or another tablespoon of cream for a looser one.

Note: Pair this with an almond meringue and include a layer of peeled and sliced ripe peaches, apricots or nectarines.

Lemon Rose Buttercream

1 cup unsalted butter, at room
 temperature

4½ cups / 540 grams confectioners'
 sugar, plus more if needed

1-2 tablespoons rose water

2½–3½ tablespoons heavy cream, plus
 more if needed

1 teaspoon grated lemon zest

In a stand mixer or using handheld electric beaters at medium speed, beat the butter until creamy, about 2 minutes. Reduce the speed to low and add the confectioners' sugar, rose water, heavy cream and zest. Increase the speed to high and beat for 3 minutes. Taste.

Add up to ½ cup more confectioners' sugar if you'd like a thicker buttercream or another tablespoon of cream for a looser one.

Note: Some rose waters are quite strong, so add a little, taste and repeat. For a livelier lemon note, use 1 tablespoon rose water, 1 tablespoon lemon juice and 2½ tablespoons heavy cream.

Lavender Lemon Blackberry Buttercream

1 cup unsalted butter, at room
   temperature

4½ cups / 540 grams confectioners'
   sugar, plus more if needed

5 tablespoons blackberry juice, plus more
   if needed

¼–½ teaspoon lavender extract

1–2 drops natural purple food coloring

2 teaspoons grated lemon zest

In a stand mixer or using handheld electric beaters, beat the butter on medium speed
until creamy, about 2 minutes. Reduce the speed to low and add the confectioners' sugar,
blackberry juice, lavender extract, food coloring and zest. Increase the speed to high and
beat for 3 minutes. Taste.

Add up to ½ cup more confectioners' sugar if you'd like a thicker buttercream or a
tablespoon more of blackberry juice if you'd like a looser buttercream.

Praliné

This is a key pantry staple in many a French household. It's easily purchased and so not often made at home. I've never understood why it's not readily available in the United States, but it is easy to make and can be stored for three months. The recipe I use is from Gaston Lenôtre, who was, for the second half of the twentieth century, the most celebrated pastry chef in France, if not the world.

Praliné refers to almonds or hazelnuts that have been candied, like nut brittle. Sometimes the nuts are chopped and used for texture or decoration, often to add crunch to a filling or to the top or sides of a buttercream-iced génoise cake. Sometimes they are pulverized to a powder and folded directly into a buttercream. When they are finely chopped, you'll find them added to chocolate confections. Broken into large pieces, they make for a great, sweet snack.

Note that the nuts need to be both shelled and skinned and that a candy thermometer is needed.

2 ½ cups / 500 grams granulated sugar

½ cup water

3⅓ cups / 500 grams shelled and skinned almonds or hazelnuts

Line 2 baking sheets with parchment paper and set aside.

Combine the sugar and water in a large, heavy saucepan and bring it to a boil. Continue to cook until the temperature reaches 248°F on a candy thermometer, about 5 minutes. Remove from heat and immediately (and carefully) add the nuts. Using a long wooden spoon, stir the mixture until the sugar appears sandy. Return to medium heat and cook, stirring, for about 12–14 minutes, or until the sugar has darkened to a golden caramel color.

Pour the mixture onto the parchment-lined baking sheets and set aside to come to room temperature. After about an hour, break the brittle into small pieces. If you want to pulverize it, do so in a Vitamix or food processor once truly cool to the touch.

Store in a covered glass jar out of sunlight.

This recipe will yield about 5 cups or 750 grams of praliné. To make a praliné buttercream, fold a scant cup / 150 grams of powdered praliné into 4 cups buttercream.

Buds and Petals

———•———

A scattering of rose petals has a nonchalant beauty that will catch anyone's eye. But for baking, try rose and lavender sugars, both easily made. I also stir these into tea and tisanes for a subtle floral note and, in larger quantity, when making lemonade.

DRIED, SLIGHTLY SWEETENED ROSE PETALS

There's so little to this. Make five or fifty. Make them with roses or any other edible flower so long as they've not been sprayed with pesticides.

Preheat the oven to 100°F. Line a baking sheet with parchment paper. Cover with as many petals as you are using. The petals must not overlap. Use a sieve to lightly dust the petals with confectioners' sugar. Place in the oven for about an hour. The petals should be dry and slightly crisp. Set aside to cool to room temperature.

CANDIED ROSE PETALS

Brush rose petals lightly on both sides with a little room-temperature simple syrup. Ideally, use a watercolor brush, as you want a delicate, faint touch. The faint mist from a spray bottle works, too. Alternatively, dip into beaten egg whites, then let the excess egg drip off. Drag lightly through superfine sugar or confectioners' sugar, then lift for a moment, to let the excess fall away. Leave to dry overnight on a parchment-lined baking sheet or place in a 100°F oven for an hour. If not using right away, it's best to freeze them.

ROSE SUGAR

Combine the dried rose petals in the Candied Rose Petals recipe with a small amount of granulated sugar in a small food processor or a Vitamix and pulse to break down the petals. Add more sugar and pulse until you have a fragrant sugar. This is delicious on the rim of a glass filled with lemonade. It is also lovely sprinkled on yogurt and even raita. Roses vary so much in intensity that there's no point in suggesting an exact ratio. But assume something close to ½ cup whole dried rose petals (not packed) to 1 cup / 200 grams granulated sugar. Another technique is to layer granulated sugar with fresh rose petals in a glass jar. Cover the jar and store for a few weeks in a cool, dark cupboard or pantry.

LAVENDER SUGAR

When using lavender, which is a bit stronger than rose, I use about 2 tablespoons dried culinary lavender buds and about 2 cups / 400 grams granulated sugar. Process the lavender with about ½ cup / 100 grams sugar to break down the lavender. Add the remaining sugar and pulse to create a fragrant sugar.

Mousse au Chocolat

Chocolate Mousse

This is the mousse my mother and I have always made. It's adapted from Julia Child's *Mastering the Art of French Cooking*. I can see, in my mind's eye, the page in my mother's copy with its several chocolate stains, all made by me. Their shapes read to me like a map of the years we made this together. The moment we'd pour the melted chocolate from its pot, I'd run my fingers round and round the sides, then lick them clean. Not clean enough, however, to keep from dotting the page with my prints like an edible finger painting. Her copy is falling apart, but we both know that replacing it with a clean copy would leave us bereft.

Unlike Julia, my mother makes this with Poire Williams, not rum. The delicate taste of pear gives a soft elegance to the chocolate that we both love. I use a darker chocolate than Julia, who calls for semisweet. No matter how dark you like yours, however, stay under 70% cacao or you will adversely alter the texture of the mousse.

This classic French dessert can, of course, be eaten solo, and this recipe will serve about six. But it is also a key component in turning many a cake into something celebratory. Sandwiched between layers of chocolate génoise, you have the makings of a gâteau opéra, for example, or a birthday cake. Rolled in a pistachio, chocolate or coffee génoise, and you are well on your way to a sumptuous bûche de Noël. Tucked into a ladyfinger-lined bowl, and all you need is whipped cream to make a chocolate charlotte or whipped mascarpone to riff in French on an Italian tiramisu. Perfume it with Grand Marnier or Cointreau and orange zest instead of coffee and rum and set it on an almond génoise flavored with more orange or dark chocolate, and you have the magic that makes people *ooh* and *aah* in blissed-out gratitude.

I will often make this mousse a day before dinner parties. If I have time to use it in a cake, all the more fun. If I don't, the adult chocolate lovers at the table will grow quiet in the intense pleasure of eating it straight up, and the kids will dilute it with great billowing clouds of whipped cream. There is no wrong here, only right and double right.

170 grams dark chocolate, 62%–70% cacao, chopped

12 tablespoons unsalted butter, cut into small pieces

¼ cup strong coffee or espresso

4 large eggs, separated, at room temperature

⅔ cup / 170 grams plus 1 tablespoon granulated sugar

2 tablespoons dark rum or other liqueur

1 tablespoon water

¼ teaspoon fine sea salt

½ teaspoon vanilla extract

Melt the chocolate, butter and coffee together in the top of a double boiler and stir well to combine. Remove the pot containing the chocolate from heat and set aside to cool slightly. Keep the water in the bottom pot at a low simmer.

Fill a large metal bowl with ice and the coldest water your faucet will allow and set aside.

Place the egg yolks, ⅔ cup of the granulated sugar, the rum and water in a medium metal mixing bowl and set it over the pot of simmering water. Whisk by hand or with handheld electric beaters for about 3 minutes, or until the mixture is nearly as thick as mayonnaise. Immediately set the bowl in the bowl of ice water. Continue to whisk until the mixture is cool to the touch. Remove from the ice water and, using a rubber spatula, fold the chocolate mixture into the egg yolk mixture.

In a stand mixer or using handheld electric beaters, beat the egg whites with the salt for 2 minutes. Add the remaining sugar and continue to beat until the whites are thick and shiny, but not dry and stiff. Add the vanilla and beat to combine.

Using a rubber spatula, fold one-third of the beaten egg whites into the chocolate mixture to lighten it, then gently but decisively fold this chocolate mixture into the remaining whites until no streaks of white remain. Don't overfold or the mixture will lose its volume.

Transfer the mousse to a clean bowl and refrigerate for 30 minutes. Cover the bowl with plastic wrap and chill for at least another 4 hours and up to 24. Serve chilled, but not cold—about 10 minutes at room temperature should take the edge off.

Acknowledgments

Those of you who have loved a dog will understand why I begin with Griffin. A Bouvier des Flandres, Griffin was ninety pounds and had eyes of extraordinary depth, ears the softest I've known and a pure, noble and wise soul. To call him attentive would be to miss the point entirely. He was connected to us every moment, ever attuned to even the slightest shift in our unspoken thoughts. He was fair, too; knowing he was needed and loved by all of us, he was careful to travel between my husband's side and mine, moving from one study to the next during the day and one side of the bed to the other at night. And moments before dying, he seemed to wake with a last look of sudden awareness upon hearing the name of our son, Garrick. None of this is to suggest his massive presence in our lives was only of the deep and profound variety. Not at all. Griffin had a playful joyousness, a love of ritual, and a larger-than-life character that filled our home. How lucky we were. How much he is missed.

In Memoriam

Griffin

April 6, 2010–February 27, 2022

Books are mere intangible fragments of hopes and ideas until someone confirms that they could and should be solid things in the world for all to read. For this, I must thank my agent and very dear friend, Eric Simonoff. His affirmation works like alchemy, turning tentative tiptoeing into bold purpose.

Kara Watson edited this book with the loveliest mix of generosity, grace, excitement and warmth. Her fine editorial eye is exactly what every writer wants—precision and perception delivered in discreet pencil but considered with great care and nuance. Working with Kara has been an absolute pleasure. A wholehearted thanks to Valerie Steiker, who first saw something promising in my proposal and decided Scribner should take a leap, and my sincerest gratitude to and admiration for the great Nan Graham, for allowing a book of cakes a spot on what is otherwise a distinguished and literary list.

So many people at Scribner have helped bring this book to life visually. Jaya Miceli and Jaime Putorti, most notably. Emily Polson and Jamie Selzer have kept the train on the tracks through thick and thin, including my getting Covid the week everything needed to be finalized.

In Cassandre Montoriol, a Parisian illustrator, I found an artist whose witty, colorful and whimsical art had me instantly enamored. Her talent is abundant, her intuition spot-on and I've loved our long-distance Zooms.

Thanks to the wonderfully generous Denise and Terry Denson for the loan of their enchanting apartment. Thanks, too, to Chrissy Tkac, intern extraordinaire, for giving me her precious free moments whenever she could. And, of course, to the many fabulous writers and bakers, professional and not, who allowed me to include their treasured recipes.

Nothing in this book hasn't been lovingly tasted, debated and edited by my husband, John Burnham Schwartz. A beautiful novelist and screenwriter, he also happens to be a masterful editor. I can't imagine sending a book into the world without it passing through his hands. The many marks and lines in blue ink he makes on every manuscript of mine fill me with a sense of calm that's quite hard to describe but is akin to feeling protected.

And last, but really first, my loving thanks go to Garrick, our son, who must have wondered many an evening why the kitchen was a mess and no actual dinner was in sight. I hope that one day he will bake something from these pages and have a Proustian moment, a taste memory of childhood, and that what will be conjured won't be the mere taste of butter, sugar and lemon, but the immediate memory of his mother's love.

Index

Note: Page references in color indicate named recipe variations.